Organizational Opportunity and Deviant Behavior

Organizational Opportunity and Deviant Behavior

Convenience in White-Collar Crime

Petter Gottschalk

Professor, Department of Leadership and Organizational Behavior, BI Norwegian Business School, Oslo, Norway

 Edward Elgar
PUBLISHING

Cheltenham, UK • Northampton, MA, USA

Published by
Edward Elgar Publishing Limited
The Lypiatts
15 Lansdown Road
Cheltenham
Glos GL50 2JA
UK

Edward Elgar Publishing, Inc.
William Pratt House
9 Dewey Court
Northampton
Massachusetts 01060
USA

A catalogue record for this book
is available from the British Library

Library of Congress Control Number: 2017947259

This book is available electronically in the **Elgar**online
Business subject collection
DOI 10.4337/9781788111881

ISBN 978 1 78811 187 4 (cased)
ISBN 978 1 78811 188 1 (eBook)

Typeset by Servis Filmsetting Ltd, Stockport, Cheshire
Printed and bound in Great Britain by TJ International Ltd, Padstow

Contents

Figures

Tables

Tables

Introduction

This book summarizes the theoretical knowledge on the important subject of white-collar crime and offers a novel theoretical perspective of convenience as introduced in earlier books (Gottschalk, 2016, 2017). Despite eight decades of research on white-collar crime and criminals, our accumulated knowledge of its occurrence is still limited. In this book, our accumulated knowledge is described from the perspective of convenience. Convenience in white-collar crime relates to savings in time and effort by privileged and trusted individuals in reaching goals, exploring and exploiting opportunities, avoiding collapse and pain, and in illegally benefiting individuals and organizations.

In an empirical study of white-collar crime by Bucy et al. (2008), they found that typical white-collar criminals might be characterized as people who are intelligent, arrogant, cunning, successful, greedy, willing to take risks, aggressive, narcissistic, determined, and charismatic. This is in line with the eight personality characteristics that fuel white-collar criminal activity:

1. Need for control
2. Tendency to bullying
3. Being charismatic
4. Having a fear of failing
5. Possessing company ambition
6. Lacking integrity
7. Having narcissism
8. Lacking social conscience.

Ever since Sutherland presented his thoughts before World War II and later documented his theory in his book *White-Collar Crime* (Sutherland, 1949), a number of researchers have contributed to our understanding of white-collar crime occurrence. This book summarizes the current status of our knowledge about white-collar crime from the perspective of convenience. Convenience is introduced as an organizing concept in this book. A number of well-known theories from criminology, sociology, and other disciplines are organized under the umbrella term of convenience theory.

Since Sutherland (1939) coined the term "white-collar crime", researchers have struggled to understand and explain why some members of the elite in society abuse their privileged positions and trust from others to commit financial crime. Among the explanations we find opportunity and greed, lack of self-control, and neutralization of guilt. In this book, we build on the concept of convenience to explain white-collar crime occurrence.

This book presents research on convenience theory, which suggests that there are three dimensions that lead to white-collar crime: financial desire, organizational opportunity, and deviant behavior. These three dimensions influence each other, and a set of six relationships between the three dimensions are explored in this book.

Convenience theory suggests that financial crime is a convenient option for top executives and others in the elite in society when there are major challenges or great possibilities for personal or organizational profits. Rather than giving up on a contract in a corrupt country, a bribe may be a convenient option to get the contract anyway. Rather than going bankrupt, bank fraud may be a convenient option to try to save the business. Rather than giving up the desire to own a house in a rich neighborhood, embezzlement at work may be a convenient option to realize the dream.

Hopefully this book is helpful to academic researchers and students interested in white-collar crime and crime in general. Also, practitioners belong to the target group for this book, including government officials interested in and responsible for reducing crime levels. This book is also aimed at an audience that works with informality (shadow, informal, gray economy and its components). It might also be useful for a wider audience in entrepreneurship, business management areas, and beyond.

Just like the concept of white-collar crime is continuously debated, so is the concept of theory. Two decades ago, there was an important debate about what theory is and what it is not, where the main contributors were DiMaggio (1995), Sutton and Staw (1995), and Weick (1995). Sutton and Staw (1995: 378) define theory in the following way:

> Theory is about the connections among phenomena, a story about why acts, events, structure, and thoughts occur. Theory emphasizes the nature of causal relationships, identifying what comes first as well as the timing of such events. Strong theory, in our view, probes underlying processes so as to understand the systematic reasons for a particular occurrence or nonoccurrence. It often burrows deeply into microprocesses, laterally into neighboring concepts, or in an upward direction, tying itself to broader social phenomena. It usually is laced with a set of convincing and logically interconnected arguments. It can have implications that we have not seen with our naked (or theoretically unassisted) eye. It may have implications that run counter to our common sense.

Theory acts as an educational device that creates insights into criminal phenomena (Colquitt and Zapata-Phelan, 2007: 1282):

> A theory might be a prediction or explanation, a set of interrelated constructs, definitions, and propositions that presents a systematic view of phenomena by specifying relations among variables, with the purpose of explaining natural phenomena. The systematic view might be an argument, a discussion, or a rationale, and it helps to explain or predict phenomena that occur in the world. Some define theory in terms of relationships between independent and dependent variables, where theory is a collection of assertions, both verbal and symbolic, that identifies what variables are important and for what reasons, and that specifies how they are interrelated and why. It identifies the conditions under which variables should be related or not related. Other scholars have defined theory in terms of narratives and accounts.

Corley and Gioia (2011: 12) provide a shorter definition of theory:

> Theory is a statement of concepts and their interrelationships that shows how and/or why a phenomenon occurs.

Various disciplines such as criminology, sociology, psychology, strategy, marketing, and management have developed a number of theories with the aim of explaining how and why individuals involve themselves in crime, and how they get involved in crime. Some of the theories are individualistic and look at risk factors in personality traits and family conditions (Listwan et al., 2010). Other theories emphasize ideology and culture, which represent the environment in terms of economy, society, and structures.

Sociological theories of white-collar crime, for example, postulate that managers who commit economic offenses live in a social setting, that is, culture, in which a very high value is placed on material success and individual wealth. Both economic theories and sociological theories are of the opinion that striving for wealth and enjoyment in some way contributes to economic crime committed by managers (Blickle et al., 2006).

It is difficult to overstate the importance of theory to understanding prevention of white-collar crime. Theory allows analysts to understand and predict outcomes on the basis of probability (Colquitt and Zapata-Phelan, 2007). Theory also allows analysts to describe and explain a process or sequence of events. Theory prevents analysts from being bewildered by the complexity of the real world by providing a linguistic tool for organizing a coherent understanding of the real world.

Theory acts as an educational tool, which can be used to develop insights into criminal phenomena such as financial crime in general and white-collar crime in particular. A theory is an undocumented explanation of a phenomenon or relationship. The opposite of theory is not practice.

The opposite of theory is empirical findings. Both theory and empirical study are concerned with practice but while theory presents thoughts about practice, empirical study presents facts about practice.

In this book we apply the following definition of theory as summarized by Løkke and Sørensen (2014): a series of logical arguments that specifies a set of relationships among concepts. Specifically, we first introduce the main concept of convenience and describe convenience orientation. Next, we introduce three concepts as dimensions in convenience theory: desire for profit caused by threats and possibilities, organizational opportunity to commit and conceal crime, and personal willingness for deviant behavior. Finally, a set of relationships are introduced to link motive, opportunity, and willingness. Convenience theory suggests that there are mutual influences among all three concepts. For example, greater opportunity can lead to greater willingness, and greater willingness can lead to greater opportunity. The purpose of convenience theory is to explain why and how white-collar crime occurs.

1. Convenience in white-collar crime

Convenience is a concept that was theoretically mainly associated with efficiency in time savings. Today, convenience is associated with a number of other characteristics, such as reduced effort and reduced pain. Convenience is associated with terms such as fast, easy, and safe. Convenience says something about attractiveness and accessibility. A convenient individual is not necessarily bad or lazy. On the contrary, the person can be seen as smart and rational (Sundström and Radon, 2015).

In the marketing literature, convenience store is a term used to define three phases in retailing. First, retailers identified a business opportunity in offering a new retail format based on the self-service idea. Self-service replaced over-the-counter service. Next, retailers identified customers' willingness to pay a little more if the store was always open and situated in the neighborhood or with the gas station. Finally, e-commerce represents another kind of convenience, where the ordering process can take place from home (Sundström and Radon, 2015). In all three instances, there are costs associated with convenience (Locke and Blomquist, 2016). In the case of self-service, customers have to find and physically handle items themselves. In the case of online shopping, customers have to find and electronically handle items themselves. Just like convenience is a driver for consumers when shopping, convenience is a driver for executives and other members in the elite when struggling to reach personal and organizational goals.

In the marketing literature, distinctions are made between decision convenience, access convenience, benefit convenience, transaction convenience, and post-benefit convenience (Seiders et al., 2007). In our convenience theory for white-collar crime, we make distinctions between economical convenience, organizational convenience, and behavioral convenience.

CONVENIENCE ORIENTATION

Convenience orientation is conceptualized as the value that individuals and organizations place on actions with inherent characteristics of saving time and effort. Convenience orientation can be considered a value-like construct that influences behavior and decision-making. Mai and Olsen (2016) measured convenience orientation in terms of a desire to spend as little time as possible on the task, in terms of an attitude that the less effort needed the better, and in terms of a consideration that it is a waste of time to spend a long time on the task. Convenience orientation toward illegal actions increases as negative attitudes toward legal actions increase. The basic elements in convenience orientation are executives' attitudes toward the saving of time, effort, and discomfort in the planning, action, and achievement of goals. Generally, convenience orientation is the degree to which an executive is inclined to save time and effort to reach goals. Convenience orientation refers to a person's general preference for convenient maneuvers. A convenience-oriented person is one who seeks to accomplish a task in the shortest time with the least expenditure of human energy (Berry et al., 2002).

In the marketing literature, convenience orientation is, for example, measured in terms of the stage in a person's life cycle, family size, economic status, social status, and education (Sundström and Radon, 2015). Similar characteristics of convenience orientation might be developed for individuals in the elite regarding white-collar crime.

Convenience in the decision-making process is not only concerned with one alternative being more convenient than another one. Convenience is also concerned with the extent to which an individual collects information about more alternatives and collects more information about each one. Market research indicates that consumers tend to make buying decisions based on little information about few alternatives (Sundström and Radon, 2015). A similar process can be explored for white-collar crime where the individual avoids the effort of collecting more information about more alternatives that might have led to a non-criminal rather than a criminal solution to a challenge or problem.

It is not the actual convenience that is important in convenience theory. Rather, it is the perceived, expected, and assumed convenience that influences choice of action. Berry et al. (2002) make this distinction explicit by conceptualizing convenience as individuals' time and effort perceptions related to an action. White-collar criminals probably vary in their perceived convenience of their actions. Low expected convenience can be one of the reasons why not more members of the elite commit white-collar offenses.

Convenience is of value because time and effort are associated with value. Time is a limited and scarce resource. Saving time means reallocating time across activities to achieve greater efficiency. Similarly, effort can be reallocated to create value elsewhere. The more effort is exerted, the more outcomes can be expected in return (Berry et al., 2002).

Convenience in white-collar crime relates to savings in time and effort by privileged and trusted individuals to reach a goal. Convenience here is an attribute of an illegal action. Convenience comes at a potential cost to the offender in terms of the likelihood of detection and future punishment. In other words, reducing time and effort now entails a greater potential for future cost. "Paying for convenience" is a way of phrasing this proposition (Farquhar and Rowley, 2009).

Convenience is the perceived savings in time and effort required to find and to facilitate the use of a solution to a problem or to exploit favorable circumstances. Convenience directly relates to the amount of time and effort that is required to accomplish a task. Convenience addresses the time and effort exerted before, during, and after an activity. Convenience represents a time and effort component related to the complete illegal transaction process or processes (Collier and Kimes, 2012).

How privileged individuals in the elite think and feel about time and effort varies. Chen and Nadkarni (2017: 34) found that many chief executive officers (CEOs) can be characterized by time urgency where they have the feeling of being chronically hurried:

> Time urgency is a relatively stable trait. Time-urgent people are acutely aware of the passage of time and feel chronically hurried. They often create aggressive internal deadlines and use them as markers of the timely completion of team tasks. They regularly check work progress, increase others' awareness of the remaining time, and motivate others to accomplish commitments within the allotted time.

People differ in their temporal orientation, including perceived time scarcity, the degree to which they value time, and their sensitivity to time-related issues. Facing strain, greed, or other situations, an illegal activity can represent a convenient solution to a problem that the individual or the organization would otherwise find difficult or even impossible to solve. The desire for convenience varies among people. Convenience orientation is a term that refers to a person's general preference for convenient solutions to problems. A convenience-oriented individual is one who seeks to accomplish a task in the shortest time with the least expenditure of human energy (Farquhar and Rowley, 2009).

Convenience motivates the choice of action. An important element in convenience is saving time in terms of efficiency in time savings, and another element is avoiding more problematic, stressful, and challenging situations. Convenience can be both an absolute construct and a relative construct. As an absolute construct, it is attractive to commit crime as such. As a relative construct, it is more convenient to commit crime than to carry out alternative actions to solve a problem or gain benefits from a possibility. Convenience is an advantage in favor of a specific action to the detriment of alternative actions. In white-collar crime, it seems that convenience is mainly a relative construct. Decision-making implies a choice between alternatives, where one alternative might be relatively more convenient. Convenience is a matter of perception in advance of possible criminal actions. Convenience must be viewed as a significant variable whose understanding involves complexity in multiple meanings (Sundström and Radon, 2015).

For example, the flexibility to choose the exact moment for making a deal or another kind of action can be perceived as a matter of convenience. Convenience can also mean selecting a proper occasion, which, in turn, is about timing. There may be more reluctance to do something at a certain point in time than willingness to save or spend time. Thus, when something is convenient, it could mean saving time as well as spending time and doing it at the right moment (Sundström and Radon, 2015).

In addition to time convenience and timing convenience, there may be place convenience, where a potential offender finds the spatial circumstances convenient for crime (Sundström and Radon, 2015). In white-collar crime, the organizational setting is typically characterized by spatial convenience.

Three main dimensions to explain white-collar crime have emerged. All of them link to convenience (Gottschalk, 2016, 2017). The first dimension is concerned with economic aspects, where convenience implies that the illegal financial gain is a convenient option for the decision-maker to cover needs. The second dimension is concerned with organizational aspects, where convenience implies that the offender has convenient access to premises and convenient ability to hide illegal transactions among legal transactions. The third dimension is concerned with behavioral aspects, where convenience implies that the offender finds convenient justification.

Convenience orientation is introduced in this book as an explanation for white-collar crime among CEOs. This chapter thus makes a case for a specific way of explaining CEO behavior. A question worth addressing is what other explanatory hypotheses should be considered. There is a need to place the convenience perspective in a broader setting of proposed or rival explanations. The question is what other approaches exist to explain the relevant behavior, and whether the convenience approach applies in other contexts as well. Future research might focus on a discussion of what counts as a satisfactory explanation.

To address this question, it is relevant to go back to Sutherland (1949), who coined the term white-collar crime. He emphasized attitudes in society where white-collar crime is considered less serious than traditional street crime. While convenience theory emphasizes factors at the individual and organizational level, Sutherland (1949) emphasized hypotheses at the community level. Convenience theory lacks explicit representations of society-level factors such as criminal market structures (e.g., cartels), the extent of national corruption, and law enforcement mechanisms.

The notion of convenience may seem rather obvious and not especially illuminating. When convenience orientation is simply defined as the degree to which an executive is inclined to save time, effort, and pain to reach a goal, it sounds more like an aspect of prudence than deviant criminal behavior. However, as pointed out in this chapter, some CEOs will employ illegal or objectionable means in striving to reach goals. This type of behavior is not necessarily different from the behavior of others in positions of power and authority (politicians, officers of universities, church officials, heads of major philanthropies, etc.), but the degree of freedom enjoyed by many CEOs make the CEO position nevertheless very special in terms of convenience.

WHO ARE WHITE-COLLAR OFFENDERS?

Individual differences between offenders and non-offenders in regards to psychological and cognitive characteristics are important explanatory factors in the etiology of criminal behavior. Benson (2013) argues that the importance of individual differences has been made apparent by the increasingly relevant research of biosocial criminologists, as well as the theories and findings of life course and developmental criminologists. White-collar criminals are often assumed to be quite normal people who do not suffer from the personal disturbances that seem so common among street offenders. The only obvious disturbance is white-collar criminals' resistance to define their activities as crime. Other than their tendency to rationalize and excuse their crime by active application of neutralization techniques, the psychological makeup of white-collar offenders is often not visible.

However, many white-collar criminals have a mindset that will make them stop at nothing to enrich themselves and their organizations. The extent of convenience obviously varies with the mindset. Individual characteristics matter in regards to white-collar crime convenience. Personality traits may facilitate business success at one point in time and white-collar offending at another point in time. Benson (2013) finds that narcissistic self-confidence when coupled with drive, ambitiousness, and insensitivity to others may enable some people to successfully undertake risky business endeavors that more prudent and introspective individuals would never attempt. An ambitious and convenient mindset may also permit, if not drive, these individuals in the single-minded pursuit of their goals to engage in financial crime.

Almost all white-collar criminals are known to use linguistic techniques to justify or excuse deviant behavior. By applying neutralization techniques, white-collar criminals think they are doing nothing wrong. They deny responsibility, injury, and victim. They condemn the condemners. They claim appeal to higher loyalties and normality of action. They claim entitlement, and they argue the case of legal mistake. They find their own mistakes acceptable. They argue a dilemma arose, whereby they made a reasonable tradeoff before committing the act (Siponen and Vance, 2010). Such claims enable offenders to find crime convenient.

Benson and Simpson (2015: 145) found that white-collar criminals seldom think of injury or victims: "Many white-collar offenses fail to match this common-sense stereotype because the offenders do not set out intentionally to harm any specific individual. Rather, the consequences of their illegal acts fall upon impersonal organizations or a diffuse and unseen mass of people."

The idea of neutralization techniques (Sykes and Matza, 1957) resulted from work on Sutherland's (1949) differential association theory. According to this theory, people are always aware of their moral obligation to abide by the law, and they are aware that they have the same moral obligation within themselves to avoid illegitimate acts. The theory postulates that criminal behavior learning occurs in association with those who find such criminal behavior favorable and in isolation from those who find it unfavorable (Benson and Simpson, 2015). Crime is relatively convenient when there is no guilt feeling for doing something learned from others.

Evidence of neutralization can be found in autobiographies by white-collar criminals such as Kerik (2015), Bogen (2008), Eriksen (2010), and Fosse (Fosse and Magnusson, 2004). Bernard B. Kerik was the former police commissioner in New York who served three years in prison. He seems to deny responsibility, to condemn his condemners, and to suggest normality of action.

Offender-focused theories explain crime in terms of personality characteristics (Koppen et al., 2010). Self-control theory is a typical theory related to deviant behavior (Gottfredson and Hirschi, 1990). Individuals with low self-control have a tendency to be impulsive, self-centered, out for adventure, and out for immediate pleasure. Immediate pleasure may be achieved more conveniently by white-collar crime than by legal activities.

The typical profile of a white-collar criminal includes the following attributes:

- The person has high social status and considerable influence, enjoying respect and trust, and belongs to the elite.
- The elite have generally more knowledge, money, and prestige, and occupy higher positions than others in the population.
- Privileges and authority of the elite are often not visible or transparent, but nevertheless known to everybody.

- The elite can be found in business, public administration, politics, congregations, and many other sectors in society.
- The elite is a minority that behaves as an authority toward others.
- The person is often wealthy and does not really need crime income to live a good life.
- The person is typically well educated and connects to important networks of partners and friends.
- The person exploits his or her position to commit financial crime.
- The person does not look at himself or herself as a criminal, but rather as a community builder who applies personal rules for his or her own behavior.
- The person may be in a position that makes the police reluctant to initiate a crime investigation.
- The person has access to resources that enable the involvement of top defense attorneys, and can behave in court in a manner that creates sympathy among the general public, partly because the defendant belongs to the upper class similar to the judge, the prosecutor, and the attorney.

White-collar criminals are mostly men. The low female fraction can be explained by a number of factors, such as relative need for material wealth, relative opportunity to commit crime, and relative risk aversion. In addition, the detection rate for female white-collar criminals may be lower than for male criminals, for example because women are more rarely suspected of crime. The most famous US cases involve men, including Bernie Ebbers, Bernard Madoff, Raj Rajaratman, and Jeff Schilling. In Germany, Blickle et al. (2006) studied a sample of 76 convicted white-collar criminals where only 6 offenders were women while 70 offenders were men. In a US sample studied by Langton and Piquero (2007), 16 percent of criminals were women and 84 percent men. In a study in the Netherlands of 644 prosecuted white-collar criminals between 2008 and 2012, women made up only 15 percent of the sample (Onna et al., 2014).

While it is true that Bernard Madoff was the architect of a mammoth Ponzi scheme, Madoff's fraud seems different in some significant ways from the kinds of CEO criminality at manufacturing or telecommunications firms where large numbers of employees are put at risk, large numbers of shareholders are put at risk, financial markets in certain industries are misled in serious ways, and large numbers of salespeople and consumers are impacted. Furthermore, the crimes perpetrated by Ken Lay and Bernie Ebbers are different – at least in form and, in some respects, in regard to impact – from that of Bernard Madoff.

WHAT DO WHITE-COLLAR OFFENDERS DO?

White-collar criminals commit financial crime, where a great variety of options can be found, as illustrated in Figure 1.1. Fraud, theft, manipulation, and corruption are the four main categories of financial crime with a number of subcategories.

Fraud can be defined as the intentional perversion of truth for the purpose of inducing another in reliance upon that truth to part with some

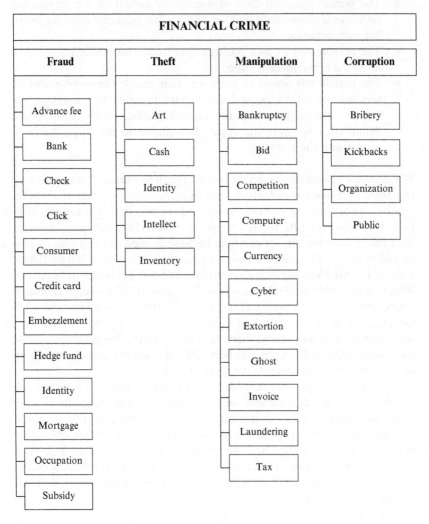

Figure 1.1   Main categories and subcategories of financial crime

valuable thing belonging to him or her or to surrender a legal right. Fraud is an intentional and unlawful making of a misrepresentation, which causes actual prejudice or which is potentially prejudicial to another. Bank fraud is a typical example. Bank fraud is a criminal offense of knowingly executing a scheme to defraud a financial institution.

Theft can be defined as the illegal taking of another person's, group's, or organization's property without the victim's consent. For example, identity theft combined with identity fraud is the unlawful use of another's personal identifying information. It involves financial or other personal information stolen with the intent of establishing another person's identity as the thief's own. It occurs when someone uses personally identifying information, such as name, social security number, date of birth, government passport number, or credit card number, without the owner's permission, to commit financial crime.

Manipulation can be defined as a means of gaining illegal control or influence over others' activities, means, and results. For example, bankruptcy crime relates to criminal acts committed in connection with bankruptcy or liquidation proceedings. A person filing for bankruptcy or a business that has gone into liquidation can hide assets after proceedings have been initiated, thereby preventing creditors from collecting their claims. However, most of the criminal acts are typically committed before bankruptcy/liquidation proceedings are initiated; for example the debtor has failed to keep accounts or has unlawfully withdrawn money from the business.

Corruption is defined as the giving, requesting, receiving, or accepting of an improper advantage related to a position, office, or assignment. The improper advantage does not have to be connected to a specific action or to not doing this action. It will be sufficient if the advantage can be linked to a person's position, office, or assignment. An individual (or group) is guilty of corruption if he or she accept money or money's worth for doing something that he or she is under a duty to do anyway, that he or she is under a duty not to do, or to exercise a legitimate discretion for improper reason. Corruption is the act of destroying or perverting the integrity or fidelity of a person in his or her discharge of duty; it is to induce to act dishonestly or unfaithfully, it is to make venal, and it is to bribe. Corruption involves behavior on the part of officials in the public or private sectors, in which they improperly and unlawfully enrich themselves and/or those close to them, or induce others to do so, by misusing the position in which they are placed. Corruption covers a wide range of illegal activity such as kickbacks, embezzlement, and extortion.

HOW DO WHITE-COLLAR OFFENDERS DO IT?

For an offense to occur there has to be an opportunity. Benson (2013) argues that social, economic, legal, and regulatory conditions or changes in such conditions influence opportunities for various types of white-collar crime. As opportunities increase or decrease, white-collar crime expands or contracts accordingly because the choice to engage in white-collar crime becomes either more or less convenient to potential offenders.

Situation-focused theories explain crime in terms of opportunity structures. Piquero and Benson (2004) proposed a middle-ground explanation of white-collar crime, which they call the punctuated situational theory of offending. This theory assumes that white-collar criminals start offending when they reach their thirties or forties. External factors, such as personal or occupational crisis, and opportunities that result from a certain occupational status, are claimed to explain crime. Situational opportunities – such as a more influential job and more important contacts – give access to illegitimate means to obtain desirable goals.

The opportunity perspective in the situation has also been stressed by Benson and Simpson (2015). They emphasize legal access to premises and resources, distance from victims, and manipulation within regular transactions.

The situation is not only characterized by opportunities in the organization, but also by the organizational environment. Criminogenic conditions in the environment make white-collar crime even more accessible. Alibux (2015) exemplifies the environment with the attitude toward banks that are considered too powerful to fail, which thus may protect the wrongdoings of bank executives. This is in line with institutional theory, which suggests that opportunities are shaped by individuals, groups, other organizations, and society at large.

Opportunity is a distinct characteristic of white-collar crime and varies depending on the kinds of criminals involved. An opportunity is attractive as a means of responding to desires. It is the organizational dimension that provides the white-collar criminal an opportunity to commit financial crime and conceal it in legal organizational activities. While possibility in the economic dimension of convenience theory is concerned with goals (such as sales and bonuses), opportunity in the organizational dimension is concerned with crime (such as corruption and embezzlement).

Aguilera and Vadera (2008: 434) describe a criminal opportunity as "the presence of a favorable combination of circumstances that renders a possible course of action relevant". Opportunity arises when individuals or groups can engage in illegal and unethical behavior and expect, with reasonable confidence, to avoid detection and punishment. Opportunity to commit crime may include macro- and micro-level factors. Macro-level factors encompass the characteristics of the industries in which the business finds itself embedded, such as market structure, business sets of an industry, that is, companies whose actions are visible to one another, and variations in the regulatory environment.

Benson and Simpson (2015) argue that many white-collar offenses manifest the following opportunity properties: (1) the offender has legitimate access to the location in which the crime is committed, (2) the offender is spatially separate from the victim, and (3) the offender's actions have a superficial appearance of legitimacy. Opportunity occurs in terms of these three properties that are typically the case for executives and other individuals in the elite. In terms of convenience, these properties may be attractive and convenient when considering white-collar crime to solve a financial problem. It is convenient for the offender to conceal the crime and give it an appearance of outward respectability.

Opportunity is dependent on the social capital available to the criminal. The structure and quality of social ties in hierarchical and transactional relationships shape opportunity structures. Social capital is the sum of actual or potential resources accruing to the criminal by virtue of his or her position in a hierarchy and in a network.

The organizational dimension of white-collar crime becomes particularly evident when financial crime is committed to benefit the organization rather than the individual. This is called corporate crime as opposed to occupational crime for personal benefit. Hansen (2009) argues that the problem with occupational crime is that it is committed within the confines of positions of trust and in organizations which prohibit surveillance and accountability. Heath (2008) found that individuals who are further up the chain of command in the firm tend to commit bigger and more severe occupational crime. On the other hand, corporate crime, sometimes labeled organizational offending, results from offenses by collectivities or aggregates of discrete individuals. If a corporate official violates the law in acting for the corporation, we still define it as corporate crime. However, if he or she gains personal benefit in the commission of a crime against the corporation, we regard it as occupational crime. A corporation cannot be subject to imprisonment, and therefore the majority of penalties to control individual violators are not available for corporations and corporate crime.

The typical modus of a white-collar criminal includes the following attributes:

- Crime is committed in an organizational context of business that shapes the economical foundation for deviant acts.
- Crime is committed by non-physical means and by dark activities

through the manipulation and hiding of activities and general secrecy.
- Crime is committed on purpose, with intention and planning, and the act represents a breach of trust.
- The act is organized within legal activities, such that the act itself is disguised, rather than the offender.
- When suspicion occurs, the offender influences witnesses and potential whistleblowers by applying formal and informal authority in the organizational setting.

White-collar criminals commit offenses in their professional setting, where criminal activities are concealed and disguised in organizational work of otherwise law-abiding behavior. The criminals have power and influence, form relationships with other persons or professionals that protect them from developing criminal identities, and enjoy trust from others in privileged networks (Kempa, 2010; Podgor, 2007).

Brightman (2009) emphasizes that white-collar offenders commit crime without violence. Very different from burglars, killers, and possibly thieves, there is no physical violence involved in criminal activity. On the contrary, typical cases are characterized by individuals who behave nicely and properly. They tend to use their charm, charisma, and influence to commit and cover their illegal activities. However, psychological violence may be present in white-collar crime cases.

WHY DO WHITE-COLLAR OFFENDERS DO IT?

Benson (2013) argues that no matter how alluring or enticing a white-collar crime opportunity may be, not everyone who could offend does. Why are some people ready to take advantage of white-collar crime opportunities, while others are not? Why are opportunities more tempting to some people than others? Answers to these questions must lie in the nature or characteristics of the people involved as well as their personal situation. We have to understand their motives. What would they like to achieve by committing crime?

An interesting starting point is to look at Maslow's hierarchy of needs. The Russian-American psychologist Abraham Maslow developed a hierarchy of human needs. Needs start at the bottom with physiological need, need for security, social need, and need for respect and self-realization. When basic needs such as food and shelter are satisfied, then the person moves up the pyramid to satisfy needs for safety and control over his or her own life situation, as illustrated in Figure 1.2. Further up in the pyramid, the person strives for status, recognition, and self-respect. While street

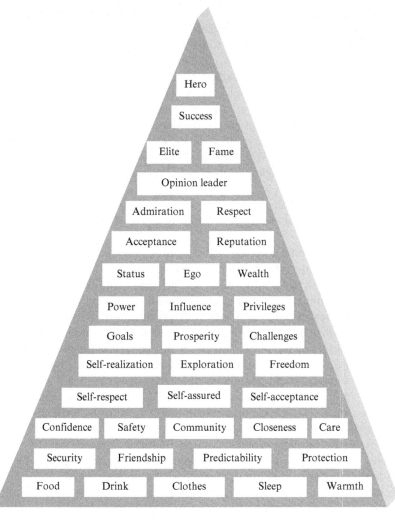

Figure 1.2   Pyramid of needs for white-collar offenders adapted from Maslow

crime is often concerned with the lower levels, white-collar crime is often concerned with the upper levels in terms of status and success.

Most individuals will want to move higher up in the pyramid when needs below are satisfied. However, there are some exceptions. An example can be found in law firms, where partners work very long hours and make a lot of money without reaching very high in the pyramid. Business lawyers tend to over-satisfy basic needs by owning large houses, several cars, boats, and shares in companies. They are not very respected and are not considered leading experts of the law.

The opposite example seems to be a university professor, who quickly tries to move up the pyramid once the basic needs of housing are satisfied. They struggle to publish in leading research journals to become famous, associated with a reputation of being leaders in their fields.

As far as money or other valuable items can help them in climbing higher in the pyramid, potential offenders may find white-collar crime convenient if other options to achieve success are more stressful and require more resources. Whether the offender wants more at a certain level or wants to climb to higher levels in the pyramid, financial crime can be a means to an end.

For some white-collar criminals, money is the goal of crime. For other white-collar criminals, money is a means to a goal of acceptance, influence, and fame.

For example, to be accepted and recognized as a successful businessperson, his or her enterprise has to grow and make money. Financial success as a businessperson can lead to influence, privileges, and status. Admiration and respect within the elite is a desirable goal for many individuals. If such a goal cannot be reached by legal means, illegal means represent an alternative.

On the other hand, the threat of bankruptcy may cause a fall from a high level to a low level in the hierarchy of needs. When a famous person in the elite has enjoyed admiration and respect for many years, but is suddenly facing a business collapse which may cause a fall in the hierarchy down to where even friendships can get lost, the person may apply illegal means such as tax evasion and corruption to save the business. By saving the business, the person can remain high up in the pyramid of needs.

Some white-collar criminals commit financial crime to benefit themselves, while others commit crime to benefit the organization. The former is labeled occupational crime, benefiting the individual, while the latter is labeled corporate crime, benefiting the larger organization (Holtfreter, 2015). Antitrust violations, securities offenses, and health care fraud are typical examples of corporate crime. Corruption is typically characterized by a briber who commits corporate crime, while the bribed commits occupational crime.

The typical motive of a white-collar criminal includes the following attributes:

- Crime is committed for illegal profit for personal or organizational gain.
- It can be greed, availability, possibility, threat, fear, or strain that cause the act.

- Threats can come from loss-making business and special market structures and forces.
- Crime is committed to climb in the hierarchy of needs or to avoid falling in the hierarchy of needs.
- White-collar crime is profit-driven crime based on favorable economic circumstances.
- Human behavior finds motivation in the self-interested pursuit of pleasure and the avoidance of pain.
- The offender considers the current gain convenient when compared to future cost, and would like to avoid additional time and effort to solve the problem.
- Crime is convenient as it often is an attempt to circumvent more difficult (legal) means of accomplishment – such as hard work, fair competition, and navigation of bureaucracy and red tape.
- The individual gets tired while dealing with complexity and thus searches for simple solutions.

Strengths and weaknesses, possibilities and threats are typical motives for white-collar crime, as discussed in the next chapter.

UNRELIABLE OFFENDER CHARACTERISTICS

Unfortunately, deciding exactly who the white-collar offender is remains a matter of dispute. Benson (2013) argues that this tension is reflected in the varying definitions of white-collar crime that are employed in research in this area. Following in the tradition of Sutherland (1949), this book focuses on high-status individuals who are involved in organizationally and occupationally based offenses. These individuals have made convenient choices, and their criminal choices are influenced by individual and psychological characteristics as well as situational characteristics and opportunity structures.

A number of theories can be explored to shed light on convenience in white-collar crime. First, we find convenience in the context of differential association and social learning. Differential association theory suggests that whether individuals engage in white-collar crime is largely based on their socialization within certain peer groups. In an elite setting, interactions with deviant others promote criminal activity. Next, strain theory suggests that people find crime convenient when they are blocked from legitimately achieving their ambitions and preventing further pain. A variety of pressures, or strains, increase the likelihood of engaging in crime (Holtfreter, 2015). Furthermore, a series of other theoretical perspectives can shed light on convenience, such as the theory of profit-driven crime, theory of goal orientation, theory of social concern, fear of falling theory, American dream theory, theory of crime forces, opportunity theory, institutional theory, agency theory, rational choice theory, self-control theory, obedience theory, negative life events theory, slippery slope theory, neutralization theory, and social conflict theory. These theories are organized in support of convenience theory in the following chapters into the economical, organizational, and behavioral dimensions of convenience.

Trust is an important factor in the convenience of white-collar crime. Dearden (2016) argues that violation of trust is at the core of white-collar crime. Trust implies that vulnerability is accepted based upon the positive expectations of the motives and actions of another.

As long as white-collar crime is a convenient option to explore and exploit opportunities, to avoid threats and uncertainty, to climb the pyramid of needs, and to reach goals, it will continue to occur among members of the privileged elite who have opportunities for deviant behavior. In a perspective of offender profiling, some characteristics can be identified, such as being a respected and often charismatic individual in temporal or permanent trouble, ambitious and short-term focused, showing distant but at the same time social behavior, as we explore in the following chapters.

When Sutherland (1939) coined the term white-collar crime, only a small percentage of the working population had white-collar positions. Sutherland made an important point that upper-class people commit crime in the course of their professions, and sometimes manipulate and cheat for vast amounts. Since Sutherland coined the term, white-collar workers now form the majority of the labor force. This is why the term now has an added attribute of elite, where the offender must belong to the elite to be classified as a white-collar criminal. The elite enjoy privileges and special access to commit financial crime.

Given this definition, a number of situations fall outside the white-collar crime category. Examples include auto mechanics who charge for services not rendered, industrial workers who steal at the plant, or restaurant workers who scam the customers or owners. Furthermore, neither computer-enabled financial crime such as CEO fraud nor social security fraud belongs in the category of white-collar crime.

White-collar crime implies elite crime by skilled offenders, often involving vast amounts of money (Felson and Boba, 2010). Crime cases involving small amounts by employees using rather simple methods without special access are not defined as white-collar crime. Although high-level white-collar offenses can do dramatic damage, these are the exceptions rather than the rule in the area of financial crime. Most organizational and occupational occurrences of financial crime are rather unskilled, easily accomplished, and modest in economic return. Such offenders without any elite status are not really that clever, and they are more frequently caught. They commit ordinary thefts or other abuses while they believe nobody is looking.

White-collar crime is not necessarily fancy and advanced. It may also be simple and unskilled. What makes it exceptional is the special access to opportunities that others do not enjoy. Based on position, profession, trust, access, loyalty from others, power, and influence, offenders can conveniently commit crime and hide it among legal activities. The tactics used by offenders may be extremely diverse. It makes sense to continue using white-collar as the defining feature.

Felson and Boba (2010) argue that white-collar crime fits within the larger system of criminal behavior, and that the systems are structured by how the offender gets to the target of crime. Typically, the offender abuses his or her specialized organizational role to gain information and access to victims. For example, an attorney may steal money from a trust fund administered for an elderly wealthy widow, a contractor may fake an insurance claim, or a building inspector may receive bribes in return for building permits. In each example, somebody uses an occupational or professional role to gain specialized access to the victim, and then commits a crime.

We define a type of crime by the people who might do more of it, and who are in a position where the situation enables them to do more of it. Felson and Boba (2010) prefer the term "crime of specialized access" over white-collar crime. Such criminal acts are defined by one key element: abusing one's job or profession to gain specific access to a crime target. Routine legal activities set the stage for illegal activities. Legitimate features of the work role – often including personal ties and privileges – provide a chance to do misdeeds.

Victims of white-collar crime are diverse. In our database of 405 convicted white-collar criminals in Norway from 2009 to 2015, this is the distribution of victims:

- 115 offenders caused harm to their employers by embezzlements, bribes, fake invoices, and so on.
- 84 offenders caused harm to society by tax evasion.
- 68 offenders caused harm to customers of the firm by overcharging services, embezzlement of collected funds, and so on.
- 57 offenders committed bank fraud by false property statements, fake contracts, stolen identities, and so on.
- 30 offenders committed insider trading, harming other shareholders.
- 51 offenders caused harm to other persons or organizations.

2. Economical dimension of convenience theory

Convenience theory as an explanation for white-collar crime suggests that offenders are attracted by convenience in three dimensions (Gottschalk, 2016, 2017). First, in the economical dimension offenders are attracted by crime as a convenient way of satisfying desires for personal and organizational profits. For some offenders, it is all about the American dream (Trahan et al., 2005). Second, in the organizational dimension offenders are attracted by organizational opportunities for financial crime in a setting where offenders enjoy professional access and trust from others. Finally, in the behavioral dimension offenders perceive their own deviant behaviors as unproblematic and justified (O'Connor, 2005).

Convenience is a term often applied in studies of consumer behavior. Convenience theory adds something important to our understanding because it:

1. disaggregates the components of a consumer's decisions about services and similarly disaggregates the dimensions of a white-collar criminal's decisions about deviant behavior
2. explains why illegitimate actions may be chosen at the detriment of legitimate actions
3. provides a way of thinking about why organizations might not do anything about being an arena for crime.

The key components of convenience theory are similar to Felson and Boba's (2010) problem triangle analysis in routine activity theory. Routine activity theory suggests three conditions for crime to occur: a motivated offender, an opportunity in terms of a suitable target, and the absence of a capable or moral guardian. The existence or absence of a likely guardian represents an inhibitor or facilitator for crime. The premise of routine activity theory is that crime is to a minor extent affected by social causes such as poverty, inequality, and unemployment. Motivated offenders are individuals who are not only capable of committing criminal activity, but are willing to do so. Suitable targets can be things that are seen by offenders as particularly attractive.

When introducing routine activity theory, Cohen and Felson (1979) concentrated upon the circumstances in which offenders carry out predatory criminal acts. Most criminal acts require convergence in space and time of (1) likely offenders, (2) suitable targets, and (3) the absence of capable guardians against crime. The lack of any of these elements is sufficient to prevent the successful completion of a crime. Though guardianship is implicit in everyday life, it is usually invisible due to the absence of violations and is therefore easy to overlook. Guardians are not only protective tools, weapons, and skills, but also mental models in the minds of potential offenders that stimulate self-control to avoid criminal acts.

When compared to convenience theory, routine activity theory's three conditions do not cover all three dimensions. The likely offenders can be found in the behavioral dimension, while both suitable targets and absence of capable guardians can be found in the organizational dimension. While routine activity theory defines conditions for crime to occur, convenience theory defines situations where crime occurs. White-collar crime only occurs when there is a financial motive in the economical dimension.

Another traditional theory is worthwhile comparing to convenience theory. Fraud theory with the fraud triangle suggests three conditions for fraud (Cressey, 1972): (1) incentives and pressures, (2) opportunities, and (3) attitudes and rationalization. Incentives and pressures belong in the economical dimension; opportunities belong in the organizational dimension; while attitudes and rationalization belong in the behavioral dimension. As such, the fraud triangle covers all dimensions of convenience theory. However, at the core of convenience theory is convenience in all three dimensions as well as opportunity found in the organizational setting based on professional role and trust by others. Furthermore, convenience theory emphasizes the relative importance of convenience, where offenders have alternative legitimate actions available to respond to incentives and pressures, but they choose illegitimate actions since these actions are considered more convenient.

Convenience theory relates to Clarke's (1999) hot products, where he studied the targets of theft. He found that hot products include residential burglary, theft from cars, theft of cars, commercial vehicle theft, and shoplifting. Hot products are targets for crime. White-collar crime is committed for economical gain, which implies that items of value that belong to others are taken over in an illegal way. The takeover can occur directly by theft or indirectly by corruption, where competitors lose because the customer is bribed by another competitor. Other ways of depriving others of assets include fraud and manipulation.

In this chapter, a number of well-known theories are introduced to explain the economical dimension of convenience theory.

The economical dimension of convenience theory is concerned with threats and possibilities where white-collar crime can help in terms of illegal financial gain. An illegal financial gain can help reduce or eliminate threats, and an illegal financial gain can help explore and exploit possibilities.

Not all members of the elite are as successful as they would like to be. Some feel that they are not provided with the ability to achieve their ambitious goals. They blame the system rather than themselves for their lack of success, and they compensate through white-collar crime (Wood and Alleyne, 2010).

MOTIVATIONAL CHARACTERISTICS

The motive for white-collar crime is simply financial gain. The motive for financial gain, however, can vary. Crime might be a response to both possibilities and threats, and it might be a response to both strengths and weaknesses. An offense can enable exploration and exploitation of a business or a personal possibility that may otherwise seem unobtainable. An offense can enable avoidance of business or personal threats. An offense can make the business or the personal situation even stronger, and it can reduce and compensate for business or personal weaknesses.

Financial gain as a motive for white-collar crime can either benefit the individual or the organization. If illegal financial gain benefits the individual, it is labeled occupational crime. The individual benefits personally from illegal economical gain in a setting where his or her occupation enables white-collar crime. The motive for personal financial gain can vary in terms of possibilities and threats, and strengths and weaknesses. Examples of possibilities include increased personal wealth to enjoy as well as enjoyment through providing others – such as relatives and friends – with gifts and benefits. Examples of avoidance of threats include avoidance of personal bankruptcy and avoidance of falling from a high-status position based on being rich. Examples of strengths include a strengthened role in the local community and increased admiration at work. Examples of compensation for weaknesses include buying friends and compensating for lack of popularity by paying for others.

When financial gain as a motive for white-collar crime benefits the organization, it can again be explained by possibilities, threats, strengths, and weaknesses. Possibilities include achieving a new contract and establishing a subsidiary in a corrupt country. Threats include avoidance of bankruptcy for the business, where tax evasion and bank fraud can be relevant forms of white-collar crime. Strengths can be improved in terms of higher share prices and better corporate reputation. Examples of weaknesses that can be compensated by illegal financial gain include avoidance of loss of key personnel, continuation of risky business practices, and growth rather than consolidation in the firm.

As discussed so far, there are all kinds of motives and motivations for white-collar crime. A motive is something that causes someone to act in a certain way and do certain things. Similarly, motivation is a theoretical construct used to explain behavior. Motivation represents the reasons for people's actions, desires, and needs. Motivation involves personality and cultural factors that induce individuals to act in ways that neutralize the strong ethical controls of society. Specific cultural factors that lead to crime and criminal behavior include the desire to make a fast buck and the fear of losing what has already been made (Aguilera and Vadera, 2008).

Motivation is different from, but at the same time linked to, opportunity (Steffensmeier and Allan, 1996: 478): "Motivation is distinct from opportunity, but the two often intertwine, as when opportunity enhances temptation. As in legitimate enterprise, being able tends to make one more willing, just as being willing increases the prospects of being able."

The various motives and reasons for white-collar crime can be summarized in a pyramid as illustrated in Figure 2.1. The figure is a simplified version of Figure 1.2. The pyramid represents a hierarchy of needs and desires that people have. As suggested by Maslow a long time ago, everyone has a desire to climb higher and higher in this pyramid (Maslow, 1943). Many white-collar criminals seem willing to risk everything for success and status at the top of the pyramid.

When starting at the bottom, people want food, clothes, and shelter. Immigrants from poor countries can be found at this level. Next, people want security and safety. Refugees can be found at this level. Higher up, we find the need for self-realization and self-respect. Then follows admiration and respect by others, before success and fame. Finally, an individual's highest level is to be a hero.

We find members of the elite in the upper half of the pyramid. They would like to climb to the top and stay at the top. White-collar crime can help them both climb to the top and remain at the top.

Maslow developed the pyramid of human needs in his motivation theory about what motivates people to action. The needs in the pyramid are physiological needs, safety needs, social needs, and needs for esteem and self-actualization. White-collar crime is motivated by the two upper levels, social needs and needs for esteem and self-actualization. Here we find needs for status, success, recognition, influence, and admiration. This is in contrast to street crime, which often is motivated by physiological needs. According to Maslow, needs for status and success are insatiable.

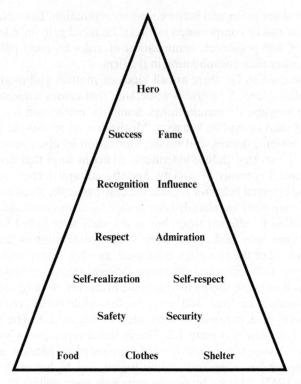

Figure 2.1   Pyramid of human needs

White-collar criminals are by definition already situated in the upper half of Maslow's hierarchy of needs, but they want to climb higher. They strive for fulfillment, self-esteem, and esteem from others. As Agnew (2014: 2) formulates it: "crime is often the most expedient way to get what you want" and "fraud is often easier, simpler, faster, more exciting, and more certain than other means of securing one's ends".

Glory and power are important to many in the elite in society. They care about status symbols that cost money. They care about being treated as very important persons (VIPs), having reserved parking spaces, and being preferred customers in noble restaurants. They care about flying first class on planes, and they care about staying in suites in hotels. At work, they care about having the corner office on the top floor with a large meeting table and comfortable chairs to show their position. Visible status symbols of all varieties are often self-perpetuating when it comes to power. It is convenient to enjoy privileges and status symbols. The maintenance of façade and personal reputation is important to keep their positions in the elite.

When their positions in the elite are threatened, some try to compensate through white-collar crime.

Many law-abiding members of the elite use their economic prosperity to climb to the top of Maslow's hierarchy of needs. Rich people want respect and reputation as well as status and admiration in the community. This can be achieved by giving away money through philanthropic behavior. A philanthropist is someone seemingly without self-interest willing to help the disadvantaged while ignoring financial gain. The richest person in the city of Bergen in Norway gave substantial sums to research at the University of Bergen. He was rewarded with the title of Doctor Honoris Causa by the university, which denotes considerable prestige. A shipowner was also awarded an honorary doctoral degree after having donated large sums of money to the University of Oslo.

Words like status, privileges, recognition, fame, and admiration are all associated with both law-abiding and criminal white-collar people. Economic crime is committed by white-collar offenders to climb, to maintain position in, or to avoid falling from the pyramid.

Climbing the pyramid by both law-abiding and criminal individuals can be explained by the American dream theory. The American dream suggests that everyone in America has the possibility of becoming monetarily successful. A high white-collar crime rate can be attributed to the commitment to the goal of material success as experienced in the American dream. It is caused by an overemphasis on success in apparent assets (Schoepfer and Piquero, 2006), and it is not matched by a concurrent emphasis on what means are legitimate for reaching desired goals (Pratt and Cullen, 2005). When fewer people experience that they are able to live the American dream by means of law-abiding behavior, more will explore alternative avenues.

A white-collar criminal wrote in his autobiography about his American dream (Kerik, 2015: 146): "I had lived a version of the American dream: a high school dropout who with ambition, hard work, and a lot of good luck rose to the cusp of one of the highest positions in the land." The American dream emphasizes economic success, while at the same time society is perceived to be restricting individuals' access to legitimate opportunities for upward socioeconomic mobility, which, in turn, can result in high levels of criminogenic anomie in society (Pratt and Cullen, 2005).

The opposite of the American dream theory is the fear of falling theory. While the dream is about climbing up the pyramid, the fear is about falling down from the pyramid. Fear of falling theory suggests that people in leading positions are afraid of the consequences of failure and therefore try to survive in their positions by applying various means (Piquero, 2012). They are afraid of falling off the financial cliff and losing their wealth and status. Therefore, they work constantly to remain successful, preferably more successful than others, while not having the time to relax and enjoy their wealth because of their fear of failure. It is this struggle for financial success and the maintenance of that success which are important to them. The fear of falling leads to solutions to problems such as acute illiquidity in terms of financial crime as the only way out of the crises. Profit-driven crime is thus not only an issue of making even more money. Rather, it is an issue of survival, and it may be about rescuing a sinking ship.

THEORY OF PROFIT-DRIVEN CRIME

White-collar crime relates to profit-motivated offenses based on economical possibilities and threats. Fraud and embezzlement are two examples. Fraud is asset crime in which the offender gains access to money or other valuables by subjecting someone to an action based on false premises (Füss and Hecker, 2008). Embezzlement is gaining access to money or other valuables without any consent from the owner.

Naylor (2003) attempts to provide a general theoretical model and a clarified terminology by which profit-driven crime can be understood in economic rather than sociological terms. It proposes a typology that shifts the focus from actors to actions. Rather than focusing on profit-driven crime as a logical sequence of actions, it deconstructs a profit-driven crime into its inherent characteristics, which differ radically according to whether a crime is predatory, market-based, or commercial in nature. Among the principal characteristics is whether transfers of property occur by force, free-market exchange, or fraud; whether those transfers involve redistribution of wealth, distribution of income, or redistribution of income; and/ or whether the crime occurs in a non-business, underground network or legitimate business setting. This approach answers the how, rather than the who or why.

In conformity with the managerial perspective in business literature, which highlights the role of managers as agents in deciding enterprise strategies and operations (Lopez-Rodriguez, 2009), as well as leading the activities required to implement corporate priorities, managers can develop and implement both legal and illegal strategies. Managers' perceptions and interpretations determine their commitment to certain goals over other goals (sub-goals). The goal of business enterprises is to make a profit, which can be achieved both legally and illegally. Strong and ambitious goal orientation in competitive markets can lead to a strategic choice of white-collar crime. Profit-driven crime by both legal and criminal business enterprises should be understood mainly in economic rather than sociological or criminological terms. The amounts involved can be staggering (Menon and Siew, 2012). Leonard and Weber (1970: 408) argued that too little attention has been paid to market forces as a reason for criminal behavior: "Insufficient attention has been focused by sociologists on the extent to which market structures – that is, the economic power available to certain corporations in concentrated industries – may generate criminal conduct."

In Naylor's (2003) theory of profit-driven crime, predatory offenses involve redistribution of existing legally owned wealth from one party to another. Market-based offenses involve evasion of regulations, taxes, and prohibitions. Commercial offenses involve illegal methods to distribute goods and services. Predatory crime involves the illegal redistribution of existing wealth, market-based crime involves the illegal earning of new income, and commercial crime involves the illegal redistribution of legally earned income.

Wealth refers to a stock of assets that has been accumulated, and it is measured at a point in time. On the other hand, income refers to a flow of value per unit of time. Predatory crime is crime purely of redistribution of existing wealth. Examples include bank fraud and embezzlement. Market-based crime is crime of distribution of new income. Examples include tax evasion and environmental pollution. Commercial crime is crime of illegal methods. Examples include corruption and cartel pricing with competitors.

Profit-driven crime can occur in situations characterized by threats and situations characterized by possibilities. Threats of bankruptcy, loss of bonus, loss of position, degradation, divorce, layoff, expulsion, forced sale of cottage or house, lack of achievement, and loss of prestige can be reduced and eliminated by an unfair financial gain. Illegal appropriation of assets may cause the company to avoid bankruptcy; the sales director to get a bonus; the CEO to retain their job; the deputy director to be promoted rather than degraded; the company to reach its financial targets on the bottom line; and the company and executives to appear to be successful.

Economic threats may occur both in private life and at work. In private life it may revolve around financial disorder, soaring debt, and the striving for status in line with the hierarchy for recognition and influence. Gambling insanity can cause acute economic needs. Embezzlement at work might be a convenient solution to get rid of such a threat. On rare occasions it is not economic threats, but other kinds of threats that can be solved by economic crime. If a bank manager attended a party with criminals in the mafia, where pictures were taken while the bank manager had relations with a prostitute, the bank manager may subsequently be willing to launder money for the mafia. If a customs station manager experiences threats to his or her children from smugglers, then the manager may be willing both to inform about border controls and to fail to conduct border controls.

Threats in the workplace may stem from specific market conditions and market forces. Some business enterprises can be so dominant in an industry that others may only survive through economic crime. The threat of losing everything they have built up by working very hard over a long period of time may cause owners who once were entrepreneurs to intervene and commit value added tax (VAT) fraud and tax evasion in order to prevent their own empire collapsing. The alternative for the former entrepreneurs can be bankruptcy crime by removing all assets before bankruptcy so that creditors receive little or nothing. The purpose is to protect the economic interests of the business (Blicke et al., 2006) and possibly start up again without debts.

Threats can come from a monopoly, where potential competitors have the choice either to commit crime or to join the monopoly (Chang et al., 2005). When competitors have formed a cartel, an emerging business may have the choice of either joining the illegal collusion or going bankrupt. Economic balance, preferably excess, is a requirement in the long run to survive in all kinds of markets (Brightman, 2009).

Profit-driven crime is not only committed in situations characterized by threats. Offenses are also committed in situations characterized by possibilities. They are committed to safeguard financial possibilities. Possibilities for overseas establishment, added bonus, promotion, and prestige gain can be achieved through economic crime. By bribing local officials, successful overseas investments can take place, and the project director can receive an extra bonus for the success. The director may also be promoted, and the company can be recognized as a global player. Also in private life, the need to explore and exploit possibilities can arise. Greed leads to a need for an increasingly larger house, several cabins, bigger boats, and more expensive holidays. Again, the solution can be to commit embezzlement at work.

Goldstraw-White (2012) defines greed as socially constructed needs and desires that can never be completely covered or contented. Greed can be a very strong quest to get more and more of something, and there is a strong preference to maximize personal wealth. The more, the better.

In our sample of 405 convicted white-collar criminals to be presented later in this book, most of them pursued possibilities rather than avoided threats when they committed financial crime. Few of them give an impression of being in distress and thus having basic needs in Maslow's pyramid. The vast majority had a motive reminiscent of status and self-actualization at the top of the hierarchy of needs.

THEORY OF GOAL ORIENTATION

Profit orientation becomes stronger in goal-oriented organizations, whose aim tends to be an ambitious financial bottom line (Jonnergård et al., 2010). In such organizations, goals tend to justify means – even criminal means – to achieve desired profit at the bottom line. For example, corruption may seem acceptable to achieve long-term profit goals. In goal-oriented businesses, increased profits can be expedient both for the business (corporate crime) and for executives (occupational crime), who retain their jobs, enjoy promotion, and receive bonus payments. There is a greater degree of criminogenity – that is, propensity for financial crime – in organizations that are primarily or exclusively controlled and managed by ambitious financial goals, because a failure to achieve these goals may have very negative consequences, while achievement of them may have very positive consequences for the organization as well as for executives.

Dodge (2009: 15) argued that it is tough rivalry that makes executives in the organization commit crime to attain goals: "The competitive environment generates pressures on the organization to violate the law in order to attain goals."

Profit-oriented crime is less likely in organizations that do not aim to make money. Therefore, we expect less white-collar crime in the public sector compared to the private sector. Most of the public sector is managed by rules rather than objectives. When rules – such as zero tolerance against corruption – emerge in conflict with goals, then rules are mostly followed in the public sector. The situation is the opposite in the private sector, where rules are ignored if they prevent the achievement of objectives.

As expected, only 8 percent of the convicted 405 white-collar criminals worked in the public sector in Norway. In addition to management by rules rather than objectives, another explanation for the low percentage can be found in public service motivation theory. This theory suggests that people who enter into job positions in the public sector do it for reasons other than to make money.

THEORY OF STRAIN AND STRUGGLE

Threats cause strain and struggle to reduce and compensate for the threats. The central concept of strain theory is that society sets universal goals for its population and then offers the ability to achieve them to a limited number of people. Similarly, an organization often sets ambitious goals, and then very few members are able to achieve them. The resultant inequality of opportunity causes strain and creates a motive for white-collar crime (Wood and Alleyne, 2010).

The strain of pursuing goals within diverse opportunity structures, such as in an organizational context, may lead to adaptations of crime, delinquency, and other deviant behavior. The disjunction between goals and means creates strain that an individual wants to overcome. Unrealistic expectations may come from a number of sources, including families, friends, media, life events, and self (Hoffmann, 2002).

Agnew (2005) identified three categories of strain: failure to achieve positively valued goals, the removal of positively valued stimuli, and the presentation of negative stimuli. Strain theory posits that each type of strain ultimately leads to deviance for slightly different reasons. All three types tend to increase the likelihood that an individual will experience negative emotions in proportion to the magnitude, duration, and proximity of stress. Strains most likely to result in crime are those seen as unjust and high in magnitude, associated with low social control, proximity of threat and consequence, and the creation of some incentive to engage in criminal behavior.

Strains are defined as events and conditions which are disliked by individuals. Strains lead to negative emotions and thereby create pressure for corrective action. Crime is one possible action, which might be perceived as a means to escape from or reduce strains (Froggio and Agnew, 2007). The strain of pursuing goals within diverse possibility structures may lead to adaptations such as crime, delinquency, and other deviant behaviors (Hoffmann, 2002). Delinquency results when individuals are unable to achieve their goals through legitimate channels (Agnew, 2012).

Sources of strain include failure to achieve inspiration, failure to achieve aspiration, and failure to achieve a fair and just outcome. Individuals who suffer strongly from failure to achieve goals will be more likely to commit financial crime because they want to reclaim their position.

In an empirical study by Langton and Piquero (2007), they found that strain theory was useful for predicting a select group of white-collar offenses. Using data about convicted white-collar offenders, they examined the ability of strain theory to explain white-collar offenses. First, they found that strain was positively and significantly related to financial motivations for offending. Second, they found that individuals reporting higher levels of strain were more likely to engage in more complex types of financial crime. Third, they found that strain was related to negative emotions. Finally, they found that strain among white-collar offenders was negatively related to business-type motivations for offending.

Strain among white-collar criminals can be measured in terms of (Langton and Piquero, 2007):

1. number of legal marriages, where two or more legal marriages are assumed to imply more strain
2. neighborhood, where lower-class or lower middle-class neighborhoods are assumed to imply more strain
3. academic performance, where failure to achieve positively valued goals is assumed to imply more strain
4. total assets, where less wealth is assumed to imply more strain
5. total liabilities, where more debts are assumed to imply more strain
6. employment history, where failure to achieve positively valued goals is assumed to imply more strain.

Levels of white-collar crime can be measured in terms of offense types, which form a hierarchical pattern in terms of their organizational complexity and the harm they inflict (Langton and Piquero, 2007):

1. low-level white-collar crime such as embezzlement, tax offenses, and credit fraud
2. mid-level white-collar crime such as mail fraud, bribery, and false claims
3. complex large-scale corporate crime such as antitrust and securities violations.

By means of logistic regression, Langton and Piquero (2007) attempted to predict crime level by strain factors. They proposed that more strain would lead to a higher level of white-collar crime. Overall, however, they found no significant support for this explanation.

Strain has many potential causes. The theory of crime forces suggests that the market is such that the only way to survive is to implement financial practices similar to the ones applied by competitors (Leonard and Weber, 1970). If corruption is the name of the game, every business has to provide bribes to stay in business.

Strain typically occurs in times of economic failure and inability to achieve class status. Strain triggers negative emotional states such as anger, fear, or depression, with anger being potentially the most criminogenic emotion. Of course, not all strained individuals resort to illegitimate coping strategies because there are often legitimate – but less convenient – coping mechanisms they could turn to. Different types of strain appear to influence different types of negative effects which in turn influence whether a legitimate or illegitimate method of coping is used to adapt to strain. Angry responses to strain seem to increase the likelihood of illegitimate coping while no angry responses to strain appear to decrease the probability of illegitimate coping (Ngo and Paternoster, 2016).

THEORY OF RATIONAL SELF-INTEREST

The economic perspective is concerned with the influence of rational self-interest in explaining the development of white-collar crime (Pillay and Kluvers, 2014). The economic model of rational self-interest is all about weighing up the pros and cons of alternative courses of actions. The model considers incentives and probability of detection (Welsh et al., 2014). This applies to both private and professional life. Human behavior finds motivation in the self-centered quest for satisfaction and avoidance of suffering (Hirschi and Gottfredson, 1987). The rational approach to white-collar crime finds support in an empirical study by Bucy et al. (2008), which identified a number of motives for white-collar crime. According to their survey, greed is the most common cause of criminal acts (Hamilton and Micklethwait, 2006). Money and other forms of financial gain are always the target of crime.

The economic model implies that white-collar individuals pursue their goals, make tradeoffs between likely consequences and select actions from several available options. When crime is attractive as a means to fulfill desires and satisfy needs, a rational actor chooses that option. The white-collar individual conducts an assessment of the benefits and costs, where crime is chosen if the benefits of crime exceed the costs of crime. Included in the costs of crime is the damage suffered by the individual in case of detection multiplied by the perceived probability of detection. Since the perceived probability of detection usually is very low, the costs associated with crime are also very low.

Because the economic model implies that crime can be a rational choice, the crime rate will be lower where the risk of detection is perceived to be greater, and where the punishment is stricter (Pratt and Cullen, 2005). Rational choice theorists have taken a position that assumes that the standard economic theory of individual preferences will determine whether crime is committed. The greater the benefits of crime and the less the costs of crime, the more attractive it is to commit criminal acts.

However, Kamerdze et al. (2014) argue that impulses, emotions, and feelings play a role in individuals' preferences and utility functions, and therefore are relevant to the theory of rational choice, because cognitive processes of decision-makers will be affected. For example, the feeling of discomfort may prevent a white-collar person from committing crime, even if he or she has a great need for financial gain to achieve personal goals and/or objectives for the business.

The economic model of rational self-interest does not imply that every individual in the same situation will conclude and act in the same way. There will be different choices in the same situation because rationality is a subjective matter. For example, the objective detection risk will be the same in the same situation, while the subjective detection risk will vary with individual variations in risk willingness and risk aversion. A person with high risk willingness and low risk aversion will tend to perceive the detection risk as very low, while a person with low risk willingness and high risk aversion will tend to perceive the detection risk as not so low. Research suggests that there is a gender gap in terms of subjective detection likelihood. For example, women tend to have a stronger belief in speed control when driving on the highway. Therefore it is argued that men tend to drive faster than women on the highway. The explanation for why women more often adhere to speed limits is thus not necessarily that they prefer to be more law-abiding than men.

The economic model of rational self-interest is affected by many factors. An interesting factor is the extent of economic benefits after disclosure, sentencing, and prison. If a potential criminal expects that illegal financial gain will be tracked down and confiscated, there is little to look forward to after imprisonment. On the other hand, a potential criminal can calculate that a five-year prison stay will attract an annual salary of 200,000 dollars if a million dollars are waiting on release. Especially for white-collar criminals with greed as their main motive, concealment of financial gain is critical in the case of crime disclosure. Therefore, many white-collar criminals invest much effort in hiding and concealing illegal financial gain both to avoid detection and to avoid confiscation. Tax havens and faithful family and friends are means of succeeding in such efforts. On the other hand, law enforcement is committed to confiscating most profit from economic crime in terms of asset recovery. If law enforcement succeeds to a greater extent in terms of withdrawal of illegal profits, then the economic model suggests that criminogenity will decline among white-collar people. An interesting example is Norway, where legislation was introduced to change the burden of proof. Earlier, law enforcement had to prove that assets were acquired in illegal ways. Now, prosecuted individuals and firms have to prove that assets were acquired in legal ways. If they are unsuccessful in providing such proofs, then assets will be confiscated.

If the individual assesses economic crime as an attractive action in the form of gain now (profit for the realization of current ambitions) compared to possible future cost (punishment, isolation, loneliness), and the individual prefers to avoid the use of more time and effort to solve problems preventing the realization of ambitions, then convenience theory says that crime will occur. White-collar crime is not the emotional abuse of power and influence. Such crime is rarely spontaneous or emotional. It is based on calculated risks. It is a consequence of the selection of a convenience solution for a challenge or a problem.

While the economic model of rational self-interest considers personal benefits versus detection risk and associated costs for the offender (Welsh et al., 2014), Agnew (2014) suggests that economic crime can also be committed when the individual thinks more of benefits for others than for themselves. An entrepreneur can commit financial crime to ensure that all employees have a job to return to. A trusted employee can pay bribes to make sure that the company will have new orders to survive in the future. An executive may commit embezzlement to be able to help his or her adult children recover after personal bankruptcy.

Agnew (2014) believes that social concern consists of four elements, namely that individuals (1) care about the welfare of others, (2) want close ties with others, (3) are likely to follow moral guidelines such as innocent people should not suffer harm, and (4) tend to seek confirmation through other people's actions and norms. That a person puts others before himself or herself will initially lead to less crime. But economic crime may be committed where the welfare of others and their success is the motive.

The theory of rational self-interest suggests that people who commit crime do so after considering the risks of detection and punishment (risk assessment) to be less important to them than the rewards (financial gain) of completing criminal acts successfully. Persons who do not commit crime decide that completing the act successfully is too risky and not worth the benefits (Lyman and Potter, 2007). In other words, if the rationally expected utility of an action clearly outweighs the expected disadvantages resulting from the action, thereby leaving some net material advantage, then every person would commit the offense in question (Blickle et al., 2006).

In organized crime, Shvarts (2001) suggests that rational choice theory can explain the growth of the Russian mafia. Because of low income and financial difficulties at the individual level, combined with a corrupt police force, it seems rational to move into organized crime to improve the standard of living for members joining the criminal organization.

Rational choice theory suggests that humans are selfish, focused on achieving their own individual happiness directly or indirectly through the enjoyment of helping others. Happiness is considered the highest moral purpose of rational existence. Altruism, in contrast, is thus irrational and determinative of undesirable outcomes. Here, sacrifice is the antithesis of rationality, where the individual chooses an action independent of personal utility. Self-interest is defended in the rational choice theory by contrasting it with irrational sacrifice (Barry and Stephens, 1998).

Rational choice theory adopts a utilitarian belief that the economical individual is a reasoning actor who weighs means and ends, costs and benefits to make a decision whether or not to commit white-collar crime.

For example, an increase in detection rate will cause a decrease in crime rate (Hefendehl, 2010).

Rational choice by individuals can sometimes be explained by their actions and by their reactions to others' actions. White-collar crime can be both an act of actions and an act of reaction. The choices individuals make are determined by the anticipated utility, viewed as an indication of individuals' beliefs and preferences that behavioral strategies are expected to produce.

The theory of rational self-interest adopts a utilitarian belief that the economical individual is a reasoning actor who weighs means and ends, costs and benefits to make a decision whether or not to commit white-collar crime. Utility theory suggests that a criminal will attempt to maximize the utility from criminal behavior. An expected utility maximizing criminal commits an illegal act and, if he or she is neither caught nor punished, increases personal or organizational wealth.

In conclusion, the economical dimension of white-collar crime emphasizes the motive, which is financial benefit for the purpose of avoiding pain (such as bankruptcy) or gaining advantage (such as market share). Within convenience theory, profit-driven crime is explained by goal orientation, strain and struggle, rational self-interest, and other perspectives from management and criminology. Illegal profit can be an end or a means to an end, as we have illustrated using the hierarchy of needs.

3. Organizational dimension of convenience theory

The organizational dimension sets white-collar criminals apart from other financial criminals. Abusing social security benefits, committing tax evasion, or committing Internet fraud on a personal level is not considered white-collar crime. White-collar crime is defined as financial crime committed in a professional capability in an organizational context.

While possibilities in the economical dimension are concerned with convenient abilities for the achievement of goals (avoid threats and gain benefits such as real estate and foreign establishment), opportunities in the organizational dimension revolve around how crime can be committed conveniently. The economical dimension answers the why, while the organizational dimension answers the how of white-collar crime. We distinguish between the economic ability to realize wishes, meet needs, and fulfill desires, and the professional opportunity to implement white-collar crime in connection with regular business activities. Corruption, bank fraud, and embezzlement are typical examples of financial crime in professional settings.

An organization is a system of coordinated actions among individuals and groups with boundaries and goals (Puranam et al., 2014). An organization can be a hierarchy, a matrix, or a network or any other kind of relationship between people in a professional work environment (Dion, 2008).

PROFESSIONAL CHARACTERISTICS

Ahrne and Brunsson (2011) argue that an organization is characterized by membership, hierarchy, monitoring, and sanctions. Organizations decide about membership; about who will be allowed to join the organization as employees. Membership brings a certain identity with it, an identity that differs from that of non-members. Organizations include a hierarchy; a duty to oblige others to comply with decisions. Hierarchy entails a form of organized power. Organizations can issue commands, and can also decide upon rules that its members are expected to follow in their actions. An organization has the right to monitor compliance with its commands and rules. Organizations have the right to decide about sanctions, both positive and negative. They can decide to change a member's status by using promotions, grading systems, awards, diplomas, and medals.

Organizational members have different roles that lead to different degrees of power and influence. Some organizational members have to do, and indeed do, what they are told. Other members decide what should be done. Power and influence is associated with level in the organizational hierarchy, tasks to be performed, and individual freedom. Some members enjoy substantial individual freedom even though they can be found at lower levels of the organization.

White-collar crime is committed by privileged individuals in the elite. They typically enjoy substantial individual freedom in their professions, with little or no control. A typical example is the chief executive officer (CEO). The CEO is the only person at that hierarchical level in the organization. Below the CEO, there are a number of executives at the same hierarchical level. Above the CEO, there are a number of board members at the same hierarchical level. But the CEO is alone at his or her level. The CEO is supposed to be controlled by the board, but the board only meets once in a while to discuss business issues. Executives below the CEO are typically appointed by the CEO and are usually loyal to the CEO.

Power, influence, and freedom are typical professional characteristics not just of CEOs; some politicians, government officials, heads of religious organizations, and other leading figures in society also enjoy trust without control. Some independent professions, such as lawyers and doctors, enjoy the same kind of freedom.

The organizational anchoring may result in some revealed white-collar criminals avoiding investigation, prosecution, and conviction. The business may be too powerful or important to collapse (such as banks), and the criminals may be too powerful to jail. After the downturn in the US economy in 2008, many expected bank executives to be prosecuted, but they were not. Pontell et al. (2014: 10) explain why it did not happen:

> From a criminological standpoint, the current financial meltdown points to the need to unpack the concept of status when examining white-collar and corporate offenses. The high standing of those involved in the current scandal has acted as a significant shield to accusations of criminal wrongdoing in at least three ways. First, the legal resources that offenders can bring to bear on any case made against them are significant. This would give pause to any prosecutor, regardless of the evidence that exists. Second, their place in the organization assures that the many below them will be held more directly responsible for the more readily detected offenses. The downward focus on white-collar and corporate crimes is partly a function of the visibility of the offense and the ease with which it can be officially pursued. Third, the political power of large financial institutions allows for effective lobbying that both distances them from the

criminal law and prevents the government from restricting them from receiving taxpayer money when they get into trouble.

A similar lack of prosecution and punishment can be found in private fraud investigations. For example, Valukas (2010) identified executive misconduct as the reason for the bankruptcy of Lehman Brothers, but the investigation nevertheless concluded that executives were legally not to blame. Therefore, they were never prosecuted.

The organizational setting focuses on the profession and position associated with a business or other kinds of entity that makes it possible to carry out criminal acts. A profession is an occupation for which a person is eligible by virtue of education and experience. In a narrow sense, a profession is a group of professionals with the exclusive right to perform certain work because they have completed a special education. Examples are medical doctors and attorneys. This definition is too narrow in our context. Profession is here broadly defined as a qualified occupational practice based on knowledge and experience. Dion (2009) argues that organizational culture makes it possible to adopt organizational purposes and objectives, which are basically deviant in comparison with social norms yet in line with the competition. Deviant purposes can be chosen when business corporations are trapped by doubtful, immoral, or disloyal means that are used by competitors. They could also be trapped by the business milieu as a social institution. Furthermore, they could be trapped by their own sector-based morality, which is oriented toward profit maximization.

THEORY OF CRIME OPPORTUNITIES

Organizational opportunity is a distinct characteristic of white-collar crime that varies with the persons who are involved in crime (Michel, 2008). An opportunity is attractive as a way of responding to needs (Bucy et al., 2008). It is the organizational dimension that gives white-collar criminals the opportunity to commit economic crime and hide it in seemingly legal activities in the business.

Aguilera and Vadera (2008: 434) describe a criminal opportunity as "the presence of a favorable combination of circumstances that renders a possible course of action relevant". Opportunities for crime occur when individuals and groups can engage in illegal and unethical behavior and expect, with a certain confidence (Haines, 2014), that they will avoid detection and punishment. Opportunity to commit white-collar crime can be found at the community level, the business level, and the individual level. At the community level, control regimes might be absent, and entire industries may be available for financial crime. An example here could be the construction industry, where one can find instances of both cartels and undeclared work. Another example could be tax collection authorities that are unable to trace and control accounting figures from businesses, thereby opening up the possibility of tax evasion with minimal risk of detection and punishment.

Huisman and Erp (2013) argue that a criminal opportunity has the following five characteristics: (1) the effort required to carry out the offense, (2) the perceived risks of detection, (3) the rewards to be gained from the offense, (4) the situational conditions that may encourage criminal action, and (5) the excuse and neutralization of the offense.

At the business level, ethics and rules can be absent, while economic crime is a straightforward business practice. An example here is subsidy fraud, where ferry companies report lower traffic numbers to ensure greater government transfers. Another example is internal invoice fraud, where the accounting department lacks the overview of who is allowed to approve what invoices.

At the individual level, greed can dominate where the business does not have an adequate reaction to economic crime. One example here might be law firms where partners abuse money in client accounts. Another example is corruption, where the bribed person receives money from the bribing person without anybody noticing on either side.

Benson and Simpson (2015) write that the organizational opportunity to commit white-collar crime manifests itself through the following three characteristics: (1) the offender has lawful and legitimate access to the premises and systems where crime is committed, (2) the offender is geographically separated from his or her victim, and (3) criminal acts appear to be legitimate business.

This is very different from street crime such as violence and burglary, where the offender has no legal access, the offender is in the same location as his or her victim, and the offense does not appear to be legal. A fundamental difference between white-collar crime and street crime is that while white-collar criminals conceal their crime but do not hide themselves, street criminals do not conceal their crime but hide themselves. Street crime is easily detected, while street criminals are not always easy to find. White-collar crime is difficult to detect, but white-collar criminals are easy to find.

White-collar crime does not take place privately; it takes place on the job. The organization is the venue for crime. McKendall and Wagner (1997) describe the opportunity as context and environmental conditions that facilitate rather than prevent the carrying out of criminal activities. For example, in the case of corruption, both the briber and the bribed are linked to a job context. The briber typically uses company money to pay, while the bribed receives the money personally because his or her organization is attractive to the bribing company.

The organizational dimension through work represents the offender's crime scene. By virtue of employment, ownership, position, relations, and knowledge, the offender can explore and exploit his or her association with the organization to commit financial crime. As sales executive, the person can pay bribes, and as procurement executive, the person can receive bribes. As finance executive, the person may safely commit embezzlement by fixing accounting figures, and as chief accountant, the person can manipulate accounting to perform tax evasion. As chief executive, the person can sign fake contracts or order fraudulent appraisals that open up possibilities for bank fraud by asking the bank to finance future income expected from contract partners and the sale of real estate. There are ample opportunities for economic crime by executives and others linked to enterprises. Examples of these others include administrative managers, attorneys, auditors, bank managers, board members, boat dealers, car dealers, concert organizers, councilmen, district managers, entrepreneurs, investors, management consultants, mayors, medical doctors, members of parliament, nursery owners, property developers, real-estate agents, shipbrokers, stockbrokers, and surveyors.

White-collar crime opportunities occur through the three characteristics described by Benson and Simpson (2015). The opportunities are greatest for top executives and other members of the elite in society. In relation to convenience theory, the three characteristics make it comfortable, easy, and convenient to commit financial crime to solve a problem or overcome a challenge. It may be relatively simple and thus convenient for white-collar elite members to hide criminal activities in the stream of legal activities, and thus give crime an outer semblance of credibility in a respectable business (Pickett and Pickett, 2002).

Opportunity makes a thief, it is sometimes stated. If the availability of legal opportunities to solve problems and exploit possibilities deteriorates, while illegal opportunities flourish and are considered convenient, then white-collar individuals will become less law-abiding. If fraud, theft, manipulation, and corruption are easily docked in the enterprise, while law-abiding alternatives are invisible or hard to implement, then opportunity creates an offender.

Organizational opportunity for economic crime depends on the intellectual and social capital that is available to the potential white-collar criminal. Intellectual capital is knowledge in terms of understanding, insight, reflection, ability, and skill. Social capital is relations in hierarchical and transactional exchanges. Social capital is the sum of actual and potential resources available for white-collar individuals by virtue of his or her position in formal and informal hierarchies, networks, and matrices (Adler and Kwon, 2002). Formal as well as informal power means influence over resources that can be used for crime.

White-collar offenders are often not alone when committing financial crime. They may cooperate with people internally as well as with people externally. If there is internal crime cooperation, then it may be more convenient for each individual to participate. An environment where crime is accepted strengthens the organizational opportunity. If there is external crime cooperation, then it may again be more convenient for each individual to participate. External actors who, for example, submit fake invoices or receive bribes, enter into a relationship with the internal actor(s) with a code of silence.

The organizational dimension of white-collar offenses is particularly evident when crime is committed on behalf of the business. A distinction is often made between white-collar criminals who commit financial crime for personal gain and white-collar criminals who do it for their employer (Trahan, 2011). The first is labeled occupational crime, while the second is labeled corporate crime. Examples of corporate crime include manipulation of financial figures for tax evasion and unjustified government subsidies, bribery to obtain contracts, false loan applications to obtain credit from banks, and money laundering in tax havens to recruit securities clients. The organizational anchoring of crime is evident in corporate offenses as crime takes place within the business and to the benefit of the business (Bradshaw, 2015).

While occupational crime is often hidden by the individual to enrich himself or herself by abusing corporate resources (Hansen, 2009), corporate crime is often hidden by a group of individuals to improve business conditions. In both cases, crime is committed by virtue of position and trust in the organization, which prevents monitoring, control, and accountability.

Heath (2008) found that individuals who are higher up on the ladder in the company, tend to commit larger and more serious occupational crime. The same is probably the case for corporate crime. Empirical studies by Gottschalk (2016, 2017) show that corporate criminals are older, commit crime for larger sums of money, and are connected to larger organizations than occupational criminals. The studies support the assumption that white-collar criminals at the top of the ladder commit financial crime for far larger amounts of money than white-collar collar offenders further down the hierarchical ladder. This finding applies to both occupational and corporate crime.

Corporate crime, often called organizational offenses or business crime (Reed and Yeager, 1996), typically results from the actions of several individuals in more or less rooted cooperation. If a business representative commits crime on behalf of the organization, it is defined as corporate crime. If the same person commits crime for personal gain, it is defined as occupational crime. At criminal prosecution in the criminal justice system, both occupational crime and corporate crime are individualized, because a company cannot be sentenced to prison. A business can only be fined (Bookman, 2008). The Norwegian database with 405 convicted white-collar criminals contains 68 offenders (17 percent) who committed financial crime on behalf of the organization. Corporate crime represents violations of integrity as well as failure to comply with moral standards, as in the example of corruption managed by Siemens in Germany as described by Eberl et al. (2015).

The organizational dimension implies that the business is the basis for deviant acts. Sometimes the organization is also a victim of crime. In the Norwegian study, 28 percent of all convicted white-collar criminals victimized their own employers; 19 percent caused damage to society at large, for example by tax evasion; 18 percent caused harm to customers; 15 percent caused bank losses; 8 percent caused loss among shareholders; and the remaining 12 percent hurt others.

The organizational dimension of white-collar crime also becomes evident when several people from the same enterprise are involved in offenses (Ashforth et al., 2008), and when the organization is characterized by a criminal mindset (O'Connor, 2005), whether it concerns occupational crime or corporate crime. A single, stand-alone white-collar criminal can be described as a rotten apple, but when several are involved in crime, and corporate culture virtually stimulates offenses, then it is more appropriate to describe the phenomenon as a basket of rotten apples or a rotten apple orchard, like Punch (2003: 172) defines it: "The metaphor of 'rotten orchards' indicates that it is sometimes not the apple, or even the barrel that is rotten but the *system* (or significant parts of the system)."

White-collar crime is characterized by opportunism. There must be an opportunity to commit elite crime. If opportunities are limited, there will be less crime. This is evident when looking at the distribution of white-collar crimes between women and men. There are far fewer women than men in positions of trust with privileges and little control. Therefore, it is not surprising that there are far fewer white-collar offenders among women than men. In Norway, women constitute only 7 percent of white-collar inmates, while the rest are men.

Opportunity arises out of certain jobs. For example, the opportunity to engage in health care fraud is obviously facilitated if one has a job in the health care system. Individuals who are in key positions and involved in networks based on trust have increased access to criminal opportunities. The opportunity perspective is important, because these offenses usually require special business-related access to commit conspiracies, frauds, embezzlements, and other kinds of financial crime (Benson and Simpson, 2015).

Offenders take advantage of their positions of power with almost unlimited authority in the opportunity structure (Kempa, 2010), because they have legitimate and often privileged access to physical and virtual locations in which crime is committed, are totally in charge of resource allocations and transactions, and are successful in concealment based on key resources used to hide their crime. Offenders have an economic motivation and opportunity (Huisman and Erp, 2013), linked to an organizational platform and availability, in a setting of people who do not know, do not care, or do not reveal the individual(s) with behavioral traits who commit crime. Opportunity includes people who are loyal to the criminal either as followers or as silent partners.

THEORY OF PRINCIPALS AND AGENTS

The principal–agent theory (or simply agency theory) can illuminate white-collar crime in an organizational context. Principal is a term for a person or a body that leaves work to an agent. The agent carries out the work for the principal. The principal may be a board of a company that leaves the corporate management to the CEO. The CEO is then the agent in the relationship. The CEO may in turn entrust tasks to other executives, where the CEO becomes the principal, while people in positions such as chief financial officer (CFO), chief operating officer (COO), and chief tecnology officer (CTO) are agents. Agents perform tasks on behalf of principals.

The agency perspective describes problems that may arise between principal and agent because of diverging preferences and different values, asymmetry in knowledge of activities and performance, and different attitudes to risk. Principals must always suspect that agents make decisions that benefit themselves at the expense of the principals. For example, a CEO may cheat and defraud owners (Williams, 2008), and a purchasing manager can fool the CEO when selecting vendors (Chrisman et al., 2007), by taking bribes that can cause the company to pay more for inferior quality, for instance.

Agency theory is based on the assumption of narrow self-interest. The problem arises whenever one party (a principal) employs another (an agent) to carry out a task. The interests of principal and agent diverge, and the principal has imperfect information about the agent's contribution (Bosse and Phillips, 2016). According to principal–agent analysis, exchanges encourage private gain (Pillay and Kluvers, 2014).

In agency theory, managers are treated as opportunistic agents motivated by individual utility maximization. Taking an economic model of man that treats human beings as rational actors seeking to maximize individual utility, when given the opportunity, executives will maximize their own utilities at the expense of shareholders. Based on an analysis of the evolution of CEOs' leadership and power, Shen (2003) proposes that boards need to focus on CEO leadership development in early CEO tenure, but should then shift their focus toward the control of managerial opportunism as CEOs prove their leadership on the job.

In agency theory, there are three problems: preferences (principal and agent may have conflicting values or goals), knowledge (principal and agent may not have the same information and insights), and risk (principal and agent may not have the same kind of risk aversion or risk willingness). In terms of preferences, the principal's and the agent's best interests may not align. The desires and goals of the principal and the agent may be in conflict. In terms of knowledge, it is difficult or expensive for the principal to verify what the agent is actually doing. When it comes to risk, the principal and the agent may have different attitudes.

Shareholders employ some agents in the form of board members. Board members recruit an agent as CEO. The CEO employs a number of top executives. Top executives recruit middle managers. Thus, principals and agents can be found at different levels of the corporate hierarchy, and some individuals are in the role of principal in one relationship and in the role of agent in another relationship.

Principals expect agents to make decisions in the best interests of the principals. However, due to agency problems, agents may not make these decisions. On the contrary, agents may succumb to self-interest, opportunistic behavior, and lack of understanding of requests from principals.

Generally, corruption and other forms of economic crime are in agency theory considered to be a consequence of the principal's inability to control and prevent the agent from abusing his or her position for personal gain (Li and Ouyang, 2007). However, the principal may as well be the criminal. For example, the CFO may provide inside information to a board member who abuses the information for insider trading. The point here is that the principal and the agent have different roles in an organizational context, where they both have little information about each other's activities.

While occupational crime is an agency problem where the criminal abuses agency roles for personal benefit, corporate crime is a structural problem where the enterprise is to benefit. Most countries' jurisdictions make a similar distinction between a natural person (individual) and a juridical person (organization), and demand criminal liability in terms of prison versus fine.

Agency theory is a management theory often applied to crime, where normally the agent, rather than the principal, is in danger of committing crime. White-collar crime is thus illegal and unethical actions usually by agents of organizations (Vadera and Aguilera, 2015). Agency theory describes the relationship between principal and agent using the concept of work-based interactions. The agent carries out work on behalf of the principal in an organizational arrangement. Principal–agent theory holds that owners (principals) have different interests from administrators (agents), such that principals must always suspect agents of making decisions that benefit themselves, to the cost of principals. In a principal–agent perspective, there is an opportunity for the white-collar offender to carry out the regular job at the same time as crime is committed, because the principal is unable to monitor what the agent is doing, what knowledge the agent applies, and what risk the agent is willing to take (Chrisman et al., 2007; Li and Ouyang, 2007; Williams, 2008). Agency theory argues that the principal is unable to control the agent because of lack of insight and lack of access to the activities performed by the agent in roles such as mayor, chairperson, or CEO (Eisenhardt, 1985).

Agency theory has broadened the risk-sharing literature to include the agency problem that occurs when cooperating parties have different goals and division of labor. The cooperating parties are engaged in an agency relationship defined as a contract under which one or more persons (the principal(s)) engage one or more persons (the agent(s)) to perform some work-based service on their behalf, which involves delegating some decision-making authority to the agent (Jensen and Meckling, 1976). Agency theory describes the relationship between the two parties using the metaphor of a contract about work-based interactions.

Goal conflict typically occurs when the two parties do not share productivity gains. The risk-sharing problem might, for example, result from different attitudes toward the use of new technologies (Eisenhardt, 1985). Because the unit of analysis is the contract governing the relationship between the two parties, the focus of the theory is on determining the most efficient contract governing the principal–agent relationship given assumptions about people (e.g., self-interest, bounded rationality, risk aversion), organizations (e.g., goal conflict of members), and information (e.g., information is a commodity that can be purchased).

Agency theory has long been applied to crime. Garoupa (2007) applied the theory to criminal organizations. He modeled the criminal firm as a family business with one principal and several agents. He had an illegal monopoly in mind, where it is difficult to detect and punish the principal unless an agent is detected. Furthermore, it is assumed that agents work rather independently so that the likelihood of detection of one agent is fairly independent from that of another. An example of such agents is drug dealers in the street with the principal being the local distributor. Another example would be agents as extortionists or blackmailers distributed across a city with the principal being the coordinator of their activities, providing them with information or criminal know-how.

A similar principal–agent relationship to that in criminal organizations can be found in legal organizations. For example, when the principal asks an agent to succeed for the company in a market in a corrupt country, the principal stays away from all activities that could link him or her to corruption. The principal simply does not want to know how the agent succeeded in the market.

Gross (1978: 65) discussed criminals as agents for a criminal organization in the following way:

> Although organizations are here held to be criminogenic and although courts no longer exhibit much hesitation in charging the organization itself with crime, organizations of course cannot themselves act – they must have agents who act for them. Who will the persons be who will act for organizations in their criminal behavior?

Agency theory in management studies is primarily used for situations where two parties enter into a contract, but the reasoning of the theory is also relevant when no formal contract is signed or, what might be more relevant, when the contract does not deal with issues brought forward by agency theory. An agency relationship arises whenever an individual or an organization is authorized to act for or on behalf of another individual or organization (Benson and Simpson, 2015).

Agents often provide principals with some sort of specialized service based on the agent's expertise and training. They do things that principals may not have the ability, expertise, time, or willingness to do for themselves. Principals place their trust in agents and hope that they will act in their best interests (Benson and Simpson, 2015).

Arnold et al. (2012) argue that one reason for corruption is that inappropriately installed incentive systems produce outcomes in which both principals and agents act in a harmful manner in society. Organizational complexity allows criminals to hide their activities within legal transactions.

Deception is closely related to the abuse of trust. Abuses or violations of trust occur in agency relationships. Agents sometimes abuse trust placed in them by their principals. The relationship is unbalanced, and the agent's actions may be based on factors that the principal has no way of knowing about (Benson and Simpson, 2015). Therefore, white-collar crime in an organizational context may be a convenient opportunity.

THEORY OF SOCIAL DISORGANIZATION

Social disorganization leads to the breakdown of conventional social norms. The gradual erosion of conventional relationships weakens the organization and makes it unable to satisfy the needs of its members. The organization gradually loses the ability to control the behavior of its members. There is no functional authority over potential white-collar criminals in the organization (Wood and Alleyne, 2010). As a consequence of social disorganization, organizational opportunity to commit white-collar crime increases.

Lack of social control attenuates bonding mechanisms by making supervision and interpersonal attachments more tenuous. Social disorganization weakens the ability of social bonds to circumscribe delinquent behavior. Instability, heterogeneity, and broken relationships reduce the likelihood of supervision. Social disorganization negatively affects the ability to reduce delinquent behavior (Hoffmann, 2002).

Decisions are made in the organization by people with decision-making powers. A decision may be defined as a choice between two or more alternative courses of action. In convenience theory there are two options: the legal option and the illegal option. Decision-makers often choose the option that is most convenient. In a socially disorganized enterprise, the regular decision-making structure has disappeared, and everyone tries to make decisions at their own discretion.

Teleworking reduces the ability to track what others are doing in the organization. While meetings have a role in establishing who is in charge, the lack of meetings leads to personal initiatives and freedom that conveniently can be exploited. Teleworking is characterized by tasks performed using information and communication technology at other places and often at other times than when colleagues perform their tasks. Modern technology enables work to be completed whenever the worker would like to. Independence in time and space makes work more individualized and less subject to control. This includes tasks performed by trusted and privileged people in the enterprise. Social bonds disappear and create a vacuum that can be perceived as social disorganization.

The organizational opportunity for financial crime can be particularly evident when an executive handles a business problem all by himself or herself. For example, a CFO of a publishing house was to liquidate the publisher's involvement in a chain of bookstores. Upon liquidation of the involvement and receipt of the settlement, it was very tempting for the CFO to channel some of the proceeds to himself or herself. Another example is the president (and priest) in a religious foundation that was to establish retirement homes and nursing homes in Spain for old

Norwegians. The president had sole rights to manage money in an account in a Spanish bank. It was tempting for him to misuse some of the money. In fact, he lived a double life in the economical dimension of convenience theory. While being a proper family man and priest in Norway, he organized wild parties with prostitutes in Spain.

Socially disorganized enterprises culturally transmit criminal traditions that are transmissible as any other cultural elements. When executives and other privileged individuals are exposed to delinquent traditions, some of them succumb to delinquent behavior. In such a cultural climate, white-collar crime becomes a satisfying alternative to unsatisfactory legitimate conventions. If the organization fails to adequately provide for its members, they will absorb alternative cultural traditions. The cultural formation and the criminality that emanates from it are passed from experienced executives to newcomers via socialization, motivating young people to deviate from conventional norms (Wood and Alleyne, 2010). As a consequence of cultural deterioration, the organizational opportunity to commit white-collar crime increases.

Some organizations have a culture where they only selectively comply with regulatory mandates. They buffer against and resist external forces. They ignore regulatory enforcement and other external pressures, and they select response strategies such as symbolic forms of action, window dressing, or outright ignorance. Desai (2016) found that one reason for ignorance is that new regulatory mandates create uncertainty regarding how, when, and in what ways the organization should respond to these external pressures. An organization's prior history of compliance influences its ability and motivation to satisfy future compliance requirements.

Some new laws are broad enough to allow organizations significant discretion in the nature or timing of their compliance responses. Some regulatory mandates can be misinterpreted, mistranslated, or misconstrued by executives. Information asymmetries between regulators and regulated organizations, and the lack of knowledge sharing between these distinct parties, discourage organizational compliance efforts (Desai, 2016). A culture where compliance is not important makes delinquency and white-collar crime more convenient.

Crime may occur, for example, when the organization is dysfunctional in its collaborative relationships (Dion, 2008), where individuals' needs and feelings are completely ignored. In many organizations, people are left completely to themselves, and as a consequence, they take what they think they deserve. In a matrix organization, the vertical activities may operate legally, while the horizontal activities may operate illegally. In a network organization, the core, the peripherals, or parts of the network may be open to financial crime.

Social disorganization increases offenders' opportunities to commit financial crime without being detected. Offenders have unrestricted and legitimate access to the location in which the crime is committed without any kinds of controls. Offenders' actions also have a superficial appearance of legitimacy internally, since both legal and illegal actions in the organization are characterized by disorganization (Benson and Simpson, 2015).

Social disorganization theory argues that crime is a function of people dynamics in the organization and between organizations, and not necessarily a function of each individual within such organizations. Business enterprises experiencing rapid changes in their social and economic structures will experience higher crime rates. Management mobility is another structural factor or antecedent that can be held to produce organizations that are socially disorganized. Conventional mechanisms of social control are weak and unable to regulate the behavior within organizations (Pratt and Cullen, 2005).

Especially in knowledge organizations, where the hierarchical structure tends to be weak, social controls among colleagues are of importance to prevent financial crime. An unstable and disorganized unit will suffer from lack of knowledge exchange and collaboration to prevent and detect white-collar crime (Swart and Kinnie, 2003).

Structural antecedents include not only management instability and rapid organizational changes, but also external factors such as family disruptions and no intelligence about life outside work. Social disorganization can be found at the very top of organizations, where chief executives have created large business spaces for themselves without allowing access to others. There are no ties allowing others to act collectively to fight problems (Pratt and Cullen, 2005).

Social control is the opposite of social disorganization. Social control theory argues that individuals will restrain from committing white-collar crime if society and the organization has processes that prevent them from doing so (Abadinsky, 2007: 22):

> Social control refers to those processes by which the community influences its members toward conformance with established norms of behavior. Social control theorists argue that the relevant question is not, Why do persons become involved in crime, organized or otherwise? but, rather, Why do most persons conform to societal norms? If, as control theorists generally assume, most persons are sufficiently motivated by the potential rewards to commit criminal acts, why do only a few make crime a career? According to control theorists, delinquent acts result when an individual's bond to society is weak or broken. The strength of this bond is determined by internal and external restraints. In other words, internal and external restraints determine whether we move in the direction of crime or of law-abiding behavior.

Social control theory is also concerned with relationships between the individuals being controlled and those that perform the controls (Tiwana and Keil, 2009: 13):

> We define attempted control as the extent to which a controller attempts to utilize a given control mechanism to influence controlee behavior. Attempted control therefore refers to the control mechanisms that the controller implements in a given project, independent of whether or how they are exercised. We define realized control as the extent to which the controller is able to successfully exercise a given control mechanism during the systems development process. An attempted control mechanism must be effectively exercised, or realized, for it to enhance systems development performance.

Corporate disorganization weakens the ability of social bonds to circumscribe delinquent behavior. In enterprises characterized by instability and heterogeneity, the likelihood of effective socialization and supervision is reduced. The impact of social bonds varies by type of organization and disorganized units negatively affect the ability of social bonds to reduce delinquent behavior (Hoffmann, 2002).

Social disorganization can be a result of one or more deviant cultures in the organization. Deviant culture theory argues that joining a criminal subculture in the upper class will increase the likelihood of white-collar crime (Lyman and Potter, 2007: 70): "The subculture shares a lifestyle that is often accompanied by an alternative language and culture. The lower-class lifestyle is typically characterized by being tough, taking care of one's own affairs, and rejecting any kind of governmental authority." Cultural deviance theories are based on the assumption that, for example, slum dwellers violate the law because they belong to a unique subculture that exists in lower-class areas. The subculture's values and norms conflict with those of the upper class on which criminal law is based (Lyman and Potter, 2007).

Social networks may play an important role in the incidence of white-collar crime. An example of social networks is people sharing a common religion, religious language, and history composed of stories of events, a homeland, and oppression. They may have ancestors who emigrated from the same regions in the world, and they may have settled in certain population clusters (Corcoran et al., 2012).

THEORY OF STRATEGIC RESOURCES

White-collar offenders have access to resources to commit financial crime in convenient ways. Furthermore, they have access to resources to conceal crime as well as to prevent prosecution if they are detected. Resource-based theory postulates that differences in individuals' opportunities can be explained by the extent of resource access and the ability to combine and exploit resources. A resource is an enabler that is used to satisfy human needs. A resource has utility and limited availability.

Resource-based theory applied to white-collar crime implies that executives and other members of the elite are potential white-collar offenders that are able to commit financial crime to the extent that they have access to resources that can be applied to criminal actions. Strategic resources are characterized as being valuable, unique, not imitable, not transferable, combinable, exploitable, and not substitutable:

1. *Valuable resource.* Application of the resource provides a highly appreciated outcome. For example, a supplier can be a valuable resource if the vendor is willing to participate in fictitious invoicing.
2. *Unique resource.* Very few have access to this resource, because it is exceptional and rare. For example, an outstanding attorney can be a unique asset if the counterparty has inferior legal assistance.
3. *Not imitable resource.* It is not possible to imitate or copy this resource. For example, an accounting system for subsidy fraud is difficult to copy.
4. *Not transferable resource.* The resource cannot be released from its context or be moved in any way. For example, price fixing in a cartel is difficult to move to a different industry.
5. *Combinable resource.* The resource can be combined with other resources in such a way that it results in an even more highly appreciated outcome. For example, a frayed property appraiser can be combined with a criminal property developer to commit bank fraud.
6. *Exploitable resource.* The white-collar individual is able to apply the resource in criminal activities. For example, a corrupt son of a government minister may be bribed to influence his father so that the business is successful in obtaining local licenses and contracts.
7. *Not substitutable resource.* The resource cannot be replaced by another resource to achieve a correspondingly high-valued result. For example, only the corrupt son of a government minister and no one else is available for corruption to successfully obtain local licenses and contracts.

Organizational opportunity to commit economic crime depends on the social capital that is available to white-collar offenders. The structure and quality of social relations in hierarchical and transaction-oriented relationships determine the degree of social capital that the offender can exploit. Social capital is the sum of the actual and potential social resources available in a hierarchy and in a network (Adler and Kwon, 2002). Formal as well as informal power means influence over resources that can be used for crime.

Access to resources in the organizational dimension makes it more relevant and attractive to explore possibilities and avoid threats using financial crime. The willingness to exploit a resource for white-collar crime increases when it is perceived as convenient. The legal management of key personnel and other resources is important so that the white-collar offender has the ability to commit economic crime by virtue of his or her position in a comfortable way. The resource-based theory implies that the difference between success and failure for white-collar offenders can be explained by the efficient or inefficient ability to leverage strategic resources.

Not only do white-collar offenders have access to resources to carry out financial crime, they also have access to resources to cover criminal acts. Criminal acts are easily hidden in a multitude of legal transactions in different contexts and different locations performed by different people. The organizational affiliation makes crime look like ordinary business. Economic crime is easily concealed among apparently legal activity. Offenders leverage resources that make it convenient to conceal crime among regular business transactions. In particular, businesses that practice secrecy enable convenient concealment of financial crime. For example, many multinational companies do not disclose what they pay in taxes in various countries. This kind of secrecy makes it easy to conceal economic crime such as corruption, since regular financial statements are not accessible. Secrecy combined with sloppy and opportunistic accounting can make financial crime even more attractive. Accounting is no mathematical discipline. Rather, the value of accounts receivable, business contracts, and warehouse stocks are subject to personal judgments. Auditors are often criticized in the aftermath when financial crime is disclosed.

Chasing profits leaves people more creative in finding ways to make more legal as well as illegal profits for themselves and the organization, and people become more creative in concealing crime in various ways (Füss and Hecker, 2008). Crime is carried out in such a way that the risk of detection is minimal and even microscopic (Pratt and Cullen, 2005).

In the rare case of detection of potential crime, the possible offender has access to strategic resources like few others. Available resources include better defense, private investigations, and presentation in the media. The suspected offender can hire the best attorneys, paid by the organization or personally. The best attorneys do not limit their efforts to substance defense, where legal issues are at stake. The best defense lawyers also conduct information control and symbolic defense. Information control is concerned with the flow of damaging information about the client. A defense attorney will attempt to prevent police from exploring and exploiting various sources of information collection. Information control implies taking control over the information sources that are most likely to be contacted by the police. The police have many information sources when they investigate a case, and these sources can, to a varying extent, be influenced by a defense attorney.

Information is the raw material in all police work. The relative importance of and benefits derived from pieces of information are dependent on the relevance to a specific crime case, the quality of information, and the timeliness of information. Information value in police work is determined by information adaptability to police tasks in an investigation. A smart defense lawyer can reduce information value by lowering its fitness for policing purposes. Information quality can be reduced in terms of accuracy, relevance, completeness, conciseness, and scope.

In addition to substance defense and information control, a white-collar defense lawyer is typically involved in symbolic defense. A symbol is an object or phrase that represents an idea, belief, or action. Symbols take the form of words, sounds, gestures, or visual images. Symbolic defense is concerned with activities that represent defense, but in themselves are no defense. It is an alternative and supplement to substance defense. Substance and symbolic defense are different arenas where the white-collar attorney can work actively to try to make the police close the case, to make the court dismiss the case, and to enable the reopening of a case to allow the client to plead not guilty. The purpose of symbolic defense is to communicate information and legal opinions by means of symbols. Examples of attorney opinions are concerns about unacceptable delays in police investigations, low-quality police work, or other issues related to police and prosecution work. Complaining about delays in police investigations is not substance defense, as the complaint is not expressing a meaning about the crime and possible punishment. Complaining is symbolic defense, where the objective is to mobilize sympathy for the white-collar client.

Where a possible crime is detected, the potential offender has access not only to better defense as a strategic resource, but also to an alternative avenue of private investigation. When suspicion of misconduct and crime emerges, the organization may hire a fraud examiner to conduct a private investigation into the matter. The enterprise takes control of suspicions by implementing an internal investigation. An external law firm or auditing firm is engaged to reconstruct past events and the sequence of events. Typically, the resulting investigation report points to misconduct, while at the same time concluding that there have been no criminal offenses. The police will monitor the internal investigation and await its conclusion.

When the conclusion states that there may be misconduct, but no crime, the police and prosecution tend to settle with that.

In addition to better defense and private investigation as available resources in case of detection of possible crime, the potential offender can also hire public relations consultants. These consultants help tell a story to the media where the potential offender is presented as a victim of unfortunate circumstances.

Furthermore, a white-collar defendant may behave in court in such a way that he or she often gets more sympathy and a milder sentence than other defendants, partly because the person belongs to the same segment in society as the judge, prosecutor, and attorney. Finally, a convicted offender has the expertise and network to hide criminal profits and protect himself or herself against confiscation, so that the government will be unsuccessful in its attempts at asset recovery.

If a white-collar criminal should end up in jail, defense attorneys work hard to make prison life as easy as possible for the client. Attorneys argue that it is much worse for a member of the elite to end up in prison than for other people. After a short while, the white-collar offender, however, typically gets most of his or her freedom back in an imprisonment setting to avoid too much damage. Additionally, research indicates that it is easier for a white-collar criminal than for a street criminal to spend time in prison. White-collar offenders tend to find new friends more easily, and they are able to sleep all night, while most other inmates may have trouble sleeping and making friends in prison (Dhami, 2007; Stadler et al., 2013).

Nevertheless, defense lawyers apply the special sensitivity hypothesis, which claims that white-collar offenders are ill-equipped to adjust to the rigors of prison life (Stadler et al., 2013: 1091):

> Termed the "special sensitivity hypothesis", the claim is made that white-collar offenders experience the pains of imprisonment to a greater degree than traditional street offenders. Upon incarceration, they enter a world that is foreign to them. In the society of captives, status hierarchies found in the larger community are upended, as those with more physical prowess and criminal connections "rule the joint". White-collar offenders discover that they are no longer in the majority in a domain populated largely by poor and minority group members – in fact, prison is a place that a researcher suggests is the functional equivalent of an urban ghetto.

Furthermore, Stadler et al. (2013) found that research investigating the sentencing of white-collar offenders has revealed that federal judges often base their decisions not to impose a prison sentence for white-collar offending on a belief that prison is both unnecessary for and unduly harsh on white-collar offenders.

The essence of resource-based theory lies in its emphasis on the internal resources available to privileged individuals in the elite, rather than on external forces. Resources are available to conveniently commit crime, conceal crime, and avoid consequences in case of detection. According to the resource-based theory, performance differences can be attributed to the variance in individuals' and firms' resources and capabilities. Firms are considered to be highly heterogeneous, and the bundles of resources available to each firm are different. This is both because firms have different initial resource endowments and because managerial decisions affect resource accumulation and the direction of firm development as well as resource utilization.

Resource-based theory rests on two key points. First, resources are the determinants of individual and firm performance. Second, resources are only available to a few. Individuals and firms must continually enhance their resources and capabilities to take advantage of changing conditions.

Increased access to resources makes white-collar crime more convenient. On the contrary, reduced access to resources makes white-collar crime less convenient. From a law enforcement perspective, white-collar crime can be detected and prevented to the extent to which members of the elite are precluded from access to resources.

THEORY OF INSTITUTIONAL COLLAPSE

According to institutional theory, organizational context, behaviors, and processes may support white-collar crime. Institutional theory has been used to explain both individual and organizational actions including aspects of administrative and management practice. Organizational behaviors reflect a culture that evolves over time and becomes legitimized within an organization and society. Corruption and other kinds of financial crime become entrenched by the legitimizing process. Institutional theory assumes that there is a willingness of individuals and groups to follow predetermined and acceptable patterns of behavior that are supported by the environment. In the case of corruption, this may not be so much society's support, but its lack of support of an anti-corruption culture (Pillay and Kluvers, 2014).

An institution is characterized by values, where norms, behaviors, and ways of thinking are deeply rooted in the culture. Institutional theory seeks to explain what is normal behavior and freedom of action in an organization. The theory attempts to explain how an organization adapts to its surroundings, and how employees adapt to the organization by living the set of norms, values, and rules that are dominant in the organization.

In organizations with low morale, the propensity for unethical behavior will be greater, which can create favorable conditions for economic crime (Shadnam and Lawrence, 2011).

While the theory of social disorganization is concerned with collapse caused by internal forces, the theory of institutional collapse is concerned with breakdown caused by external forces.

As most individuals aspire to internal legitimacy by complying with their organizational context, most organizations aspire to external legitimacy by complying with their institutional context. Institutional context can be defined as customs and behavior patterns important to a society. As structures and mechanisms of social order, institutions represent stable, valued, and recurring patterns of behavior within a given community. Institutions develop and function in a pattern of social self-organization beyond the conscious intentions of the individuals involved. Institution is a word derived from Latin *institutio* from *instituere* ("to set up"), from ("in, on") and *statuere* ("to set up, establish"). An institution encompasses accepted rules and common cultural values for the community. (The term institution is also used to describe formal organizations of the government and public services, but this is not the focus of institutional theory.)

An institution is a stable set of rules supported by surveillance and sanctions. An institution is a structure that controls behaviors; it is predominantly normative, and it manifests itself in symbols such as words, gestures, and signs to convey meaning to objects and activities. Both the internal environment of organizations and the external environment may allow corruption and other forms of financial crime to develop (Pillay and Kluvers, 2014). Both the internal and external legitimacy of deviant behavior and misconduct contribute to the organizational convenience of white-collar crime.

Corruption and other forms of financial crime are encouraged when uncertainty and power concentration occur with regulation and institutional pressures, such as opaqueness, lack of transparency, injustice, and complexity. Organizational architecture, resulting from interactions between culture, structure, system, and roles, determines the extent of convenience of white-collar crime. A dysfunctional organizational architecture creates organizational deficiency and damage (Pillay and Kluvers, 2014).

A code of silence in the institution makes detection quite unlikely. Executives' solidarity is an antecedent of incivility and deviant behavior. Rather than blowing the whistle on each other, the code of silence tells everyone to keep quiet and look the other way. Solidarity refers to a situation in which the well-being of an offender or offending group is positively related to that of others, indicating mutual interdependence. Incivility refers to inappropriate social encounters representing low-intensity deviant behavior. Compared to high-intensity behaviors such as bullying or aggression, incivility represents a milder form of interpersonal mistreatment. Workplace deviance is defined as voluntary behavior that violates significant organizational norms and in so doing threatens the well-being of an organization, its members, or both (Itzkovich and Heilbrunn, 2016). The code of silence combined with solidarity with those who commit white-collar crime represents institutional deterioration where incivility and deviant behavior becomes the norm rather than the exception.

Many white-collar crime occurrences are linked to the exploitation and abuse of existing routines and practices within the organization. There may be procedures for controlling invoices, for recognition of contracts, and for accounting principles. Such routines, practices, and procedures can be abused in white-collar crime by making illegal transactions appear normal. A routine can be defined at two levels: the routine procedure and the routine application. It may be convenient to both manipulate the procedure and abuse the application. A routine is subject to interpretation by those who apply the routine. Moreover, the performance of a routine in terms of actions is dependent on the user's knowledge, skills, abilities, and attitudes (Pentland et al., 2010).

Institutional theory provides insights into organizational behavior that is influenced by individuals, other organizations, and the community that they are part of (Shadnam and Lawrence, 2011). Institutional theory applied to white-collar crime leads to criminal acts that have fertile ground in the business because of moral decay and collapse. Crime can be a natural response to the company's situation, where both the organization and the environment expect a response (Rostami et al., 2015).

Shadnam and Lawrence (2011: 379) applied institutional theory to explain moral decline and potential crime in organizations:

> Our theory of moral collapse has two main elements. First, we argue that morality in organizations is embedded in nested systems of individuals, organizations and moral communities in which ideology and regulation flow "down" from moral communities through organizations to individuals, and moral ideas and influence flow "upward" from individuals through organizations to moral communities. Second, we argue that moral collapse is associated with breakdowns in these flows, and explore conditions under which such breakdowns are likely to occur.

Shadnam and Lawrence (2011: 393) formulated several research hypotheses, which imply that the likelihood of moral decline will vary depending on several circumstances:

- Moral collapse is more likely to happen in organizations that operate in moral communities in which flows of ideology are disrupted, either through a lack of commitment to formal communication mechanisms by community leaders or the disruption of informal communication networks by high rates of membership turnover.

- Moral collapse is more likely to happen in organizations in which structures and practices diminish the organization's capacity to absorb and incorporate morally charged institutions from the organization's moral community, because the organization monopolizes the attention of its members and/or because the organization delegitimizes the morally charged institutions rooted in the moral community.
- Moral collapse is more likely to happen in organizations in which accusing individuals of misconduct creates significant social and economic costs for the organization or the moral community within which it operates.
- Moral collapse is more likely to occur in organizations to the degree that employment conditions undermine disclosure and/or work arrangements diminish the effectiveness of surveillance.

Institutional theory is mainly a sociological and public policy perspective on organizational studies. The theory sheds light on normative structures and activities. Institutional theory in public policy emphasizes the formal and legal aspects of government structures. Signs from organizations are observed as indications of values in organizational members. When activities are repeated in the same way and within the same structure, then those activities are institutionalized, and the sum of activities based on shared perceptions of reality can be defined as an institution (Hatch, 1997).

Institutional theory considers the processes by which structures, including schemes, rules, norms, and routines, become established as authoritative guidelines for social behavior. Institutional adaption is caused by political, cultural, and social influences. Behavioral patterns supported by norms, values, and expectations lead to cultural influence. A desire to equal others implies social influence. Normative institutional pressure is concerned with conformity, where deviance is disliked, disapproved of, or even dismissed (Hatch, 1997).

Structural determinants, such as the socioeconomic and political, or institutional, environmental context in which the individual engages in offenses, influence the extent of organizational opportunities to commit white-collar crime.

An organization exists in multiple institutional environments, requiring interaction with many audiences. Institutional collapse will typically lead to a lack of willingness in the environment to associate with the organization. The organization may simply be blacklisted (McDonnell and Werner, 2016).

THEORY OF SOCIAL CONFLICTS

In addition to being too big to fail and too powerful to jail (Pontell et al., 2014), professional characteristics of offenders are such that they belong to the elite in society that make the laws. When associated with powerful organizations, elite members may avoid negative attention even when they are responsible for misconduct and crime.

Social conflict theory suggests that the powerful and wealthy in the upper class of society define what is right and what is wrong. The rich and mighty people can behave like robber barons because they make the laws and because they control law enforcement. The ruling class does not consider white-collar offenses as regular crime, and certainly not similar to street crime. Nevertheless, individuals in the elite who commit crimes tend to be prosecuted if crime is detected and evidence of wrongdoing is present, as long as they are not too powerful (Pontell et al., 2014) and do not have too excellent defense attorneys.

Social conflict theory views financial crime as a function of the conflict that exists in society. The theory suggests that class conflict causes crime in any society, and that those in power create laws to protect their rights and interests. For example, embezzlement by employees is a violation of law in order to protect the interests of the employer. However, it might be argued that an employer must and should protect its own assets. Bank fraud is a crime in order to protect the powerful banking sector. However, in the perspective of conflict theory one might argue that a bank should have systems making bank fraud impossible. If an employee has no opportunity to commit embezzlement, and if a fraudster has no opportunity to commit bank fraud, then these kinds of financial crime would not occur, and there would be no need to have laws against such offenses. Law enforcement protects powerful companies against counterfeit products, although they should be able to protect themselves by reducing opportunities for the production of counterfeit products.

Social conflict theory holds that laws and law enforcement are used by dominant groups in society to minimize threats to their interests posed by those whom they perceive as dangerous and greedy. Crime is defined by legal codes and sanctioned by institutions of criminal justice to secure order in society. The ruling class secures order in the ruled class by means of laws and law enforcement. Conflicts and clashes between interest groups are restrained and stabilized by law enforcement.

According to social conflict theory, the justice system is biased and designed to protect the wealthy and powerful. The wealthy and powerful can take substantial assets out of their own companies at their own discretion whenever they like, although employed workers in the companies were the ones who created the value. The superrich can exploit their own wealth that they created as owners of corporations as long as they do not hurt other shareholders. Employees have no right to object. It is no crime to take out value from one's own enterprise and build private mansions with the money. This is no crime by the owners. Even when the owners just inherited the wealth created by earlier generations, they can dispose freely of it for private consumption. Similarly, top executives who are on each other's corporate boards grant each other salaries that are ten or twenty times higher than regular employee salaries. As Haines (2014: 21) puts it, "financial practices that threaten corporate interests, such as embezzlement, are clearly identified as criminal even as obscenely high salaries remain relatively untouched by regulatory controls". Furthermore, sharp practices such as insider trading that threaten confidence in equities markets have enjoyed vigorous prosecution, since the powerful see them as opaque transactions that give an unfair advantage to those who are not members of the market institutions.

Karl Marx, who analyzed capitalism and suggested the transition to socialism and ultimately to communism, created the basis for social conflict theory. Capitalism is an economic system in which persons privately own trade, industries, firms, shops, and means of production and operate these enterprises for profit. Socialism is an economic system characterized by cooperative enterprises, common ownership, and state ownership. Communism is a socioeconomic system structured upon the common ownership of the means of production and characterized by the absence of social classes.

Marxist criminology views the competitive nature of the capitalist system as a major cause of financial crime. It focuses on what creates stability and continuity in society, and it adopts a predefined political philosophy. Marxist criminology focuses on why things change by identifying the disruptive forces in capitalist societies, and describing how power, wealth, prestige, and perceptions of the world divide every society. The economic struggle is the central venue for the Marxists. Marx divided society into two unequal classes and demonstrated the inequality in the historical transition from patrician and slave to capitalist and wage worker. It is the rulers versus the ruled. Marx also underlined that all societies have a certain hierarchy wherein the higher class has more privileges than the lower one. In a capitalist society where economic resources equate to power, it is in the interest of the ascendant class to maintain economic stratification in order to dictate the legal order.

THEORY OF TRANSACTION COSTS

Transaction costs include efforts, time, and direct payments linked to search, development, negotiations, risks, management, and control of relationships with others. Transaction costs can reduce the profitability of white-collar crime and increase the likelihood of detection. Transaction costs occur when an offender has to deal with other individuals and organizations. White-collar criminals will attempt to minimize transaction costs and orient criminal activity toward offenses where transaction costs are low.

Transaction costs include both costs associated with conflicts and costs associated with misunderstandings (Wright, 2006: 58):

> Transaction costs apply both to legitimate business and to illicit enterprises. They include the costs of conflicts and misunderstandings that lead to delays, to breakdowns and to other malfunctions. They can include such things as the costs of incentives, of ensuring co-ordination and the enforcement of regulations, rules or customs. In the case of a criminal organization, controlling transaction costs is necessary to keep it protected from betrayal and from prosecution. This includes the need to protect the organization from informers and from others (such as law enforcement agencies) who threaten its profits and stability. For such organizations, the use of violence and coercion is often the most effective way of reducing transaction costs.

Wright (2006: 58) studied organized crime and found that, for example, mafia groups consider transaction costs before criminal acts are carried out: "Mafia groups consider the costs of each transaction in estimating the risk involved in their drug dealing operations. Betrayal of the group by informers leading to disruption of operations, seizure of drugs and arrest of group members is the predominant transaction cost in such cases." Violence and threats can here be considered both as transaction costs and as means to reduce transaction costs. By use of threats and violence a criminal might expect that the victim will behave more in accordance with criminal expectations.

Transaction costs occur when someone leaks to the police, and when someone attempts whistleblowing, as the criminal has to increase efforts for covering up and hiding traces and paths. To keep someone silent, a white-collar criminal may have to bribe someone, and in such a situation the bribe can be considered a transaction cost.

An indication of transaction costs in white-collar crime is the number of individuals involved in crime. In our sample of 369 convicted white-collar criminals from 2009 to 2014 in Norway, there were 101 criminals who operated alone, thus causing no transaction costs. We can assume that a rising number of involved persons cause an increase in transaction costs. The distribution of involved persons as a measure of transaction costs were as follows: 101 criminals operated alone, 60 criminals operated in a group of 2 offenders, 63 criminals operated in a group of 3 offenders, 56 criminals operated in a group of 4 offenders, 25 criminals operated in a group of 5 offenders, 30 criminals operated in a group of 6 offenders, 14 criminals operated in a group of 7 offenders, and 8 criminals operated in a group of 8 offenders.

According to transaction cost theory, transaction costs are influenced by the extent of deviant behavior, the extent of deviant acts, and general uncertainty in the environment. Opportunistic behavior by others can cause a rise in transaction costs for the criminal(s). Opportunism means following personal interests characterized by smartness and egoism. Opportunism includes behaviors such as lying, cheating, and stealing.

Transaction cost theory describes white-collar crime not in terms of activities but in terms of relationships. Hierarchy and market are two alternative forms of dealing with others. Hierarchy is based on power and influence, while market is based on demand and supply. Hierarchy can cause large transaction costs if the criminal is not in complete control. Market can cause large transaction costs if others ask for substantial fees to implement desired behavior.

Transaction costs will influence whether or not a white-collar criminal involves someone else in the crime. Costs will also influence the choice of who to involve in crime. Some crime types can be carried out alone, such as fraud, embezzlement, insider trading, and theft. Other crime types must involve at least one other person, such as corruption. Yet other types must involve several other persons, such as Ponzi schemes (Nolasco et al., 2013). A white-collar criminal will try to do as much as possible on his or her own if transaction costs are large.

Others who cause transaction costs can be internal as well as external persons relative to the organization where the criminal has his or her home. They can be participants in crime, neutrals in crime, and victims of crime. Costs occur because of efforts, problems, and risks.

According to Henisz and Williamson (1999), transaction cost economics is a comparative contractual approach to economic organization in which the action resides in the details of transactions on the one hand and governance on the other. Given that all complex criminal contracts are unavoidably incomplete and that contracts as mere promises – unsupported by credible commitment – are not self-enforcing (by reason of opportunism), the question for the criminal is which transactions should be organized and how. Much of the predictive content of transaction cost economics works through the discriminating alignment hypothesis, according to which transactions, which differ in their attributes, are aligned with governance structures, which differ in their costs and competencies, so as to effect a (mainly) transaction cost economizing result. Implementing this requires that transactions, governance structures, and transaction cost economizing all be part of the criminal scheme.

Transaction cost economics concurs that the transaction is the basic unit of analysis and regards governance as the means by which order is accomplished in a relation in which potential conflict threatens to undo or upset opportunities to realize gains (Henisz and Williamson, 1999). The problem of conflict, on which transaction cost economics originally focused, is that of bilateral dependency. The organization of transactions that are supported by generic investments is considered easy: classical market contracting works well because each party can go its own way with minimal cost to the other. Specific investments are where the problems arise.

Williamson (1979, 1981) identified three types of transactions according to specificity. Non-specific transactions have low asset specificity and are associated with the acquisition of commodities. Idiosyncratic transactions have high specificity. Mixed transactions have elements of both commodity and customization. Transaction specificity can be viewed alongside transaction frequency, a second major construct of transaction cost economics, which distinguishes occasional from recurrent transaction types. Recurrent transactions in crime increase the likelihood of detection, while at the same time unit transaction costs will drop.

Two frequency categories multiplied by three specificity types produces six discrete transaction classes. It can be argued that the market is better for all but two classes, which are both recurrent and idiosyncratic.

The third major determinant of transaction costs is uncertainty, compounded by the bounded rationality of humans and often associated with the complexity of the crime to be carried out. Uncertainty is recognized as a major determinant of transaction costs. It is compounded by the bounded rationality of humans and is often associated with the complexity of the product acquired. Given the cognitive limits of human actors, complex arrangements in crime are unavoidably incomplete. Relational incompleteness poses problems when paired with the condition of opportunism – which manifests itself as adverse selection, moral hazard, shirking, sub-goal pursuit, and other forms of deviant behavior. Because human actors will not reliably disclose true conditions upon request or self-fulfill all promises, contracts as mere promises, unsupported by credible commitments, will not be self-enforcing (Williamson, 2000).

Transaction cost theory received attention in 2009 when Professor Oliver Williamson received the Nobel Prize in economics for his research on transaction cost economics. Williamson builds his theory on works by earlier Nobel Laureates such as Professors Herbert Simon and Ronald Coase. A core assumption in their work is that actors behave in an opportunistic way, which means that people explore and exploit opportunities at the cost of others. Furthermore, it is difficult, almost impossible, to foresee another person's attitude toward opportunistic possibilities. Therefore, some of the transaction costs occur because actors have to control each other to detect and prevent opportunism (Dibbern et al., 2008).

In conclusion, the organizational dimension of white-collar crime emphasizes the opportunity structure in the professional setting, where the offender has the opportunity to both commit and conceal financial crime. Organizational opportunity is a distinct characteristic of white-collar crime that separates it from other kinds of financial crime such as cybercrime committed independently of occupation. Privileged individuals are not subject to efficient control, as emphasized in the principal–agent perspective. Social disorganization enables deviant behavior without anyone noticing. Institutional collapse causes a lack of reaction to misconduct and crime.

4. Behavioral dimension of convenience theory

Most theories of white-collar crime can be found along the behavioral dimension. Numerous suggestions have been presented by researchers to explain why famous people have committed financial crime. In this chapter, some of the most prominent theories are presented: differential association theory, theory of self-control and desire-for-control, slippery slope theory, and neutralization theory.

Crime is not committed by systems, routines, or organizations. Crime is committed by individuals. White-collar criminals practice a deviant behavior to carry out their offenses. White-collar crime is committed by members of the privileged socioeconomic class who are using their power and influence. Offenders are typically charismatic, have a need for control, have a tendency to bully subordinates, fear losing their status and position, exhibit narcissistic tendencies, lack integrity and social conscience, have no feelings of guilt, and do not perceive themselves as criminals.

Convenience theory argues that white-collar crime is most common among people in their forties, an age when one is most ambitious and opportunities are often the greatest. Ambitions can be significant both on behalf of oneself and on behalf of the organization. At this age, many have taken on positions that enable and make it relatively convenient to carry out financial crime. The maximum extent of criminogenity is normally reached at a time where ambitions and opportunities are at a peak.

INDIVIDUAL CHARACTERISTICS

White-collar criminals are often effortlessly reluctant to consider consequences both before and after they have committed financial crime. They feel no discomfort in relation to their crime, and they may live well with their crime. This lack of feeling of guilt and lack of bad conscience can be explained by a number of behavioral theories, such as neutralization theory and self-control theory. Neutralization techniques help remove potential guilty feelings both before and after an offense, while a lack of self-control causes the threshold for committing an offense to decline.

Many theories applied to white-collar crime and criminals are developed along the behavioral dimension. By behavior is meant human movement patterns, actions, and reactions. A person's behavior is the sum of his or her responses to external and internal stimuli. For example, criminals are often more innovative than most people (Elnan, 2016).

Researchers have introduced numerous explanations for the behavior of known white-collar offenders such as Bernard Madoff, Raj Rajaratman, and Jeff Schilling in the United States. Typical explanations include differential association theory (Sutherland, 1983), self-control theory (Gottfredson and Hirschi, 1990), slippery slope theory (Welsh et al., 2014), and neutralization theory (Sykes and Matza, 1957). Deterrence theory (Comey, 2009), obedience theory (Baird and Zelin, 2009), and negative life events theory (Engdahl, 2015) are other relevant theories.

The theories help illustrate how financial crime may be the most convenient action from a behavioral perspective to exploit an opportunity for profit. It is convenient for offenders to abuse their positions, resources, and power to inflict losses on others, while at the same time enrich themselves or their organization (Pickett and Pickett, 2002).

Research by Ragatz et al. (2012) is an example of work that explores psychological traits among white-collar offenders. Their research results suggest that white-collar offenders have lower scores on lifestyle criminality, but higher scores on some measures of psychopathology and psychopathic traits compared to non-white-collar offenders. Similarly, McKay et al. (2010) examined the psychopathology of the white-collar criminal acting as a corporate leader. They looked at the impact of a leader's behavior on other employees and the organizational culture developed during his or her reign. They found narcissism, and narcissistic behavior is suggested to be often observed among white-collar offenders (Ouimet, 2009, 2010). Narcissists exhibit an unusually high level of self-love, believing that they are uniquely special and entitled to praise and admiration.

Galvin et al. (2015) studied a number of well-known white-collar offenders in the United States and found that many of them identified themselves so strongly with the organization that they regarded themselves as the core of the business. This phenomenon can be called narcissistic identification with the organization. Such a strong identification with the organization can in itself lead to a higher level of white-collar crime. When the organization is perceived as the same entity as himself or herself, he or she may argue that he or she is entitled to enrichment at the expense of the organization.

THEORY OF DIFFERENTIAL ASSOCIATION

Criminal behavior is prevalent across all classes, and newcomers develop the attitudes and skills necessary to become delinquent by associating with individuals who are carriers of criminal norms. The essence of differential association is that criminal behavior is learned, and the main part of learning comes from within important personal groups. Exposure to the attitudes of members of the organization that either favor or reject legal codes influences the attitudes of the individual. The individual will go on to commit crime if the person is exposed more to attitudes that favor law violation than to attitudes that favor abiding by the law (Wood and Alleyne, 2010).

Differential association can occur in the organizational setting, but does not as such increase the organizational opportunity to commit white-collar crime. Rather, differential association belongs to the behavioral dimension of convenience theory, as crime learning makes it more convenient to favor law violation.

Differential association by individuals can occur outside the organizational setting, such as exposure to law-violation attitudes early in life, exposure to law-violation attitudes over a prolonged period of time in different situations, and exposure to law-violation attitudes from people they like and respect. Once the appropriate attitudes have developed, young people learn the skills of criminality in much the same way as they would learn any other skills, which is by example and training (Wood and Alleyne, 2010).

Individuals embedded within structural units by differential association are exposed to attitudes in favor of or opposed to delinquent and criminal behavior. Differential reinforcement of crime convenience develops over time as individuals are exposed to various associations and definitions conducive to delinquency (Hoffmann, 2002).

THEORY OF SELF-CONTROL AND CONTROLLING

Control theory can be used in two different ways. First, the theory of self-control proposes that individuals commit crime because of low self-control. The theory contends that individuals who lack self-control are more likely to engage in problematic behavior – such as criminal behavior – over their life course because of its time-stable nature (Gottfredsson and Hirschi, 1990). Second, the desire to control and the general wish to be in control of everything and everybody might be a characteristic of some white-collar criminals, meaning that low self-control can be combined with control of others. Desire-for-control is the general wish to be in control over everyday events related to the organization (Piquero et al., 2010).

Self-control is the ability and tendency to consider all potential implications of a particular action. Individuals with low self-control fail to carry around with them a set of inhibitions, meaning they do not consider the implications of their actions. As a consequence, these individuals who are low in self-regulation will engage in delinquent behavior (Ward et al., 2015).

Self-control is the ability to consider the consequences of actions that provide immediate rewards. The underlying assumption is that the rewards of offending are apparent to all. Individuals readily perceive the benefits of offending, but individuals with high self-control also perceive, and weigh more heavily, the costs associated with immediate gratification. Conversely, those with low self-control place more weight on the here and now and fail to consider or appreciate the long-term costs associated with satisfying one's immediate impulses. Aspects of low self-control include impulsivity, risk seeking, a preference for physical (as opposed to mental) activities, opting for simple tasks (compared with challenging ones), temper, and insensitivity to others (Jones et al., 2015).

Control theory diverts attention away from why offenders offend to why conformists do not offend. However, control theory posits that communities with a deteriorating social structure are a breeding ground for delinquency. The central contention of control theory is that people are inherently disposed to offend because offending offers short-term gains, and the central aim of those with criminal dispositions is to satisfy desires in the quickest and simplest way possible. Offending is prevented by the social bond, which operates on individuals' conscience (Wood and Alleyne, 2010).

Desire-for-control can be defined as the degree to which individuals want to be in control over whatever goes on in the organization. Those high in desire-for-control tend to manipulate events to avoid unpleasant situations and to ensure desired outcomes. They tend to attribute organizational success solely to their own hard work, while they blame failures on others. These individuals also tend to engage in more risk-taking behaviors and work harder at a challenging task (Craig and Piquero, 2016). Therefore, many executives with a high degree of desire-for-control often have a low degree of self-control.

While it is expected that a high degree of self-control is required to climb the corporate ladder, executives who have reached the top may quickly loosen up their self-control and instead develop a desire-for-control. Craig and Piquero (2016) found that both low self-control and high desire-for-control are consistent predictors of intentions to offend.

THEORY OF SLIPPERY SLOPE

Slippery slope means that a person slides over time from legal to illegal activities. Arjoon (2008: 78) explains slippery slope in the following way:

> As commonsense experience tells us, it is the small infractions that can lead to the larger ones. An organization that overlooks the small infractions of its employees creates a culture of acceptance that may lead to its own demise. This phenomenon is captured by the metaphor of the slippery slope. Many unethical acts occur without the conscience awareness of the person who engaged in the misconduct. Specifically, unethical behavior is most likely to follow the path of a slippery slope, defined as a gradual decline in which no one event makes one aware that he or she is acting unethically. The majority of unethical behaviors are unintentional and ordinary, thus affecting everyone and providing support for unethical behavior when people unconsciously lower the bar over time through small changes in their ethical behavior.

Welsh et al. (2014) argue that many recent scandals can be described as resulting from a slippery slope in which a series of small infractions gradually increase over time. Committing small indiscretions over time may gradually lead people to complete larger unethical acts that they would otherwise have judged to be impermissible.

The slippery slope theory is in contrast to individual theories such as the standard economic model of rational choice theory as described in the economical dimension. Moral behavior is shaped by psychological and organizational processes, where individuals are motivated to view themselves in a positive manner that corresponds with their moral values. Individuals tend to rationalize minor unethical acts so that they may derive some benefit without being forced to negatively update their self-concept. For example, a minor transgression such as taking a pen home from the office may seem permissible, whereas taking money out of the company cash drawer may more clearly be thought of as stealing (Welsh et al., 2014).

THEORY OF NEUTRALIZATION

In recent times, neutralization theory has been emphasized as an important explanation for deviant behavior. While the idea was presented some decades ago by Sykes and Matza (1957), its application to white-collar crime has been more recent. The theory explains why many white-collar offenders think what they will do, what they are doing, and what they have done is quite okay. They deny responsibility, damage, and victim. They condemn their critics, and they claim loyalty to overriding considerations.

White-collar offenders reduce and eliminate their feeling of guilt by claiming that everyone else does it, that it is a mistake that the act is criminalized, and that they made a tradeoff where the offense turned out to be the best alternative. There are a total of 13 identified neutralization techniques that white-collar criminals apply to rationalize their deviant behavior.

Damage denial and victim denial are two of the main neutralization techniques. These techniques find their foundation in the fact that white-collar crime is often both an impersonal and a general act without the stereotypical characteristics found in street crime (Benson and Simpson, 2015: 145): "Many white-collar offenses fail to match this common-sense stereotype because the offenders do not set out intentionally to harm any specific individual. Rather, the consequences of their illegal acts fall upon impersonal organizations or a diffuse and unseen mass of people." Some believe, and it is often argued, that white-collar offenses represent crime without victims. It is society at large that may suffer, but victims cannot be identified. However, it turns out that one can always identify a victim in any white-collar crime case. In the sample of 405 convicts in Norway, the most frequent victim categories are as follows: (1) employer where the criminal worked; (2) government revenue service because of tax evasion; (3) customers who were cheated; and (4) banks suffering fraud.

Rationalization of one's own deviant behavior and neutralization of guilt is evident when reading autobiographies written by convicted white-collar criminals. Examples include Bogen (2008), Eriksen (2010), and Fosse (Fosse and Magnusson, 2004) in Norway, and Kerik (2015) in the United States. They tend to deny responsibility, they condemn their critics, and they think that what they have done is quite normal. They claim that most people would have done the same in similar situations.

Here are 13 neutralization techniques frequently applied by white-collar criminals to rationalize their deviant behaviors (Siponen and Vance, 2010; Sykes and Matza, 1957):

1. *Disclaim responsibility for crime: Not responsible for what happened.* The offender here claims that one or more of the conditions of responsible agency were not met. The person committing a deviant act defines himself or herself as lacking responsibility for his or her actions. In this technique, the person rationalizes that the action in question is beyond his or her control. The offender views himself or herself as a billiard ball, helplessly propelled through different situations. He or she denies responsibility for the event or sequence of events.

2. *Refuse damage from crime: There is no visible harm from the action.* The offender seeks to minimize or deny the harm done. Denial of

injury involves justifying an action by minimizing the harm it causes. The misbehavior is not really serious because no party suffers directly or visibly as a result of it.

3. *Refuse victim from crime: There is nobody suffering from the action.* The offender may acknowledge the injury, but deny any existence of victims or claims that the victim(s) are unworthy of concern. Any blame for illegal actions is unjustified because the violated party deserves whatever injury he or she receives.

4. *Condemn those who criticize: Outsiders do not understand the relevant behavior.* The offender tries to accuse his or her critics of questionable motives for criticizing him or her. According to this technique of condemning the condemners, one neutralizes one's own actions by blaming those who were the target of the misconduct. The offender deflects moral condemnation onto those ridiculing the misbehavior by pointing out that they engage in similar disapproved behavior. Also, the offender condemns the procedures of the criminal justice system, especially police investigation with interrogation, as well as media coverage of the case.

5. *Justify crime by higher loyalties: It was according to expectations.* The offender denies the act was motivated by self-interest, claiming that it was instead done out of obedience to some moral obligation. The offender appeals to higher loyalties. This technique is employed by those who feel they are in a dilemma that must be resolved at the cost of violating a law or policy. In the context of an organization, an employee may appeal to organizational values or hierarchies. For example, an executive could argue that he or she has to violate a policy in order to get things done and achieve strategic objectives for the enterprise.

6. *Claim blunder quota: It was a necessary shortcut to get things done.* The offender argues that what he or she did is acceptable given the situation and given his or her position. The person feels that after having done so much good for so many for so long, he or she should be excused for more wrongdoings than other people are normally excused for. The crime should be considered an acceptable mistake. This is in line with the metaphor of the ledger, which uses the idea of compensating bad acts by good acts. That is, the individual believes that he or she has previously performed a number of good acts and has accrued a surplus of goodwill, and, as a result of this, can afford to commit some bad actions. Executives in corporate environments neutralize their actions through the metaphor of the ledger by rationalizing that their overall past good behavior justifies occasional rule-breaking.

7.   *Claim legal mistake: This should never have been illegal.* The offender argues that the law is wrong, and what the person did should not be illegal. One may therefore break the law since the law is unreasonable. The offender may argue that behaviors are sometimes criminalized and sometimes decriminalized more or less randomly over time. For example, money involved in bribing people was treated as legal expenses in accounting some decades ago, while corruption today is considered a misconduct and therefore criminalized.

8.   *Claim normality of action: Everyone else does and would do the same.* The offender argues that it is so common to commit the offense that it can hardly be defined as an offense at all. The offense is not deviant behavior, since most people do it or would do it in the same situation. What should be defined as deviant behavior is when people in the same situation obey the law.

9.   *Claim entitlement to action: It is sometimes a required behavior in this position.* The offender claims to be in his or her right to do what he or she did, perhaps because of a very stressful situation or because of some misdeed perpetrated by the victim. This is defense of necessity, which is based on the justification that if the rule-breaking is viewed as necessary, one should feel no guilt when carrying out the action.

10. *Claim solution to dilemma: The benefits of the action outweigh the costs.* The offender argues a dilemma arose whereby he or she made a reasonable tradeoff before committing the act. Tradeoff between many interests therefore resulted in the offense. Dilemma represents a state of mind where it is not obvious what is right and what is wrong to do. For example, the offense might be carried out to prevent a more serious offense from happening.

11. *Justify necessity of crime: It was necessary to carry out the offense.* The offender claims that the offense must be seen in a larger context, where the crime is an illegal element among many legal elements to ensure an important result. The offense was a required and necessary means to achieve an important goal. For example, a bribe represents nothing in dollar value compared to the potential income from a large contract abroad. Or a temporary misrepresentation of accounts could help save the company and thousands of jobs.

12. *Claim role in society: It is a natural maneuver among elite members.* The offender argues that being a minister in the government or a CEO in a global company is so time-consuming that little time can be spent on issues that are perceived as trivial. Shortcuts are part of the game. Some shortcuts may be illegal, but they are nevertheless necessary for the elite member to ensure progress. If someone is to

blame, then it is subordinates who are supposed to provide advice and control what the elite member is doing.

13. *Perceive being victim of incident: Others have ruined my life.* The incident leads to police investigation, prosecution, and possible jail sentence. Media is printing pictures of the offender on the front page, and gains from crime are taken away from the offender. Previous colleagues and friends have left, and so has the family. The offender perceives being a loser and a victim of those who reacted to his or her crime after disclosure.

Justifications are socially constructed accounts that individuals who engage in criminal acts adopt to legitimate their behavior. Justifications are beliefs that counteract negative interpretations by articulating why the acts are justifiable or excusable exceptions to the norms (Aguilera and Vadera, 2008).

Personal neutralization of misconduct and crime is not limited to white-collar criminals. However, it seems that these techniques are applied to a very great extent by such criminals. An example is politically exposed persons. It is related to the role that the criminal or potential criminal occupies at that point in time. An example of a role theory is the theory of politically exposed persons. A politically exposed person (PEP) is an individual who is entrusted with prominent public functions. It is argued by Gilligan (2009) that, as such individuals pose a potential reputation risk to regulated entities, financial institutions must track them. Most of the high-profile media PEP-related coverage in recent years relates to persons such as the former president of the Philippines, Ferdinand Marcos, and the former president of Nigeria, Sani Abacha, who were accused of fostering corruption within their countries and transferring millions of dollars of public funds out of their home countries into bank accounts overseas.

Neutralization theory is linked to attribution theory, where criminals have a tendency to attribute causes of crime to everyone else but themselves. Attribution theory is about identifying causality predicated on internal and external circumstances (Eberly et al., 2011: 731): "Identifying the locus of causality has been at the core of attribution theory since its inception and has generated an extensive research stream in the field of organizational behavior. But the question emerges whether the 'internal' and 'external' categories capture the entire conceptual space of this phenomenon." Based on this argument, Eberly et al. (2011) suggest there is a third category in addition to internal explanation and external explanation, which is labeled relational explanation. These three categories of attributes can be explored to seek causal explanations regarding how persons react in criminal situations.

Attribution theory is a part of social psychology, which studies how humans spontaneously attribute reasons, guilt, and responsibility in situations that arise. The fundamental attribution error is a term used to designate overemphasis on personal factors rather than situational factors in order to explain behavior.

THEORY OF DARK SIDES OF LEADERSHIP

The theory of double bind leadership suggests that mixed messages from a leader creates a double bind for a colleague or subordinate. Individuals are caught in double bind situations in organizational relationships when the criminal leader is expressing two orders of message and one of these denies the other. Individuals are unable to comment on the message being expressed to correct their discrimination in terms of which order of messages to respond to, since the situation in double bind leadership is such that they cannot make a meta communicative statement (Hennestad, 1990).

An individual is not able to comment on the ambiguity of the message by being critical in an assessment of the consequences of double bind because it cements the ambiguity of the situation. A simple example of double bind is a child being exposed to signals of both love and hate from a parent. The child is trapped (Hennestad, 1990: 268): "If the situation is defined as one of hate, the child could be punished for her reaction. On the other hand, if the child defines the signal as one of love, the reaction could be rejection of her affection." A double bind is a dilemma in communication in which an individual receives conflicting messages, with one message negating the other. This creates a situation in which a successful response to one message results in a failed response to the other message, so that the person might be wrong regardless of response. The nature of a double bind is that the person is unable to confront the sender of the messages with the inherent dilemma. The double bind theory is seen as part of the human experience of communication that involves intense relationships and the necessity to discriminate between orders of messages (Gibney, 2006).

The double bind theory can be applied to both individuals and organizations. A double bind organization is a social system where mixed messages are the rule rather than an exception. An organizational schizophrenia occurs in the organization, where mixed messages cannot be revealed, which has a negative effect on an employee's initiatives and learning situation. The result is a lack of authentic dialogue, which can freeze the horizon of meaning in the organization, thereby rendering infertile the soil of growth of vitality of organizational dynamics (Hennestad, 1990).

Glasø and Einarsen (2008) studied emotion regulation in leader–follower relationships. They found that negative emotions such as disappointment, uncertainty, and annoyance are typically suppressed, while positive emotions such as enthusiasm, interest, and calmness are typically expressed or faked. When leaders and followers referred to experienced or expressed emotions, the most highly scored emotions were "glad", "enthusiastic", "well", and "interested". The reported level of emotion regulation was higher for leaders than for followers.

According to Glasø et al. (2006), emotional control can be defined as a process in which individuals influence the emotions that they experience, when they arise, and how they perceive and express them. In this line of reasoning, people can modify their emotions and the emotional expressions connected with them. Emotional control in the workplace is called emotional labor or emotion work. Emotion work takes place in face-to-face or voice-to-voice interactions, and its purpose is to influence other people's perceptions, emotions, attitudes, and behavior.

Obedience theory has the potential to explain follower behavior. Obedience theory is related to the fraud triangle that consists of pressure, opportunity, and rationalization (Baird and Zelin, 2009; Hollow, 2014). The pressures to commit crime are often overt requests of management, but can also be based on perceptions from reward and incentive structures.

An even stronger argument for follower behavior can be found when obedience theory is linked to self-control theory. Self-control theory proposes that individuals commit crime because of low self-control. Except in rare cases of mass fraud such as the Enron scandal, not all elite individuals within a given organization or industry will commit crime. Hence, although the elite at the top of their profession and corporation differentially associate with the people of equal status in their own and other corporations, not all corporate elites commit crimes and behave in an overtly deviant manner (Hansen, 2009).

Leaders tend to be more domineering and assertive, and less social avoidant, distrustful, and exploitable than followers. Glasø et al.'s (2010) study shows that 30 percent of the leaders exhibit elevated profiles of personality characteristics regarding interpersonal problems, on a level comparable to that of a sample of psychiatric patients, thus indicating that severe problems may arise in social interactions between leaders and followers.

Leaders can employ different behaviors, actions, and practices that they direct at followers in order to make them cooperate. Bullying and harassment by leaders are examples of practices reported to happen on a regular basis in many work organizations. Bullying and harassment are carried out deliberately to cause humiliation, offense, and distress (Hoel et al., 2010).

Dark sides of leadership are associated with counterproductive work behaviors, misconduct, and crime. At the same time, characteristics of followers can make the situation even worse. For example, narcissistic employees have been found to be less satisfied with their jobs. Narcissistic followers ruthlessly pursue aggrandizement of the individual self, even at the price of diminishing others and at the risk of sacrificing interpersonal bonds. Narcissistic followers tend to score their supervisors more negatively than non-narcissistic individuals (Mathieu, 2013). Negative consequences of narcissistic individuals in the workplace are mostly related to damages in interpersonal relationships. Followers scoring highly on neuroticism rated their leaders lower on positive leadership. Followers' perceptions of their leaders, such as trust and satisfaction, fear and respect, influence their willingness to participate in misconduct (Salter et al., 2009).

The leadership trait perspective is an important intellectual tradition in leadership research. For white-collar criminals, we may find both light and dark sides of leader traits, although the dark sides may be the most prominent when white-collar criminals commit financial crime. Judge et al. (2009) identified four dark side personality traits:

1. *Narcissism* is a personality trait that is characterized by arrogance, self-absorption, entitlement, and hostility. Narcissists exhibit an unusually high level of self-love, believing that they are uniquely special and entitled to praise and admiration. As a self-regulatory defense mechanism against a grandiose yet shallow self-concept, narcissists tend to view others as inferior to themselves, often acting in insensitive, hostile, and self-enhancing ways. Narcissist leaders are more likely to interpret information with a self-serving bias and make decisions based on how those decisions will reflect on their reputations.
2. *Hubris* exists when an individual has excessive pride, an inflated sense of self-confidence, and makes self-evaluations in terms of talent, ability, and accomplishment that are much more positive than any reasonable objective assessment would otherwise suggest. Leaders who carry an exaggerated sense of self-worth are likely to be defensive against most forms of critical feedback, and respond to negative feedback by questioning the competence of the evaluator and the validity of the evaluation technique. When subordinates or peers disagree with hubristic leaders, these leaders deny the credibility and value of negative evaluations.
3. *Social dominance* represents a preference for hierarchy and stability to achieve control. Dominant individuals tend to control conversations, put pressure on others, and demand explanations for otherwise normal activities. Dominating individuals tend to be prejudiced, power hungry, and manipulative.

4. *Machiavellianism* is a term used to define a personality trait character-
    ized by cunning, manipulation, and the use of any means necessary to
    achieve one's political ends. These kinds of leaders are concerned with
    maximizing opportunities to craft their own personal power.

Most chief executive officer (CEO) research has traditionally tended
to take a rather one-sided view of leadership, emphasizing its positive
and constructive aspects while avoiding its darker sides (e.g., Bigley and
Wiersma, 2002; Fanelli and Misangyi, 2006; Shen, 2003). A possible
reason for this one-sided attention may be that leadership research has primarily focused on leader effectiveness, strategic thinking, and factors that
contribute to optimal performance and results (Glasø et al., 2010).

At the same time, many business school curricula are rich with case
studies of CEO failure of various types and cases of poor leadership.
Negative stories about CEOs tend to be those which attract media coverage, generally and within the business press.

There are indeed several dark sides of leadership that merit attention by
researchers. One of the darkest sides of leadership is white-collar crime,
where the CEO exploits criminal options for corporate and/or personal
gain. This constitutes the main topic of our statistical analysis.

However, dark sides of leadership can be found in less severe forms.
One example is bullying and harassment, which may or may not be linked
to crime. Bullying and harassment by CEOs are reported to happen on
a regular basis in many work organizations. Bullying and harassment at
work may be defined as repeated behavior, actions, and practices directed
at one or more colleagues, which may be conducted either deliberately or
unconsciously, but which are unwanted by the targets, causing humiliation,
offense, and distress, and which may interfere with job performance and/or
create an unpleasant working environment (Hoel et al., 2010).

The heroic perspective on leadership has been shown to be part of a
frequently held romantic illusion of leadership which, in turn, it has been
argued, attracts people with narcissistic personality. Leadership positions
prove tempting to narcissists since they provide legitimate exposure to
attention from others, a sense of importance and power, and also gratification in terms of the sense of entitlement that narcissists seem particularly
prone to.

Entrepreneurial theory can be applied to white-collar crime, whereupon
we look at the dark side of entrepreneurialism. To understand entrepreneurial behavior by white-collar criminals, important behavioral areas
include modus essendi, modus operandi, and modus vivendi. Modus
essendi is a philosophical term relating to modes of being. Modus operandi is method of operating, which is an accepted criminological concept

for classifying generic human actions from their visible and consequential manifestations. Modus vivendi represents the shared symbiotic relationship between different entrepreneurial directions (Smith, 2009).

In conclusion, the behavioral dimension of white-collar crime emphasizes the willingness of elite members to commit financial crime in the course of their occupation. When white-collar criminals apply neutralization techniques, they tend to convince themselves that they have done nothing wrong that they should be blamed for. They associate with those who agree with them, and distance themselves from those who disagree.

Chapters 2, 3, and 4 have presented the three dimensions of convenience theory. As we shall explore later in this book, it is not just the dimensions, but the interrelations between dimensions, that explain the occurrence of white-collar crime.

5.　Empirical study of white-collar criminals

Convenience theory suggests that white-collar crime is committed because of convenience in the economical, organizational, and behavioral dimensions. Gottschalk (2017) found evidence of convenience in a sample of 405 white-collar criminals sentenced to prison in Norway from 2009 to 2015. Gottschalk (2016) found evidence of convenience in a number of reports of investigations by fraud examiners in the United States and Norway.

In this chapter, we explore evidence of convenience among the most serious white-collar criminals in Norway. We define serious white-collar criminals as those who receive the most severe prison sentences.

RESEARCH METHOD

To examine convenience theory in practice, we need an empirical sample for study. An empirical sample of white-collar crime cases can be obtained as either primary or secondary data. Interviews with criminals are a typical example of primary data. Court records are a typical example of secondary data. Interviews could easily lead to biased responses, since a number of white-collar criminals tend to deny that they have committed offenses and to deny that they are responsible for possible damage or for creating victims. As evidenced in newspaper interviews with criminals and autobiographies by such criminals, they tend to see themselves as unlucky losers of a blame game. They tend to reflect on themselves as victims rather than offenders. Therefore, interviews may not be suitable for empirical testing of convenience theory.

For example, Bernard Kerik was police commissioner of New York City. He was detected, prosecuted, and sentenced for white-collar crime. He went to prison in 2010 and got out in 2014. The following year, Kerik's (2015) book was published. Throughout the 288-page book, there is ample evidence of neutralization: denial of responsibility ("my accountants made mistakes"), condemnation of condemners ("accusing me of having connections to organized crime"), normality of action ("the indictment criminalized minor ethical issues and accounting errors"), legal mistake ("everything I was charged for – tax, fraud, false statements – could have been handled ethically or civilly, without criminal charges"), acceptable mistake ("Feds were taking honest mistakes by me and my accountants and alleged they were crimes"), dilemma tradeoff ("this was one of those ethical moments that any person in public office faces repeatedly"), victim of crime ("they would subpoena and harass my friends, family, colleagues, and just about everyone I knew"), and role in society ("I have defended, worked, fought, and nearly died for our country many times in the past thirty years and was now being jailed"). These quotes from Kerik's (2015) book are certainly useful to find evidence of the behavioral dimension, but it is more difficult to find evidence of the economical and organizational dimensions in convenience theory.

Secondary data in terms of court documents are more reliable. When these documents are supplemented by media coverage, crime stories become more colorful. Media as a source of information is, of course, not without problems and the use of newspaper reports to assess convenience in white-collar crime is similar. Williams (2008) found that media coverage of white-collar crime cases tries to make sense of stories by selectively coding and communicating information to a variety of audiences. He argues that the media is not simply a device for reproducing narrowly hegemonic views of white-collar crime, but rather an active player that shapes regulatory meanings, moves markets, and sometimes encourages the very types of practices that may lead to corporate scandals.

In addition to court records about convictions, our data come from content analysis of reports about white-collar criminals in the two main financial newspapers in Norway: *Dagens Næringsliv* and *Finansavisen*. Both of these papers are conservative-leaning business newspapers. In addition, the business-friendly national daily newspaper *Aftenposten* regularly reports news of white-collar criminals, and so it was included in the study. Left-wing newspapers such as *Klassekampen* very seldom cover specific white-collar criminal cases, although they do report on the problems of white-collar crime in general.

Some white-collar criminals remain silent after they have been detected, prosecuted, and convicted. Others seem to enjoy interviews in the media, where they can present their side of the story. A few write their own autobiographies to present their own version of what happened, such as Kerik (2015). Norwegian examples include Bogen (2008) and Eriksen (2010).

SAMPLE OF CRIMINALS

As listed in Table 5.1, we have selected the eight top white-collar criminals with a maximum of 9 years in prison. In comparison, the average prison sentence for all 405 white-collar criminals was 2 years and 4 months.

All eight criminals in the table are men. There are 375 men and 30 women among the 405 white-collar criminals in Norway. The fraction of women is only 7.4 percent. But there are no women at the top of the list.

The white-collar crime for each offender is listed in Table 5.2. A variety of financial crime was committed. Given the main categories of fraud, theft, manipulation, and corruption, there are five cases of fraud, one case of theft, two cases of manipulation, and no case of corruption among the top criminals.

Table 5.1   White-collar criminals with longest jail sentences in Norway

#	Criminal	Case	Prison	Position
1	Trond G. Kristoffersen	Finance Credit	9 years	CEO
2	Fred A. Ingebrigtsen	Acta Capital	9 years	CEO
3	Henry Amundsen	Taxi Accountant	8 years	Chief accountant
4	Alain Angelil	Eltek Components	8 years	CEO
5	Ivar T. Henriksen	Waterworks	8 years	CEO
6	Frank Murud	School Buildings	7 years	Property manager
7	Birger Østraat	TS Marine	7 years	CFO
8	Torgeir Stensrud	Finance Credit	7 years	Chairman

Table 5.2   Types of white-collar crime with longest jail sentences in Norway

#	Criminal	Crime
1	Trond G. Kristoffersen	Bank fraud by misrepresentation of financial statements
2	Fred A. Ingebrigtsen	Insider trading involving family members
3	Henry Amundsen	Tax evasion by manipulative cab accounting system
4	Alain Angelil	Insider trading involving family members abroad
5	Ivar T. Henriksen	Fraud involving procurement of personal property
6	Frank Murud	Fraud involving fake invoices from suppliers
7	Birger Østraat	Embezzlement
8	Torgeir Stensrud	Bank fraud by misrepresentation of financial statements

Most of these individuals have been exposed extensively in the media. Often, they were willing to give interviews where they criticized prosecutors and told their own versions of events including their own business success stories. None of them wrote autobiographies, but journalists have presented complete stories for most of them in the media.

Court documents are substantial in most cases. All the white-collar criminals were first prosecuted in Norwegian district courts, resulting in a verdict of over 2,000 pages. Most of the criminals appealed, leading to new court documents of the same length from courts of appeal. A few criminals were able to appeal their case to the Supreme Court, leading to even more court documents that were then available for this research.

ECONOMICAL DIMENSION

All 405 white-collar criminals had profit as the motive for their crime. The average amount of money involved was 45 million Norwegian kroner (about 7 million US dollars). The smallest amount was a few thousand; the largest amount was 1.2 billion Norwegian kroner (about 200 million US dollars).

Trond G. Kristoffersen (# 1) and *Torgeir Stensrud* (# 8) were involved in financial crime amounting to the largest sum of money: 1.2 billion Norwegian kroner. The collapse of Finance Credit – a collection agency that had borrowed heavily from a number of banks based on misleading financial statements – caused heavy bank losses. The chairman of Finance Credit, Torgeir Stensrud, was convicted to seven years in prison, while the CEO, Trond Kristoffersen, was sentenced to nine years in prison. The shorter sentence for Stensrud came about because Stensrud was more cooperative during the police investigation. Finance Credit's external auditor, John Haukeland, was convicted to ten months in prison. It is likely that it was the threat of bankruptcy that caused Stensrud and Kristoffersen to manipulate accounting figures to enable Finance Credit to stay afloat on hundreds of millions of kroner from banks. Since they were unable to save the firm, which they had built themselves through hard work, the bank fraud was detected first by the media and then as part of the bankruptcy.

The main motive for chairman Stensrud was probably not loss of income. It was his fear of falling (Piquero, 2012). Financial crime is sometimes perceived as the only way out of a crisis. Profit-driven crime is thus not only an issue of making even more money. Rather, it is an issue of survival. Stensrud's fear of falling can be understood in the context of his background. His high prestige and status were at stake. Stensrud was formerly a lieutenant colonel in the Norwegian army. He was president of the NATO reserve officer organization Confédération Interalliée des Officiers de Réserve (CIOR) with more than 800,000 members from 1990 to 1992. He was also president of the Norwegian Reserve Officers' Federation from 1992 to 1998. Stensrud was then appointed honorary member of the Norwegian Reserve Officers' Federation. He was a Freemason of XII grade. In sum, he was a well-connected person in the elite of Norwegian society. A collapse of his new financial empire, Finance Credit, would also destroy his reputation. To avoid falling from on high, white-collar crime in terms of bank fraud emerged as a convenient option.

Fred A. Ingebrigtsen (# 2) enjoyed doing good deeds with his money. Acta Capital was a successful company, and Ingebrigtsen became a wealthy co-founder of the company. He was a philanthropist who donated money to the local football club and to other social purposes. He enjoyed the admiration and fame that resulted from his generous nature. He wanted to help friends and family to make money on Acta shares, so he told them when to buy and when to sell. Based on inside information, family and friends were able to make profitable transactions.

Ingebrigtsen was detected by the Financial Supervisory Authority of Norway. Five family members and friends were also sentenced to prison.

Ingebrigtsen was probably driven by the need for respect and self-realization, which is at the top of Maslow's hierarchy of human needs. He wanted satisfaction in terms of achievement, recognition, admiration, reputation, and fame from belonging to the successful business elite. His success should ensure him status and make him a hero. Money should enable him to climb higher in the hierarchy of needs.

It seems that Ingebrigtsen was both self-interested and socially concerned. His social concern may have led him to help others and give more consideration to others than to his own potential misconduct. His personal inclination may have included caring about others, forming close ties to others, and cooperating with others. This is in line with Agnew's (2014) theory of social concern, where social concern can have direct, indirect, mediating, or conditioning effects on misconduct and crime.

Henry Amundsen (# 3) established and operated an accounting firm. His main clients were taxi owners. After some years, he had close to 300 taxi owners as his clients. Not only did he offer regular accounting, he also offered a special computer program that made tax claims disappear. Because of this extra feature, his firm was attractive to many taxi owners. Most of the taxi owners were first or second generation Norwegians from Pakistan. Their extra income was often spent building vacation palaces back in Pakistan. Amundsen's economic motive for his crime was to grow his accounting business. He attracted more and more clients to his firm. He could also share some of the saved tax payments with his clients.

Both the theory of profit-driven crime (Naylor, 2003) and the American dream theory (Pratt and Cullen, 2005) seem to apply to Amundsen. Profit-driven crime by legal business enterprises should be understood mainly in economic rather than sociological or criminological terms. The American dream suggests that everyone in America (and elsewhere) has an opportunity to become monetarily successful, and being monetarily successful is the only thing that counts.

The theory of crime forces (Leonard and Weber, 1970) also seems applicable to this case, since Pakistani taxi owners were not only willing, but also pushing for tax evasion. Many of them were convicted together with Amundsen and given substantial prison sentences.

Alain Angelil (# 4) was convicted of tax evasion and insider trading. He was the founder of Eltek, an electronics company that grew to a substantial size and became quite profitable in the city of Drammen outside Oslo. Angelil became quite wealthy, but he seems to have suffered from greed. Greed is defined as a desire to own more and more, where you never become satisfied. Angelil let his family prosper, but more importantly for him was to have estates in places such as Scotland for himself.

Alain Angelil was born in Egypt and went to study engineering in Switzerland. There he met his future wife Wenche from Drammen. They moved to Drammen where he established Eltek. For many years, there were no reasons to suspect white-collar crime. When he retired, Wenche's and Alain's son, Morten Angelil, took over as chief executive officer (CEO). Soon after, it was detected that both father and son were involved in various forms of financial crime. Both father and son were finally convicted and sentenced to prison. While the father received a sentence of 8 years, the son received a sentence of 1.5 years. Four more individuals were sentenced to prison in the same Eltek criminal cases: Lars Jervan, Gunnar Sverre Nilsen, Øyvind Hagen, and Andre Sylvester Fossmark.

Hamilton and Micklethwait (2006) argue that greed is the most common reason for white-collar criminal acts. Money and other forms of financial gain are frequent motivators documented in many studies. Criminals pursue desired goals, weigh up likely consequences, and make selections from various options. When criminal opportunity is attractive as a means to fulfill one's desires, rational actors choose it. Goldstraw-White (2012) defines greed as socially constructed needs and desires that can never be completely satisfied. As individuals move up the social-class ladder, need is replaced by greed as the motivating factor behind crime. Greed is a very strong wish to continuously get more of something; it is a strong preference for maximizing wealth.

Ivar T. Henriksen (# 5) was an entrepreneur in the water supply and water waste business in one of the larger municipalities outside Oslo. He developed efficient services for inhabitants. He also did good deeds for the local community. For example, he linked a water fountain to the water supply outside a nursing home that patients could enjoy watching. After some years he was recommended for and received a medal from the King of Norway. He became a local hero. He enjoyed it very much and wanted to improve his status among close allies, friends, and family by providing them with goods and services. His motive seems to have been recognition, admiration, respect, and influence. His motive was also to enjoy privileges for himself.

He started to spend money from the waterworks on goods and services that were further and further away from the water business. He bought a number of vehicles that could hardly be used in the water business. Shortly after procurement, he let colleagues and friends buy the vehicles at a heavily reduced price. He bought a hunting farm in South Africa, which he enjoyed himself and let others in his circle enjoy.

Driven by success, he continued to expand into all kinds of endeavors. For example, he let his son establish an engineering firm financed by the waterworks. The son bought equipment, and invoices were met by his father at work. He enjoyed the status of solving whatever problems others brought forth. After a while, he built himself a new large family house, an estate that was the biggest in the whole region.

Some questioned his behavior. They were immediately silenced by powerful people. Finally, a subordinate of Henriksen called an investigative journalist at the Norwegian newspaper *Aftenposten*, and the story started to unfold. Henriksen was surprised and denied all allegations. He argued that he had provided excellent water services to inhabitants over the years.

The story of Ivar T. Henriksen resembles the American dream, where success in all aspects of life is important. The American dream suggests that everyone in America has an opportunity to become monetarily successful. A high white-collar crime rate can be attributed to the commitment to the goal of material success as experienced in the American dream. It is caused by an overemphasis on success in visible assets (Schoepfer and Piquero, 2006), and it is not matched by a concurrent emphasis on what means are legitimate for reaching the desired goal (Pratt and Cullen, 2005). Henriksen tried to make the American dream a reality within public service in Norway.

Frank Murud (# 6) was sentenced to prison for seven years for corruption and embezzlement. Murud was property manager for the Oslo City school district. His motive in the economical dimension of convenience theory was greed. He just could not get enough material wealth. His fraud amounted to 90 million Norwegian kroner (equivalent of 12 million US dollars). He spent the money on a noble property in the best neighborhood in Oslo, on luxury cars, and on luxury boats. He really enjoyed all his valuable things and commodities.

After Murud had been arrested, prosecuted, and sentenced to prison, he was not very upset about his time in jail; nor was he upset about all the negative publicity in the media. He did not really care about his family breaking up and his wife leaving him. All he cared about was all the valuables that had been taken away from him. He said he would miss his house, his cars, and his boats. He would not miss his wife, he said.

It had been convenient for him for many years to participate in corruption and to carry out embezzlement in his position as property manager to enable him to spend multiple times what he actually earned in his position. He knew of no other way to satisfy his greed for more and more wealth.

Some quotes from the internal investigation report by Kommunerevisjonen (2006) illustrate convenience in the economical dimension:

- "Another reason why the fraud was not detected was that the additional resource drain on the maintenance budget did not reduce the magnitude of planned maintenance" (page 31).
- "The chairman of the board received in 2006 a message of concern from a person who argued that the property manager had too much money privately to be employed in the public sector. The chairman asked for a check of the property manager. No alarming findings occurred" (page 32).

Murud had managed a wide variety of real estate projects for the city of Oslo at Undervisningsbygg (= Educational Construction). He earned 500,000 Norwegian kroner (70,000 US dollars) in 2004, but somehow managed to afford a 10 million kroner villa in the exclusive Holmenkollen district of the city. He also had a holiday cabin in the mountains at Geilo, two plots and an apartment in Geilo, an apartment in Lillehammer, and a house in Fredrikstad. Murud had purchased property worth tens of millions of Norwegian kroner. He was also an investor in technology company Birdstep, owning a 5.9 percent stake through shares purchased for 6.6 million Norweign kroner. He told friends and family that he was extremely successful in all kinds of money games and bets.

Birger Østraat (# 7) lived in extreme luxury for many years before he was detected. He enjoyed buying champagne for 30,000 US dollars per bottle. Østraat managed an investment fund that went bankrupt, and bankruptcy auditors detected his fraud.

ORGANIZATIONAL DIMENSION

Trond G. Kristoffersen (# 1) and *Torgeir Stensrud* (# 8) were CEO and chairman of the board, respectively, at Finance Credit. They had structured the company into a number of subsidiaries linked to a web of similar businesses that was only transparent to insiders in the company. Outsiders – even experienced banking people and auditors – were unable to understand the true financial situation of the network. This lack of transparency was exploited by Kristoffersen and Stensrud by presenting misleading financial statements. One way of misleading banks was to argue that Finance Credit and its subsidiaries had substantial accounts receivable. However, accounts receivable were from internal sister organizations in the network, not from external debtors. Accounts receivable were created in a number of exchanges in the web of businesses that created confusion among outsiders.

Because of the reputation of Torgeir Stensrud in society generally, and in terms of special contacts in the elite in Norway particularly, bank executives trusted Kristoffersen and Stensrud when they told a story of large sums of external accounts receivable that were coming in the following year. No bank executive dared to question the integrity and accountability of Torgeir Stensrud, who had held a number of important official positions in Norway and at NATO.

The attractive opportunity structure for white-collar crime in this case can be found both internally and externally (Benson and Simpson, 2015). Internally, the confusing web of businesses in Finance Credit represented an attractive organizational structure for fraud. Disorganization within Finance Credit probably led to the breakdown of conventional norms (Wood and Alleyne, 2010). Organizational complexity created an arena for convenient white-collar crime (Pillay and Kluvers, 2014).

Externally, the almost limitless trust enjoyed by Stensrud could be exploited by him. It was almost institutionalized among banks to trust individuals in the elite based on their past performance, and not on their current issues. Finance Credit and Torgeir Stensrud enjoyed external legitimacy of deviant behavior on false premises (Pillay and Kluvers, 2014). An investigative journalist finally questioned the financial performance of Finance Credit.

Fred A. Ingebrigtsen (# 2) was a self-made man who established Acta Capital with his friend Alfred Ydstebø in 1990. The capital management firm merged with a brokerage firm in 1998. His personal assets were estimated at 200 million US dollars in 2007. He was sentenced to prison in 2015.

In the media, Ingebrigtsen was presented as a nontraditional and extrovert executive. He seemed to laugh a lot. People liked his personality and believed in what he was doing. They trusted and never questioned his behavior. He was always a little different from most others. In this way, he expanded his opportunity structure far beyond what is common in the position of a chief executive. Some found him charismatic and a person easy to follow. People who had placed their assets to be managed by Ingebrigtsen at Acta trusted him completely.

From the perspective of agency theory (Bosse and Phillips, 2016), rich people had no way of monitoring how Acta was managing their assets. In a perspective of social disorganization theory (Wood and Alleyne, 2010), few if any had an overview of firm activities, and management lacked social control among themselves. In terms of institutional theory (Pillay and Kluvers, 2014), the financial business sector is very different from other industrial sectors in terms of unconventional and individual-based approaches where the most successful brokers treat their rich clients personally.

Ingebrigtsen's leakage of inside information from Acta was easy, since he knew what was going on as a prime insider. His leakage was not suspicious, since he talked about all kinds of things with all kinds of people. He went into alliances with family and friends so that they could make some extra money.

Henry Amundsen (# 3) had been employed in the internal revenue service at Oslo public tax office. He knew exactly how tax statements from cab owners were controlled in the tax office. After having left the public tax office and established his own accounting firm, he hired a computer programmer to develop accounting software to reduce income reported by cab owners. Specifically, the program created false lists from each cab work shift. A cab work shift list documents how many miles a cab has covered in a shift.

Amundsen felt quite safe by doing this, since he was convinced it would never be detected. Even if it was detected, he felt quite safe, because he did not report cab incomes to tax offices in Norway. Rather, cab owners themselves had to file their own income statements. Therefore, Amundsen was convinced that he himself would never be charged, since cab owners were responsible for fraud, while he was not.

From an opportunity perspective (Benson and Simpson, 2015), Amundsen had ample opportunity to produce income statements for his clients any way they wanted.

From an agency perspective (Eisenhardt, 1985), Amundsen was the agent while cab owners were principals. Agency theory points to three areas where the two parties may differ. They may be dissimilar in the following aspects: (1) preferences (agent and principals may have conflicting

values or preferences); (2) available knowledge (agent and principals do not have the same knowledge; we say that the situation is characterized by asymmetry between the two parties); and (3) attitude toward risk (agent and principals may have different risk aversions, i.e., they dislike exposure to risks to different degrees). While there certainly was a knowledge asymmetry between the accountant and cab owners, there is no indication that they differed in their preferences or their attitude toward risk.

From an institutional perspective (Bradshaw, 2015), the values and attitudes of both the accounting firm and the cab firms were similar in that tax was to be avoided. There was no good reason to pay more taxes than necessary to the Norwegian state, which was already very rich and spending tax revenues on all kinds of meaningless things.

Alain Angelil (# 4) was founder, CEO, and later chairman at Eltek in Drammen outside Oslo. When he became chairman, his son Morten took over the position of CEO. While some illegal transactions occurred in the organizational context, other transactions involving tax evasion and insider trading occurred outside the firm. However, illegal transactions cannot be classified as private, since Angelil took advantage of all the contacts from his founder, CEO, and chairman positions. For example, insider trading in Eltek stocks was enabled through a bank in Luxembourg where Eltek already was a client. Tax evasion as a private taxpayer was also possible by using advisors who normally worked for Eltek. His inside trade in Eltek stocks through helpers in Luxembourg was also possible because he was updated on potential mergers and acquisitions by Eltek long before other shareholders learned about the news.

From an opportunity perspective, Angelil obviously had ample opportunities to satisfy his greed. From an agency perspective, Angelil, as the criminal principal, manipulated agents to carry out illegal transactions for him, including his own brother.

From a resource perspective, Angelil had access to ample resources, including top attorneys. First, he hired attorneys to fight the claim from the internal revenue service that he should pay much more in taxes than he had done in the past. Next, he hired attorneys to fight the prosecution against him for tax evasion. When a person in Norway is prosecuted for crime in court, the person has the right of free defense. The person may hire whoever he or she desires, and the state will pay the attorney. In addition, a wealthy defendant may pay for extra defense by hiring more defense lawyers. Even though Angelil spent a lot of money to avoid prison, he was finally sentenced, after the Supreme Court refused to look at his case. This is a very rare outcome. Several white-collar defendants have been successful in getting their cases dismissed from courts partly because of privately funded defense.

Ivar T. Henriksen (# 5) was the boss at the waterworks in the district of Romerike outside Oslo. He practiced double bind leadership that made people do exactly what he wanted. Although Henriksen reported to a board, board members felt they were subordinates of the CEO. He provided board members with favors, and Henriksen was a hero nobody dared to challenge. CEO Henriksen was in charge, which is not uncommon. If a CEO is perceived of as having a more influential position than board members, the members tend to accept whatever is presented by the CEO to them. In the waterworks case, board members were recruited from local municipalities without any business or management experience.

Frank Murud (# 6) did not feel bad about his crime. He blamed lack of controls at his employer for letting him carry out his fraud scheme. In the organizational dimension, he was only allowed to approve invoices of minor amounts. Invoices of larger amounts had always to be approved by two executives or one executive higher up in the organization. When he asked a friend to send an invoice of a substantial amount, he then approved the invoice, and sent it to the accounting department, which reimbursed his friend for the amount on the invoice. Murud argued in court that because the accounting department was so sloppy, they were to blame for his fraud.

The fraud employed was reportedly a simple classic, with Murud paying fictitious bills sent in by his accomplices. Murud then collected most of the money for this kind of criminal billing service. Murud's motive for crime was greed, where greed is socially constructed needs and desires that can never be completely satisfied.

The organizational opportunity for Murud's fraud can be found in the numerous invoices that arrived at work every day for a number of maintenance services carried out by suppliers on school buildings owned by the city of Oslo. There was a flow of invoices that all looked more or less the same. When an invoice with fake contents arrived, it simply entered the flow as any other invoice.

The organizational opportunity for Murud's fraud can also be explained by his personality. He was an open-minded colleague who was always friendly and helpful at work. He socialized a lot at work, and he had many friends outside work. He told them all that he had been lucky at gambling, and they all believed him. He created an impression that he found public service very important, where professional school buildings were at his heart. He had previously worked in the private sector, but argued that it was much more important for him to serve the public sector.

This is in line with public service motivation theory suggesting that individuals work in the public sector based on values different from people in the private sector. The theory seeks to explain why individuals choose public service, given the perceived disparities in pay scale, advancement

opportunities, and overall work environment. Individuals working in the public sector have a desire to contribute to the well-being of society in general through their work. Public service motivation represents an individual's predisposition to respond to motives grounded primarily or uniquely in public institutions or organizations. While job positions in the private sector can be financially more lucrative, they tend to be very limited in scope with little or no impact on society. While job positions in the public sector can be less financially lucrative, they tend to have a wider scope with potential impacts on society. For many experts and leaders, it can be more attractive to work on bigger issues that matter for people, rather than working on smaller issues that only matter for the bottom line in a company.

Birger Østraat (# 7) managed Effex International, a fund consisting of money from many rich people. It was not noticed that he lived a life of luxury, because so many others in the financial services business lived similar lives. Making money and spending money was the name of the game in the securities industry.

BEHAVIORAL DIMENSION

Trond G. Kristoffersen (# 1) and *Torgeir Stensrud* (# 8) were CEO and chairman of the board, respectively, at Finance Credit. Strain characterized their struggles to rescue the company Finance Credit. Failure to achieve positive goals created strain and led to deviance (Agnew, 2005). Strain characterizes a condition that both individuals disliked. Strain theory argues that strain weakens the ability of normative standards to regulate behavior (Pratt and Cullen, 2005). Kristoffersen's strain resulted in frustration and resignation, where he personally spent lots of company money on expensive champagne and women in foreign cities. Stensrud's strain resulted in lies and manipulated documents in an effort to sustain and maintain the cash flow from banks. He played throughout his influential network. Both lost their self-control (Gottfredson and Hirschi, 1990).

Chairman Stensrud moved down the slippery slope over time (Welsh et al., 2014). He tried to be honest at the beginning of the crisis, but discovered it did not work. He told stories and gave presentations where he assured that the company was in a temporary slump. Maybe he believed it himself. To overcome the temporary slump, he needed financial help from banks, and several Norwegian banks were eager to help him. Banks' eagerness to help Finance Credit may have reinforced Stensrud's belief that it was only a matter of a temporary slump. Banks almost supported him in his belief that it was only a challenge of temporary illiquidity. The slide down the slippery slope occurred over time as banks needed stronger and stronger reassurance, which Stensrud could only provide by overemphasizing the positive signs and underemphasizing the negative signs at Finance Credit.

To the extent Stensrud believed it was a matter of temporary illiquidity, and Finance Credit would pay back all the millions to the banks, he felt he did nothing wrong. He thought there would be no injury and no victim. To the extent he did not believe it, he may still have felt he did nothing wrong. In terms of neutralization (Sykes and Matza, 1957), he as chairman denied responsibility for the poor business performance and put the blame on executives in the company. Because of his prominent role in society, and the desperate situation in the company, Stensrud felt entitled to use unorthodox methods to save it. He was convinced that other rules and procedures applied to his case.

Fred A. Ingebrigtsen (# 2) seems to have a number of deviant personality traits. The boss with an unstable personality type shows unstable behavior, is erratic, moody, reacts in a childish manner, is emotionally unstable, insecure, and has an immature self-image. At the same time, narcissism is a personality trait that is characterized by arrogance, self-absorption, entitlement, and hostility. Narcissists exhibit an unusually high level of self-love, believing that they are uniquely special and entitled to praise and admiration. A paradoxical combination of instability and narcissism might be observed in the case of Ingebrigtsen.

Ingebrigtsen's level of self-control seems to be low. Self-control theory contends that individuals who lack self-control are more likely to engage in problematic behavior over their life course because of its time-stable nature (Gottfredson and Hirschi, 1990). In addition, the desire to control and the general wish to be in control of everything and everybody might be a characteristic of some white-collar criminals, meaning that low self-control can lead to strong control of others (Piquero et al., 2010).

According to deterrence theory, crime can be thwarted by the threat of punishment (Comey, 2009). However, as a self-made man, Ingebrigtsen was afraid of nothing. The threat of punishment did not appear in his mind. If it did, he found it extremely unlikely and therefore it could be ignored.

Ingebrigtsen was convicted of having leaked inside information, carried out market manipulations, and violated the obligation to report insider trading related to helping friends and family members who traded in shares in the company. But he thought he had done nothing wrong, and criticized prosecutors: "They are lying and keep information away from the court" and "This is miscarriage of justice". Ingebrigtsen felt like a victim rather than an offender in his own trial. The situation and other actors turned him involuntarily into a criminal. He perceived himself as being a victim of poor treatment after disclosure and arrest. He continued to be a victim of the criminal justice system through investigation, prosecution, sentencing, and imprisonment. He may be a victim because of conspiracies created by others to hurt him. This thinking style is in line with neutralization theory (Sykes and Matza, 1957).

Henry Amundsen (# 3) created a fraudulent accounting practice for his clients. It is unclear whether Amundsen started his accounting firm with fraud in mind, based on his experience from public tax collection, or whether he slid into crime over time. Certainly, he was fully aware of what he was doing when he hired a computer programmer to create fraudulent income statements for his clients. It was a rational choice for him to help his clients, since the benefits for his firm far exceeded expected costs in terms of possible prosecution. To his surprise, his misconduct was detected, and he was prosecuted together with cab owners. Amundsen then went on appealing his case and making all kinds of statements about his innocence, which seem to indicate lack of self-control.

In terms of neutralization techniques (Sykes and Matza, 1957), Amundsen denied responsibility by arguing that he did what his clients (cab owners) asked him to do. He presented himself as lacking responsibility for whatever misrepresentations of income reported by his clients to the internal revenue service in Norway. Amundsen strongly condemned his condemners and spent a lot of effort from his prison cell arguing that the police and prosecution were after him all the time. Amundsen also claimed appeal to higher loyalties, where his clients were his customers who should be satisfied.

While Pakistani cab owners learned about tax evasion by differential association, Amundsen was probably disillusioned from his background at the internal revenue service. When they met, they had no problems figuring out how to avoid income tax that would benefit both parties.

Alain Angelil (# 4) wanted to be a tax refugee. Long before he was revealed as a white-collar criminal, he expressed his anger about Norwegian taxes in the media. He presented in the media his new hunting castle in Scotland, and told the reporter that he had formally moved to Scotland from Norway to reduce his tax burden.

Angelil obviously claimed a legal mistake in Norway, where taxes in his opinion are far too high. Claiming legal mistake is a neutralization technique implying that the offender argues that the law is wrong. Therefore what he did, others should indeed consider quite acceptable. One may violate the law because the law is unreasonable. There is something wrong with the law and the tax brackets, since the offender perceives his or her own act as sensible and correct. It may seem that the law is there to enable law enforcement on a general basis, while it is wrong to apply the law to his specific situation. Angelil's specific situation can be characterized by double taxation, where the firm Eltek first paid tax on its profits, and then a dominant owner, Alain Angelil, had to pay income tax.

It seemed like a rational choice by Angelil to commit financial crime given his greed. Organizational access and access to resources enabled him to manipulate both income statements and stock trades. He felt he was protected from prosecution based on the competence of all his advisors.

In terms of differential association, Angelil avoided interactions with people who disagreed with him. He associated mainly with people who accepted his deviant and unlawful mores, values, and norms.

Maybe the slippery slope applies to Angelil, as his greed may have led him from the right to the wrong side of the law. Slippery slope means that a person slides over time from legal to illegal activities (Arjoon, 2008). It is the small infractions that can lead to the larger ones. An organization that overlooks the small infractions of its executives creates a culture of acceptance that may lead to its own demise. This phenomenon is captured by the metaphor of the slippery slope. Many unethical acts occur without the conscience awareness of the person who engaged in the misconduct.

Ivar T. Henriksen (# 5) rose in reputation and influence over the years. Nobody objected to what he was doing, and he felt that whatever actions he took, they were a success. His self-control disappeared, and he was all over the place in making transactions and influencing people. He was on a slippery slope without noticing. When local police finally started investigations and involved national police in economic crime investigations, he seemed surprised. He applied a neutralization argument of claiming that nobody had objected to whatever business transactions he had carried out. He blamed the board for approving and silently accepting a number of transactions that implicitly represented fraud.

It seems that Henriksen suffered from narcissistic personality traits. This is a pattern of grandiosity, need for admiration, and lack of empathy. Individuals with this disorder have a grandiose sense of self. They routinely overestimate their abilities and inflate their accomplishments, often appearing boastful and pretentious. They may blithely assume that others attribute the same value to their efforts and may be surprised when the praise they expect and feel they deserve is not forthcoming.

While being equipped with low self-control, Henriksen had a strong desire-for-control. Those with high desire-for-control are, given the opportunity, more likely to offend than those possessing low desire-for-control. Desire-for-control is defined as the wish to be in control over everyday life events. In our organizational context, desire-for-control is concerned with desire-for-control of corporate offending (Piquero et al., 2010). The desire to control and the general wish to be in control of everything and every-body might be a characteristic of some white-collar criminals. Those high in desire-for-control may be decisive and assertive, and may strongly dislike unpleasant situations or failures. They try to avoid negative situations by manipulating events to ensure desired outcomes. They tend to attrib-ute success to their own hard work, while they blame failures on others. Similarly to individuals with low self-control, individuals with high desire-for-control tend to engage in risk-taking behaviors, though only when the task is important to them.

Ivar Thorer Henriksen at Romerike Water Supply and Waste felt enti-tled to abuse company funds and get into kickback schemes with suppli-ers because he was successfully running the municipality's water supply and water waste companies. He had built up and led the waterworks. For his efforts in building these plants for 35 years he was in 2002 awarded the King's Medal of Merit in gold. In 2005, he was forced to resign after Norwegian newspaper *Aftenposten*, through a series of articles, revealed irregularities concerning the operation of these enterprises. *Aftenposten* revealed that Henriksen, through a company he controlled in South Africa, had acquired nine farms and turned them into a 100,000 acre hunting farm. Henriksen was sentenced to eight years in prison for corruption and misappropriation of funds.

The revelations in *Aftenposten* started when the newspaper wrote about economic collusion via his son Pål Henriksen's companies which the father controlled. The father found it quite acceptable to spend company money on enterprises that had nothing to do with the waterworks. When asked where he got the money to buy farms in South Africa, he told investigators that it was none of their business.

Among employees at the waterworks there were rumors of fraud. But no one dared to speak out. They feared reprisals from the boss, Ivar Thorer Henriksen, who was known for his whimsical mood and his authoritarian leadership style. The waterworks chief used his power to punish active union leaders with lower wages than others, while loyal employees were rewarded with gifts and free trips. This is documented in an investigation report.

Anyone who delivered something to the waterworks also had to give something to Henriksen. All frequently used vendors ended up contribut-ing to the private enrichment of Henriksen. Employees at the waterworks worked privately on Henriksen houses and cottages, but they did not dare raise the alarm, for Ivar Henriksen was "King of Romerike" after he received the King's Medal of Merit.

Henriksen was non-bureaucratic to the point of being nerve-wracking for detail-oriented councilors. He could be a hardliner with his authoritarian

style. But he was also the epitome of human charm and disarming persua-
siveness. Nobody said anything against him. He was the King of Romerike.

Investigators write in their report that Henriksen undoubtedly put a
great deal of effort into running the water companies. He managed to
build and operate facilities within the water sector that are solid, efficient,
and ready for the future. Henriksen had great technical insight and was
energetic and innovative in his aim of developing the companies further.
The same applied to his interest in searching for new opportunities for the
utilization of energy, especially from sludge and wastewater. He put these
opportunities in a broader context, which he said needed to be interesting
for both the region and society as a whole.

Henriksen conveyed the view to investigators that he had not gained the
acceptance and respect he deserved for what he had contributed throughout many years of his life. He argued that nobody understood his visions
of modern water supply and waste. He said his allocation of funds, even to
himself, had to be viewed in a larger context of great plans for the future.

The investigation team received numerous independent statements
showing that Henriksen often had an authoritarian behavior, especially
toward employees, but also toward representatives of suppliers. Toward
locals and municipalities served by his waterworks, however, he was always
friendly and helpful. For example, outside a nursing home in Romerike, he
had built a water fountain that the residents very much enjoyed. When the
police was lacking the space for a landing platform for its helicopter, he got
a free space paved for it.

Henriksen's changing mood created uncertainty and distance between
himself and employees. Several interviewees stated that on days when he
was in a bad mood, it was best to stay away from him. Henriksen unleashed
his temper in the presence of employees and others. A representative of a
foreign supplier was physically attacked because Henriksen was annoyed
at something. A hired consultant reported that he one day came to work to
find his office door locked with all his belongings lying on the floor in the
corridor. The consultant assignment was abruptly and definitely ended.

On the other hand, Henriksen could be generous to those who made
special effort and showed a high degree of loyalty. These persons could, for
example, receive gifts of various kinds. Henriksen on one occasion gave a
big outboard motor to an employee as a thanks for good work. In another
case, two office employees went on a spa trip to Poland as a reward for,
according to the employees, overtime work without payment and otherwise well-completed work. The journey was recorded as a business trip and
not reported to the tax authorities. Many had also been permitted to buy
used cars at a subsidized rate. Henriksen decided who should be allowed
to buy and at what price. Private purchases where the employee benefited

from discounts, were common. Other employees who had problems of one kind or another, could also find that Henriksen was generous and willing to assist in various ways. In this manner he undoubtedly secured himself many faithful supporters in the organization, and employee loyalty to Henriksen grew.

In interviews with investigators, Henriksen expressed his opinion that he had no respect for political games that often led to a lack of decisions and bureaucratic dilatoriness. His impatience and result-oriented attitude, combined with what appears to have been a lack of respect for democratic decision-making in inter-municipal companies, led him several times to choose to act first and then afterwards ensure that the respective boards approved his dealings.

Henriksen was successful in influencing political processes that affected working conditions for the companies he was running for the municipalities. He was willing to spend substantial resources to get his views across, to stop what he disliked and to initiate what he liked.

Frank Murud (# 6) did not feel bad about his crime. He blamed lack of controls at his employer for letting him carry out his fraud scheme. Murud argued in court that because the accounting department was so sloppy, they were to blame for his fraud. Therefore, in the behavioral dimension, Murud applied a neutralization technique of blaming others for his own crime. He did not carry responsibility for his fraud.

When asked what was worst, (1) media coverage, (2) family breakup, (3) prison, or (4) losing all the material things, he replied that: (1) I did not notice all the stories that were written about me before and during the trial, so no problem; (2) I found out that my wife had been unfaithful to me for many years, so no problem; (3) I have met many nice guys here in prison, so no problem; but (4) I will miss very much all the cars, boats, cabins, and houses when I get out, so a big problem there.

Murud found it to be a rational choice when he could so easily satisfy his greed. There were no safeguards stopping him, and there were no mechanisms for detecting him. The benefits of fraud seemed to far exceed the costs of crime, where the costs were so low because of the microscopic probability of detection. Murud moved onto a slippery slope when he experienced that it was indeed possible to embezzle more and more money from his employer by means of close allies outside the organization. In the aftermath, Murud gives an impression of low self-control, where he tries out new ways of escaping attention.

Birger Østraat (# 7) wanted to be a successful investment banker. But he was not. Nevertheless, he spent money like most successful investment bankers do. He felt entitled to the lifestyle enjoyed by the successful ones.

CRIMINAL CHARACTERISTICS

As evidenced in this chapter, convenience orientation can be identified among convicted white-collar criminals. Their convenience orientation was frequently present in all three dimensions of convenience theory.

We suggest that executives with a greater degree of convenience orientation will be more inclined to implement convenient strategies to achieve personal and business goals. If crime is a more convenient option to reach a goal, then executives with a greater degree of convenience orientation will have a stronger tendency to break the law. In this line of reasoning, the extent of white-collar crime can be reduced if executives with strong convenience orientation are identified. Executives and others in the elite who strongly dislike spending time and effort on time-consuming and complicated procedures, might be identified by implementing review procedures and surveillance mechanisms to prevent them from committing crime.

Individual convenience orientation can be reduced by an increased subjective likelihood of detection. Simply stated, if you think you will get caught, you do not commit crime. Subjectivity relates to a perceived detection probability that might be very different from the objective likelihood of detection. For example, you may drive at 55 miles per hour because of the speed limit as long as you think there are speed controls on the highway. If you are convinced that there are no speed controls, and when there are almost no other cars on the road, then if you are in a hurry you may be inclined to break the law by driving at 70 or even 80 miles per hour.

In addition to subjective detection probability, more severe consequences of criminal offenses may further reduce the number of white-collar crime incidents. If a potential offender is convinced that detection will lead to certain and severe punishment in terms of job loss, income loss, family loss, and loss of friends – in addition to spending several years in prison – then the attraction of crime is reduced.

6. Student survey on convenience theory

Convenience theory suggests that members of the elite in society commit financial crime in their professional roles when alternative actions require too much effort. Convenience is a relative concept where white-collar crime is chosen over legitimate actions when there is a strong economical motive, ample organizational opportunities, and acceptance of deviant behavior. To study convenience theory, a group of students were asked to express their opinions using a questionnaire. The students participated in an elective class on white-collar crime in a business school in Norway. Student responses support the concept of convenience as well as the three dimensions of economical motive, organizational opportunity, and deviant behavior, respectively. In this chapter, two empirical studies are presented based on two different questionnaires presented to students in class.

STUDENT ELICITATION

Convenience theory suggests that financial crime is a convenient option for top executives and others in the elite in society when there are major challenges or great possibilities for personal or organizational profits (Gottschalk, 2017). Rather than giving up on a contract in a corrupt country, a bribe may be a convenient option to get the contract anyway. Rather than going bankrupt, bank fraud may be a convenient option to try to save the business. Rather than giving up the desire to own a house in a rich neighborhood, embezzlement at work may be a convenient option to realize the dream.

To study convenience theory empirically, this chapter presents a student elicitation on white-collar crime. Student elicitation is derived from expert elicitation, where experts are asked to say something about the unknown. Expert elicitation seeks to make explicit and utilizable the unpublished knowledge and wisdom in the heads of experts, based on their accumulated experience as well as their interpretation and reflection in a given context (Valkenhoef and Tervonen, 2016). Elicitation is defined as collecting information from people as part of human intelligence. An elicitation technique or elicitation procedure is applied to collect and gather information from people. Expert elicitation is defined as the synthesis of opinions of experts on a subject where there is uncertainty due to insufficient data (Heyman and Sailors, 2016; Valkenhoef and Tervonen, 2016).

Expert elicitation is a systematic approach to include expert insights into the subject and also insights into the limitations, strengths, and weaknesses of published studies (Slottje et al., 2008: 7):

> Usually the subjective judgment is represented as a "subjective" probability density function (PDF) reflecting the experts' belief regarding the quantity at hand, but it can also be for instance the experts' beliefs regarding the shape of a given exposure response function. An expert elicitation procedure should be developed in such a way that minimizes biases in subjective judgment and errors related to that in the elicited outcomes.

Meyer and Booker (2001) argue that expert elicitation is invaluable for assessing products, systems, and situations for which measurements or study results are sparse or nonexistent. When experts disagree, it can mean that they interpreted the question differently or that they solved it using different lines of thought. Expert judgment can be considered relevant information in the sense that it is data based on qualified opinions. The validity or quality of expert judgment, like any data, can vary. The quality of expert judgment depends on both the completeness of the expert's mental model of the phenomena in question and the process used to elicit, model, analyze, and interpret the data.

In Scandinavia, expert elicitation has been applied to estimate the magnitude of social security fraud. While the estimate for Sweden was 6–7 percent (Delegationen, 2008), the estimate for Norway was 5 percent (Proba, 2013). Slottje et al. (2008) also applied expert elicitation in the Netherlands to assess environmental health impacts.

Expert elicitation faces some of the same challenges as elite interviewing, where there are issues associated with anonymity and confidentiality produced through power relations between the researcher and the participant (Lancaster, 2017). Expert elicitation also has similarities to expert provocation, where critical reflection is stimulated among participants on issues that are often otherwise overlooked (Pangrazio, 2017).

We define a group of students as experts because the group has particular characteristics. First, they are second-year bachelor students in a business school where they have been introduced to the issues of ethics in business. Second, they have themselves chosen an elective course on white-collar crime. Finally, the student elicitation took place in the very first meeting of the class, before they were exposed to theories such as convenience theory.

MODEL FOR HYPOTHESES

Empirical means based on, concerned with, or verifiable by observation or experience rather than plain theory or pure logic. Empirical testing and confirmation of a theory is considered to occur whenever one proposition is linked to another proposition, and the first proposition lends support to the second proposition. It is a matter of theory by evidence. Empirical research is concerned with gaining knowledge by means of direct and indirect observation or experience.

Colquitt and Zapata-Phelan (2007) define theory testing as the application of existing theory in an empirical study as a means of grounding a specific set of a priori hypotheses. Existing theory is used to formulate hypotheses before testing those hypotheses with observations. Data are then gathered to explicitly test theories.

The test of convenience theory is concentrated on establishing the validity of the theory's core propositions. However, we describe the current research as an empirical study of convenience theory, rather than an empirical test of convenience theory. Ideally, testing convenience theory as an explanation of white-collar crime would imply empirical evidence from convicted white-collar criminals, which is hard – if not impossible – to obtain. Therefore, this is not empirical theory testing, only empirical theory study.

The model in Figure 6.1 illustrates the following hypotheses to study convenience theory:

A. Economical dimension hypothesis: *Increased desire for convenient profit is positively related to increased tendency to commit white-collar crime.*

B. Organizational dimension hypothesis: *Increased convenient organizational opportunity to commit financial crime is positively related to increased tendency to commit white-collar crime.*

C. Behavioral dimension hypothesis: *Increased convenient deviant criminal behavior is positively related to increased tendency to commit white-collar crime.*

D. Hypothesis from economical dimension to organizational dimension: *Increased desire for convenient profit is positively related to increased convenient organizational opportunity to commit financial crime.*

E. Hypothesis from economical dimension to behavioral dimension: *Increased desire for convenient profit is positively related to increased convenient deviant criminal behavior.*

F. Hypothesis from organizational dimension to behavioral dimension: *Increased convenient organizational opportunity to commit financial*

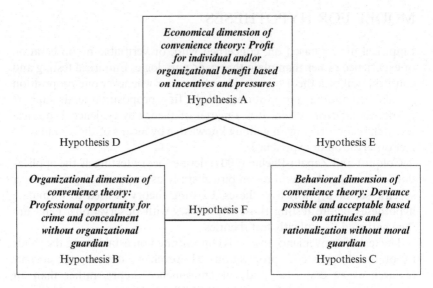

Figure 6.1   Model for hypotheses to study convenience theory

crime is positively related to increased convenient deviant criminal behavior.

In addition, we can formulate the following hypothesis that captures the overall assumptions of convenience theory:

G.   Hypothesis about convenience as a relative construct: *The more inconvenient it is to respond legitimately to financial pressures and incentives, and the more convenient it is to respond illegitimately to pressures and incentives, the stronger the tendency to commit white-collar crime will be.*

EMPIRICAL STUDY

To study the last hypothesis, hypothesis G, the following statements were included in the questionnaire as listed in the table. We expect responses to move from disagree to agree, as indicated in Figure 6.2 by an arrow. This would support convenience theory as an explanation for white-collar crime.

One hundred and twenty one students in an elective bachelor class on white-collar crime filled in the questionnaire. This is an interesting group

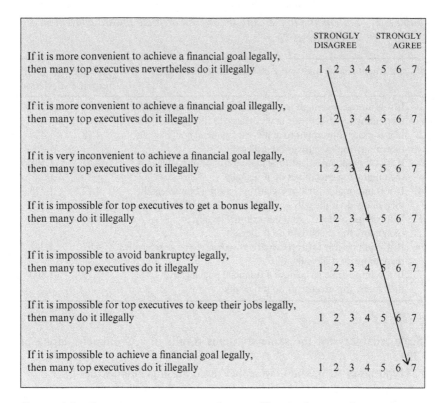

	STRONGLY DISAGREE					STRONGLY AGREE
If it is more convenient to achieve a financial goal legally, then many top executives nevertheless do it illegally	1 2 3 4 5					6 7
If it is more convenient to achieve a financial goal illegally, then many top executives do it illegally	1 2 3 4 5					6 7
If it is very inconvenient to achieve a financial goal legally, then many top executives do it illegally	1 2 3 4 5					6 7
If it is impossible for top executives to get a bonus legally, then many do it illegally	1 2 3 4 5					6 7
If it is impossible to avoid bankruptcy legally, then many top executives do it illegally	1 2 3 4 5					6 7
If it is impossible for top executives to keep their jobs legally, then many do it illegally	1 2 3 4 5					6 7
If it is impossible to achieve a financial goal legally, then many top executives do it illegally	1 2 3 4 5					6 7

Figure 6.2   Statements to measure the overall attitude toward convenience in hypothesis G

of respondents, because they are interested and motivated as evidenced by the fact they chose the elective class on "Leadership and financial crime" taught in the spring of 2017. The questionnaire was presented to them on the first day of class, before they were exposed to convenience theory.

The results are listed in Table 6.1, where the trend in Figure 6.2 is repeated in student responses. As expected, students disagree with the statement that "if it is more convenient to achieve a financial goal legally, then many top executives nevertheless do it illegally". We do not expect top executives to behave illegally when they can achieve the same results legally. Therefore, it comes as a surprise that the average score is as high as 2.96, where some respondents even agreed and strongly agreed that top executives would prefer the illegal route anyway.

Factor analysis revealed that statements 2 to 7 belong to the same factor.

Table 6.1   Statements to measure the overall attitude toward convenience in hypothesis G

#	Statements in the questionnaire on white-collar crime	Average response	Standard deviation
1.	If it is more convenient to achieve a financial goal legally, then many top executives nevertheless do it illegally	2.96	1.279
2.	If it is more convenient to achieve a financial goal illegally, then many top executives do it illegally	4.58	1.424
3.	If it is very inconvenient to achieve a financial goal legally, then many top executives do it illegally	4.61	1.508
4.	If it is impossible for top executives to get a bonus legally, then many do it illegally	4.72	1.373
5.	If it is impossible to avoid bankruptcy legally, then many top executives do it illegally	4.87	1.593
6.	If it is impossible for top executives to keep their jobs legally, then many do it illegally	4.97	1.341
7.	If it is impossible to achieve a financial goal legally, then many top executives do it illegally	5.13	1.500

Scale reliability for the same six items results in a Cronbach's alpha of .739.

Hypotheses A, B, and C were measured on single item scales:

A. *The more important the economic target, the more convenient it will be to commit financial crime.* An average score of 5.31 indicates that students agree with this statement (standard deviation 1.295).

B. *The easier it is to commit financial crime at work, the more convenient it will be to do it.* An average score of 5.27 indicates that students agree with this statement (standard deviation 1.388).

C. *The easier it is to accept one's own criminal behavior, the more convenient it will be to commit financial crime.* An average score of 5.44 indicates that students agree with this statement (standard deviation 1.352).

Hypotheses D, E, and F were measured on double item scales to represent relationships between theoretical concepts in both directions:

D. *The more ambitious an economic target is for the business, the more convenient it is to commit economic crime at work.* An average score of 4.55 indicates that students agree to some extent with this statement (standard deviation 1.240). *The more convenient it is to commit economic crime at work, the more important it is to achieve an economic target.* An average score of 4.02 indicates that students neither agree nor disagree with this statement (standard deviation 1.320).

E. *The more important the economic target, the more convenient it is to accept one's own criminal behavior.* An average score of 4.89 indicates that students agree to some extent with this statement (standard deviation 1.326). *The easier it is to accept one's own criminal behavior, the more convenient it is to achieve an economic target.* An average score of 4.54 indicates that students agree to some extent with this statement (standard deviation 1.413).

F. *The easier it is to commit economic crime at work, the more convenient it is to accept one's own criminal behavior.* An average score of 4.59 indicates that student agree to some extent with this statement (standard deviation 1.521). *The easier it is to accept one's own criminal behavior, the more convenient it is to commit economic crime at work.* An average score of 5.03 indicates that students agree with this statement (standard deviation 1.301).

Correlation coefficients were calculated for items to establish the extent of co-variation, as listed in Table 6.2.

Correlation analysis in Table 6.2 provides the following results for the three dimensions of convenience theory:

- *Economical convenience in the financial motive* varies with organizational opportunity, motive on opportunity, motive on behavior, opportunity on behavior, and behavior on opportunity.
- *Organizational convenience in the professional opportunity* varies with financial motive, deviant behavior, motive on opportunity, motive on behavior, opportunity on behavior, and behavior on opportunity.
- *Behavioral convenience in deviant willingness* varies with organizational opportunity, motive on opportunity, motive on behavior, behavior on motive, and behavior on opportunity.

Convenience orientation is conceptualized as the value that individuals and organizations place on actions with inherent characteristics of saving time and effort. Convenience orientation is measured in our six statements as a scale with acceptable reliability in Figure 6.3. A causal relationship is established in the research model in the figure, where economical, organizational, and behavioral convenience are expected to influence the extent of convenience orientation in white-collar crime.

The research model in Figure 6.3 achieves an adjusted R square of only .078, which implies that only 7.8 percent of the variation in convenience

Table 6.2 Correlation coefficients for key elements in convenience theory

	Financial motive	Organizational opportunity	Deviant behavior	Motive on opportunity	Opportunity on motive	Motive on behavior	Behavior on motive	Opportunity on behavior	Behavior on opportunity
Financial motive	1								
Organizational opportunity	.263**	1							
Deviant behavior	.100	.348**	1						
Motive on opportunity	.331**	.230*	.349**	1					
Opportunity on motive	.078	-.045	.044	.115	1				
Motive on behavior	.338**	.271*	.482**	.367**	.050	1			
Behavior on motive	.288**	.125	.269**	.270**	.214*	.395**	1		
Opportunity on behavior	.254**	.340**	.167	.205*	.227*	.399**	.234*	1	
Behavior on opportunity	.248**	.311**	.448**	.509**	.050	.629**	.294**	.431**	1

Note: * where $p<.05$ and ** where $p<0.1$.

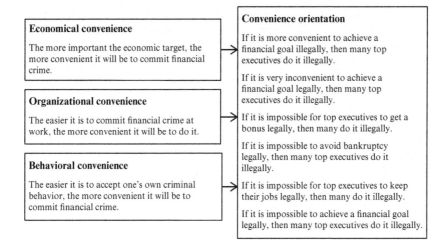

Figure 6.3   Research model to predict the extent of convenience orientation

orientation can be explained by the three predictor variables economical, organizational, and behavioral convenience. While only a small fraction of the variation can be explained by the model, the model is still statistically significant with an F-value of 4.282 and a significance of .007. When breaking down the statistics, neither economical convenience nor behavioral convenience are by themselves significant at the p<.05 level. Only organizational convenience is significant at p=.02.

This is an interesting result very much in support of convenience theory, as the theory emphasizes the organizational opportunity for crime as the main characteristic distinguishing white-collar crime from other forms of financial crime. It is the organizational connection in a professional setting that enables white-collar criminals to commit their financial crime.

A class of bachelor students who had elected to undertake a course on "Leadership and financial crime" in a business school in Norway were confronted with a short questionnaire on their first day of class in the spring term 2017. Before knowing anything about criminological, psychological, or managerial theories concerned with financial crime, they were asked to fill in the questionnaire. They had little understanding of the specific statements in the questionnaire, but they had a desire to learn how to combat crime by the elite. Therefore, they could be defined as experts in the sense of being engaged in and concerned with crime.

While many business school students may learn that top executives never commit crime because business organizations have all kinds of ethical guidelines, internal and external auditors, compliance programs, and so on, this group of students was expected to be different, and they were different. They did agree with statements such as "if it is more convenient to achieve a financial goal illegally, then many top executives do it illegally" and "if it is very inconvenient to achieve a financial goal legally, then many top executives do it illegally".

The three main elements of convenience theory were confirmed by students: the economical, organizational, and behavioral dimensions. Furthermore, correlation analysis confirms that the three dimensions are influenced by other elements as well as relationships in the conceptual model of convenience theory as illustrated in Figure 6.1. To determine convenience orientation among potential offenders, regression analysis was applied, where convenience orientation was confirmed to be significantly influenced by the set of three dimensions. However, the only significant individual dimension was organizational convenience, which supports the core distinction of white-collar crime, that is, its occurrence can be found in professional settings in organizational contexts.

INTEGRATED EXPLANATION

The behavioral dimension of crime interacts with the organizational dimension of crime. For example, executives with narcissistic or psychopathic traits (or both in the dark triad) may search for opportunities to commit financial crime in difficult situations, while conforming executives will probably not value opportunities to commit financial crime as attractive options.

The behavioral dimension of crime interacts with the economic dimension of crime as well. For example, the fear of falling (Piquero, 2012) finds causality in situations such as an acute liquidity problem, where executives perceive financial crime as the only way out of the crises. Profit-driven crime is thus not only an issue of making even more money. Rather, it is an issue of survival.

As suggested by Whetten (1989), a theoretical contribution starts by identifying factors (variables, constructs, concepts) that are parts of the explanation of the phenomenon. The phenomenon of white-collar crime finds explanation in the concepts of economics, organization, and behavior. This is the "what" of the theory.

Whetten (1989) then suggests the "how", which is how these concepts relate to each other. Figure 6.4 illustrates six integrated relationships between the economic, organizational, and behavioral dimensions. Figure 6.4 presents a model of white-collar crime occurrence, which is a presentation of convenience theory. Convenience theory represents the theoretical glue that welds the model together:

A. *It is possible to carry out and hide financial crime among legal activities in the organization.* Rational economic behavior implies individuals who consider self-interest in terms of incentives and potential costs, where detection and imprisonment are unlikely but possible costs (Welsh et al., 2014). Economic motivation exists in a self-centered search for satisfaction and avoidance of pain (Chang et al., 2005; Gottfredson and Hirschi, 1990; Hirschi and Gottfredson, 1987). Profit-driven crime in an organizational context has a superficial appearance of legitimacy (Benson and Simpson, 2015) and hides among other financial transactions (Füss and Hecker, 2008). Because the economic model implies that crime is a rational choice, crime rates will drop when likelihood of detection rises and when punishment becomes more severe (Pratt and Cullen, 2005). Impulses may play a role in distorting rational preferences and utility functions for white-collar criminals (Kamerdze et al., 2014). Crime is often the easiest and simplest way to goal achievement (Agnew, 2014). The need and desire for profit and success finds satisfaction through financial crime that offenders conveniently carry out and disguise among seemingly legal activities in the organization.

B. *Desire for profits and success makes it attractive for individuals to commit white-collar crime.* Profit-oriented offenses result from both negative and positive circumstances. The motive in situations of threats might be to protect the interests of the company and secure the survival of the enterprise (Blickle et al., 2006) or to enable down payments of personal debt (Brightman, 2009). The motive in situations of positive circumstances might be expansion into markets that are more profitable, or satisfaction of personal greed, where greed means desires and perceived needs that will always grow (Bucy et al., 2008; Goldstraw-White, 2012; Hamilton and Micklethwait, 2006). The criminal can use illegal profits to seek respect and self-realization at the top level of Maslow's pyramid of personal needs. The need and desire for profit and success makes it attractive to the individual to commit financial crime which implies convenient deviant behavior.

C. *Profession and position in the organization enables white-collar crime.* Opportunity to commit financial crime in an organizational context is a distinct characteristic of white-collar crime when compared to other financial crime offenses (Bucy et al., 2008; Michel, 2008). Executives and others in the elite have an opportunity to involve themselves in economic crime without any substantial risk of detection and punishment (Aguilera and Vadera, 2008; Haines, 2014). Opportunity manifests itself in legal access, different location, and appearance of legitimacy (Benson and Simpson, 2015; Pickett and Pickett, 2002). In a principal–agent perspective, there is an opportunity for the white-collar individual as an agent to carry out their regular job in the same situation as crime is committed. The principal is unable to monitor what the agent is doing, what knowledge the agent applies, and what risk the agent is willing to take (Chrisman et al., 2007; Li and Ouyang, 2007; Williams, 2008). A deviant organizational structure and culture can make it easier to commit financial crime and reduce the likelihood of detection and reaction (Dion, 2008; Pontell et al., 2014; Puranam et al., 2014). The profession and the position in the organization enable white-collar crime to conveniently satisfy need and the desire for profit and success.

D. *Conditions in the organization are such that the white-collar criminal can commit financial crime without others perceiving or labeling the offender as a deviant person or suspicious person.* The position occupied by the individual in relation to the organization makes it easier to practice and defend deviant behavior because of the many opportunities to commit white-collar crime (Sutherland, 1949). Social capital accumulated by the individual in terms of actual and potential resources, which are accessible because of his or her profession and position, creates a larger space for individual behavior and actions that others can hardly observe. Many initiatives by trusted persons in the elite are unknown and unfamiliar to others in the organization. Therefore, white-collar criminals do not expect consequences for themselves (Adler and Kwon, 2002). Degrees of freedom grow as individuals climb up the career ladder to the top (Heath, 2008). Degrees of freedom are particularly many when corporate crime is committed to benefit the enterprise (Bookman, 2008; Hansen, 2009; Reed and Yeager, 1996; Trahan, 2011; Valukas, 2010). Degrees of freedom are also ample when several individuals at the top of the organization participate and join forces in crime (Ashforth et al., 2008), and when the organization generally is characterized by an unethical and destructive business culture (O'Connor, 2005; Punch, 2003). The profession and position in the organization enables white-collar crime through convenient deviant behavior, which nobody notices, questions, or challenges.

E. *Acceptance and neutralization of personal deviant behavior make it easier for the white-collar offender to commit crime.* The privileged individual may feel entitled to carry out illegal acts, for example because the acts are means to reach a higher goal. The white-collar criminal belongs to the elite that makes the laws; therefore, he or she may feel free to violate the laws. The offender notices no damage and no victim. The offender does not feel sorry for banks or tax authorities. By means of neutralization techniques, the offender reduces and eliminates any feelings of guilt ahead of and after criminal acts (Sutherland, 1949; Sykes and Matza, 1957). Denial of injury and denial of victim is possible because white-collar crime is non-personal and without violence (Benson and Simpson, 2015). The acceptance and neutralization of personal deviant behavior make it convenient to commit financial crime to satisfy needs and the desire for profit and success.

F. *Deviant and criminal behavior is absorbed in an organizational context where nobody notices.* Even if unethical behavior creates reactions and suspicion develops, most internal observers will be more concerned about their own job security than blowing the whistle in situations where they are not quite sure. Criminal behavior by privileged individuals may create suspicion when the cause is visible stress that others perceive and notice as well (Agnew, 2014; Gottfredson and Hirschi, 1990; Johnson and Groff, 2014; Langton and Piquero, 2007; Pratt and Cullen, 2005). A privileged person may over time slide down a slippery slope from legal to illegal actions without really noticing or being conscious of it (Arjoon, 2008; Welsh et al., 2014). Punishment appears less likely and becomes less of a deterrent because crime occurs in professional life in an organizational context (Benson and Simpson, 2015; Comey, 2009; Gottfredson and Hirschi, 1990). Executives with an excessive desire to control others in the organization may be able to expand their own degrees of freedom by making controlled employees more passive (Piquero et al., 2010). Organizations lacking norms and common values will not notice or react to criminal behavior (Passas, 2007; Schoepfer and Piquero, 2006). The acceptance and neutralization of personal deviant behavior in terms of financial crime is conveniently absorbed in the organizational context.

CONCEPTUAL RELATIONSHIPS

Based on the research model in Figure 6.4 that captures all the conceptual relationships in convenience theory, two hypotheses were developed for each relationship:

A1. A heightened pursuit of profit to cover perceived needs increases the organizational opportunities for white-collar crime.

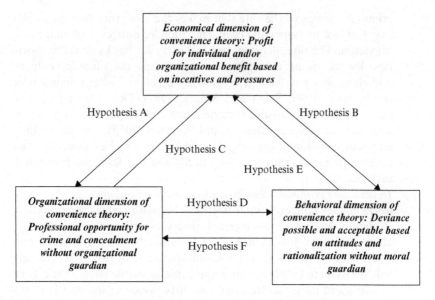

Figure 6.4   Model for hypotheses to study convenience theory

A2.   The more ambitious a financial goal is for the business, the more convenient it is to commit economic crime at work.

B1.   A heightened pursuit of profit to cover perceived needs increases the willingness to commit white-collar crime at work.

B2.   The more ambitious a financial goal is for the business, the more convenient it is to accept one's own criminal behavior.

C1.   Increased opportunity to commit white-collar crime at work strengthens the desire for profit to cover perceived needs.

C2.   The more convenient it is to commit economic crime at work, the more important it is to achieve an ambitious financial goal.

D1.   Increased opportunity to commit white-collar crime at work strengthens the willingness for a deviant behavior that includes criminal acts.

D2.   The easier it is to commit economic crime at work, the more convenient it is to accept one's own criminal behavior.

E1.   Increased willingness to commit white-collar crime at work strengthens the desire for profit to cover perceived needs.

E2.   The easier it is to accept one's own criminal behavior, the more convenient it is to achieve an ambitious financial goal.

F1.   Increased willingness to commit white-collar crime strengthens the opportunity to commit economic crime at work.

F2.   The easier it is to accept one's own criminal behavior, the more con-venient it is to commit economic crime at work.

In addition, the following issues were exposed in the questionnaire to identify respondents' perceptions of the magnitude of white-collar crime:

- I believe x% of all white-collar criminals are detected.
- I believe x% of all white-collar criminals who are detected, are investigated.
- I believe x% of all white-collar criminals who are detected and inves-tigated, are prosecuted.
- I believe x% of all white-collar criminals who are detected, investi-gated, and prosecuted, are convicted.

The above statements are concerned with the tip of the iceberg in white-collar crime. Politicians and researchers often argue that detected and con-victed white-collar criminals only represent the tip of an iceberg in terms of financial crime committed by privileged people in the elite linked to their occupations and positions in society. However, we know little about the magnitude of white-collar crime. The above statements were included in the questionnaire as potential predictors of relationships in the research model in Figure 6.4. The assumption is that lower percentages are associ-ated with stronger beliefs in the research hypotheses listed above.

REGRESSION ANALYSIS

A total of 130 students filled in the questionnaire in the class, which represents a 100 percent response rate. First, we apply descriptive statistics to study whether or not respondents agree with each relationship in the model for convenience theory. A Likert scale from 1 (completely disagree) to 7 (completely agree) was applied in the questionnaire. Therefore, a response of 4 implies neither agreement nor disagreement with the statement. Table 6.3 lists average responses as well as the standard deviation for each response.

Respondents agree with all relationships in the model of convenience theory, since all average responses are above 4. Respondents agree most strongly with the statement that "the easier it is to accept one's own crimi-nal behavior, the more convenient it is to commit economic crime at work" (F2). Respondents agree least strongly with the statement that "the more convenient it is to commit economic crime at work, the more important it is to achieve an ambitious financial goal" (C2). Respondents show the most

Organizational opportunity and deviant behavior

Table 6.3   *Statements to measure the extent of agreement or disagreement with convenience*

#	Statements in the questionnaire on white-collar crime	Average response	Standard deviation
A1.	A heightened pursuit of profit to cover perceived needs increases the organizational opportunities for white-collar crime	4.51	1.175
A2.	The more ambitious a financial goal is for the business, the more convenient it is to commit economic crime at work	4.74	1.061
B1.	A heightened pursuit of profit to cover perceived needs increases the willingness to commit white-collar crime at work	5.11	.970
B2.	The more ambitious a financial goal is for the business, the more convenient it is to accept one's own criminal behavior	4.68	1.295
C1.	Increased opportunity to commit white-collar crime at work strengthens the desire for profit to cover perceived needs	4.53	1.269
C2.	The more convenient it is to commit economic crime at work, the more important it is to achieve an ambitious financial goal	4.15	1.320
D1.	Increased opportunity to commit white-collar crime at work strengthens the willingness for a deviant behavior that includes criminal acts	4.93	1.069
D2.	The easier it is to commit economic crime at work, the more convenient it is to accept one's own criminal behavior	5.02	1.285
E1.	Increased willingness to commit white-collar crime at work strengthens the desire for profit to cover perceived needs	4.81	.969
E2.	The easier it is to accept one's own criminal behavior, the more convenient it is to achieve an ambitious financial goal	4.78	1.228
F1.	Increased willingness to commit white-collar crime strengthens the opportunity to commit economic crime at work	5.18	1.151
F2.	The easier it is to accept one's own criminal behavior, the more convenient it is to commit economic crime at work	5.65	1.054

consensus on the statement that "increased willingness to commit white-collar crime at work strengthens the desire for profit to cover perceived needs" (E1), which has the lowest standard deviation. Respondents agree the least with each other on the statement that "the more convenient it is to commit economic crime at work, the more important it is to achieve an ambitious financial goal" (C2), which has the highest standard deviation.

Next we apply correlation analysis to establish potential co-variation in responses to the 12 research hypotheses. The correlation matrix in Table 6.4 indicates significant relationships for all but one. We select randomly A1 to represent relationship A, while we compute the averages of 1 and 2 to represent relationships B–F.

The size of the iceberg as suggested by respondents is listed in Table 6.5. On average, respondents believe that only one out of five white-collar criminals is detected. They believe that one out of three detected criminals is investigated, that one out of three investigated criminals is prosecuted, and that one out of four prosecuted criminals is convicted.

The combined statements in Table 6.5 represent a multiple item scale to indicate the extent of successful law enforcement toward a specific group of criminals in society, that is, white-collar criminals. The higher the percentage, the more the respondent believes in the successful combatting of this criminal group. As a scale, the combined items achieve an acceptable reliability in terms of Cronbach's alpha of .717.

Based on these introductory statistics, we now introduce a research model in Figure 6.5 to study the extent of support for convenience theory depending on the belief in law enforcement. A stronger belief in law enforcement is assumed to result in less support for convenience theory, since more detection, investigation, prosecution, and conviction will make it less convenient to commit white-collar crime.

Regression analysis indicates that the research model is significant, with a p-value of .027 and an F-value of 2.490. The extent to which variation in law enforcement perception is determined by convenience is measured by the adjusted R square, which is only .072. This result implies that while being significant, convenience in white-collar crime only explains a minor fraction of the variation in perceived law enforcement. Among the six predictor variables, A to F, only predictor variable F is significant. This result implies that law enforcement is perceived as more successful when "increased willingness to commit white-collar crime strengthens the opportunity to commit crime at work" and when "the easier it is to accept one's own criminal behavior, the more convenient it is to commit economic crime at work".

A final statistical analysis is concerned with the correlation between convenience constructs as suggested by convenience theory. As shown in Table 6.6, most relationships correlate with other relationships in the

Table 6.4   Correlation analysis for double item scales to study theoretical relationships

Double item scale for relationships between convenience dimensions	Correlation	Average
A1. A heightened pursuit of profit to cover perceived needs increases the organizational opportunities for white-collar crime	.116	4.51
A2. The more ambitious a financial goal is for the business, the more convenient it is to commit economic crime at work		
B1. A heightened pursuit of profit to cover perceived needs increases the willingness to commit white-collar crime at work	.301**	4.89
B2. The more ambitious a financial goal is for the business, the more convenient it is to accept one's own criminal behavior		
C1. Increased opportunity to commit white-collar crime at work strengthens the desire for profit to cover perceived needs	.285**	4.34
C2. The more convenient it is to commit economic crime at work, the more important it is to achieve an ambitious financial goal		
D1. Increased opportunity to commit white-collar crime at work strengthens the willingness for a deviant behavior that includes criminal acts	.438**	4.97
D2. The easier it is to commit economic crime at work, the more convenient it is to accept one's own criminal behavior		
E1. Increased willingness to commit white-collar crime at work strengthens the desire for profit to cover perceived needs	.307**	4.80
E2. The easier it is to accept one's own criminal behavior, the more convenient it is to achieve an ambitious financial goal		
F1. Increased willingness to commit white-collar crime strengthens the opportunity to commit economic crime at work	.184*	5.41
F2. The easier it is to accept one's own criminal behavior, the more convenient it is to commit economic crime at work		

Note: * significance at p<.05, ** significance at p<.01.

Table 6.5   Statements to measure student elicitation of law enforcement

#	Statements in the questionnaire on the extent of white-collar crime law enforcement	Average response	Standard deviation
1.	Percentage of white-collar criminals detected	19%	13%
2.	Percentage of detected white-collar criminals investigated	37%	28%
3.	Percentage of detected and investigated white-collar criminals prosecuted	31%	26%
4.	Percentage of detected, investigated, and prosecuted white-collar criminals convicted	26%	26%

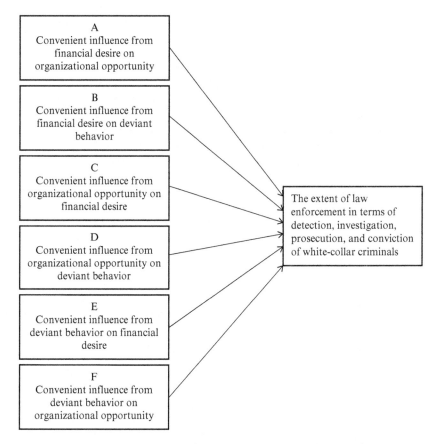

Figure 6.5   Research model predicting the perception of law enforcement dependent on convenience

Table 6.6 Correlation coefficients for key relationships in convenience theory

	Financial desire on organizational opportunity	Financial desire on deviant behavior	Organizational opportunity on financial desire	Organizational opportunity on deviant behavior	Deviant behavior on financial desire	Deviant behavior on organizational opportunity
Financial desire on organizational opportunity (A)	1	−.062	.093	.034	−.035	.000
Financial desire on deviant behavior (B)		1	.242**	.319**	.160	.383**
Organizational opportunity on financial desire (C)			1	.348**	.336**	.126
Organizational opportunity on deviant behavior (D)				1	.351**	.246**
Deviant behavior on financial desire (E)					1	.172
Deviant behavior on organizational opportunity (F)						1

Note: ** where p<.01.

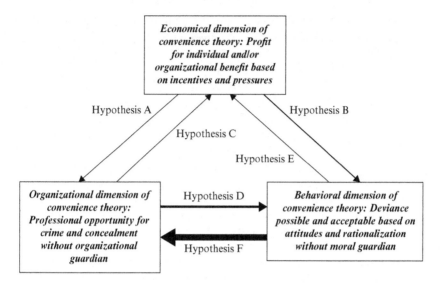

Figure 6.6   Model for hypotheses to study convenience theory

convenience model. When all six relationships are combined into a scale, Cronbach's alpha is unacceptable at .565. Thus, there is no empirical evidence to suggest that all relationships in convenience theory are linked to each other.

When we combine results from three analyses – student responses, regression analysis, and correlation analysis – then the strengths of relationships in the convenience model are as illustrated in Figure 6.6. Strongest support is found for the influence from deviant behavior on organizational opportunity in hypothesis F.

It may come as no surprise that the influence from deviant behavior on organizational opportunity is the strongest relationship in convenience theory. Neutralization theory tells us that deviant behavior is accepted by the offender based on neutralization techniques such as claiming not to be responsible, claiming there is no victim, and claiming loyalty to higher goals. While neutralization enables acceptance of criminal behavior, lack of self-control makes it easier to perform criminal acts. When the offender is both willing and able, then he or she will look for opportunities in the professional setting to conduct crime and conceal it through avoidance of organizational guardians.

In summary, a class of bachelor students who had enrolled on a course on "Leadership and financial crime" in a business school in Norway were confronted with a short questionnaire on their first day of class in the spring term 2017. Before knowing anything about criminological, psychological, or managerial theories concerned with financial crime, they were asked to fill in the questionnaire. They had little understanding of the specific statements in the questionnaire, but they had a desire to learn how to combat crime by the elite. Therefore, they could be defined as experts in the sense of being engaged in and concerned with crime.

Convenience theory suggests that members of the elite in society commit white-collar crime when alternatives to reach ambitious financial goals or avoid dangerous financial threats are too demanding. A group of financial crime students in a business school in Norway support the theory as presented in this chapter.

Hopefully, this chapter will stimulate future research into both studies of convenience theory and tests of convenience theory. Ideally, convicted white-collar criminals might be studied in future research to find potential evidence of convenience in their decisions to commit crime.

In conclusion, this chapter has reported responses from business school students to survey questions about convenience theory. Students believe that the strongest relationship within the theory is the influence from willingness in the behavioral dimension on the opportunity in the organizational dimension.

7. Whistleblowers as information sources

Whistleblowers attempt to disclose information about what they perceive as illegal, immoral, or illegitimate practices. Fraud investigators reconstruct the past after suspicions of misconduct and financial crime. Whistleblowers are an important source of information for many fraud investigators. In this chapter, characteristics of whistleblowers and their trustworthiness as information sources and the quality of pieces of information are discussed.

White-collar crime is financial crime committed by trusted people who abuse their positions in organizational settings. White-collar criminals hide their illegal activities among legal transactions (Engdahl, 2015). Victims of white-collar crime include employers, customers, investors, banks, and society at large (Alibux, 2015).

Suspicions of white-collar crime in organizations often arise when whistleblowers disclose information about potential wrongdoing (Atwater, 2006). Since white-collar crime is difficult to detect and prosecute, whistleblowers represent important information sources in the following fraud examinations and police investigations (Vadera et al., 2009). Whistleblowers may be able to provide forensic evidence in addition to witness statements (Vadera and Aguilera, 2015).

However, whistleblowers as information sources in fraud investigations are not without problems. The trustworthiness of both source (the whistleblower) and information (the facts) have to be evaluated carefully by investigators before they are included as pieces in an investigative puzzle. This chapter discusses how information from whistleblowers can be classified in fraud investigations.

CHARACTERISTICS OF WHISTLEBLOWERS

The focus on organizational members who speak out about perceived wrongdoing, also known as whistleblowers, has increased in recent years. Whistleblowing has gained recognition as an organizational social control instrument because it can terminate wrongdoing and bring offenders to justice (Bjørkelo et al., 2011).

Johnson (2005: 76) has the following definition of whistleblowing:

Whistleblowing is a distinct form of dissent consisting of four elements:
(1) the person acting must be a member or former member of the organization at issue;
(2) his or her information must be about nontrivial wrongdoing in that organization;
(3) he or she must intend to expose the wrongdoing; and
(4) he or she must act in a way that makes the information public.

Vadera et al. (2009) has the following definition of whistleblowing: "Whistleblowing is the disclosure by organizational members (former or current) of illegal, immoral, or illegitimate practices under the control of their employers, to persons or organizations that may be able to effect action." Atwater (2006) defines whistleblowing as an act by which an individual reveals wrongdoing within an organization to those in positions of authority or to the public, with hopes of rectifying the situation. Bjørkelo et al. (2011: 208) argue that the most widely applied definition in research is the one derived by Vadera et al.

Vadera et al. (2009: 555) identified the following characteristics of whistleblowers and whistleblowing:

- Federal whistleblowers were motivated by concern for public interest, were high performers, reported high levels of job security, job achievement, job commitment, and job satisfaction, and worked in high performing work groups and organizations.
- Anger at wrongful activities drove individuals to make internal reports to management. Retaliation by management shifted individuals' focus away from helping their organizations or victims and toward attaining retribution.
- Whistleblowing was more likely when observers of wrongdoing held professional positions, had more positive reactions to their work, had longer service, were recently recognized for good performance, were male, were members of larger work groups, and were employed by organizations perceived by others to be responsive to complaints.
- Whistleblowing was more frequent in the public sector than in the private.
- Whistleblowing was strongly related to situational variables with seriousness of the offense and supportiveness of the organizational climate being the strongest determinants.
- Inclination to report a peer for theft was associated with role responsibility, the interests of group members, and procedural perceptions.

Zipparo (1999) identified the following two main factors which deter public officials from reporting corruption:

- Concern about not having enough proof.
- Absence of legal protection from negative consequences.

One of the more successful whistleblowers is Michael Lissack. He worked as a banker at the Smith Barney brokerage. In 1995, he blew the whistle on a fraudulent scheme, known in municipal financing as "yield burning". Dr. Lissack filed a whistleblower lawsuit against more than a dozen Wall Street firms under the False Claims Act. In April 2000, 17 investment banks agreed to pay approximately 140 million US dollars to settle charges that they defrauded the federal government by overpricing securities sold in connection with certain municipal bond transactions. The US government has recovered more than 250 million US dollars as the result of Dr. Lissack's whistleblower action. His allegations have brought on more than a dozen civil and criminal investigations by the Securities and Exchange Commission (SEC), the Internal Revenue Service (IRS), and the US Department of Justice. Dr. Lissack has written editorials about whistleblowing for the *New York Times* and the *Los Angeles Times* and has been profiled in many international publications, including the *Wall Street Journal*, the *Financial Times*, *Fortune*, *Business Week*, *The Economist*, and *USA Today* (www.whistleblowerdirectory.com).

In 2001, Sherron Watkins, an employee in the American energy company Enron, notified her chief executive officer (CEO) Kenneth Lay about a perceived accounting scandal. Watkins did so hoping Lay would act. He did not, and was later arrested due to his involvement in the wrongdoing, because she blew the whistle (Bendiktsson, 2010).

Negative consequences after whistleblowing, suffered by some whistleblowers, are labeled retaliation. Retaliation implies to take an undesirable action against a whistleblower – who reported wrongdoing internally or outside the organization. Retaliation can be defined as taking adverse action against an employee for opposing an unlawful employment practice or participating in any investigation, proceeding, or hearing related to such a practice (Bjørkelo and Matthiesen, 2011).

The National Whistleblowers Center (NWC) in the United States lists a number of whistleblowers (www.whistleblowers.org). A few of them blew the whistle because of public procurement corruption. An example is Bunnatine Greenhouse, who stood alone in opposing the approval of a highly improper multi-billion dollar no bid contract to Halliburton for the reconstruction of Iraq. In retaliation for her courage she was removed from her position as the highest-ranking civilian contracting official of the

Army Corps of Engineers. On June 27, 2005, she testified to a congressional panel, alleging specific instances of waste, fraud, and other abuses and irregularities by Halliburton with regard to its operation in Iraq since the 2003 invasion. Vice President Dick Cheney had been the CEO of Halliburton. Criminal investigations into Halliburton were opened by the US Justice Department, the Federal Bureau of Investigation, and the Pentagon's inspector general. These investigations found no wrongdoing within the contract award and execution process. On July 25, 2011, the US District Court in Washington DC approved awarding Greenhouse 970,000 US dollars in full restitution of lost wages, compensatory damages, and attorney fees.

The Whistleblower Directory (www.whistleblowerdirectory.com) is a comprehensive database showcasing individuals who have reported financial crime. An example is Jim Alderson, who worked as an accountant for Quorum Health Services in Montana and as chief financial officer at the Whitefish hospital. In 1992 he blew the whistle on the hospital's fraudulent bookkeeping practices, wherein reimbursements were routinely sought after filing fraudulent cost reports with Medicare. In retaliation for his whistleblowing disclosure, Alderson was fired. He filed a whistleblower lawsuit against his former employer, Quorum Health Services, and its former owner, Hospital Corp. of America. Five years after Alderson filed the lawsuit, the federal government joined the case. In October 2000, Quorum settled the case. Under the False Claims law, Alderson received 11.6 million US dollars and Quorum paid a fine of 77.5 million US dollars.

Janet A. Garrison and Herb F. Hyman were procurement professionals who blew the whistle. During the course of their employment with public entities in Florida, they uncovered unethical procurement practices. They then became whistleblowers. In their jobs as government purchasers, both Garrison and Hyman believe that they are entrusted by the public to spend taxpayer dollars wisely and fairly. Each individual also notes that codes of ethics govern their membership in professional procurement associations, as well as their certifications. Thus, Garrison and Hyman felt it was their public and professional duty to report ethics breaches that clearly violated the US's laws or specific procurement statutes. However, their efforts to "do the right thing" met with unanticipated outcomes, ranging from the mixed reactions of others to a complex maze of ongoing legal proceedings (Atwater, 2006).

Janet A. Garrison's whistleblowing experience occurred when she worked as a purchasing analyst for the Florida Department of Education (DOE). Back in 2003, she was asked to help develop a solicitation for privatizing about 174 jobs in DOE's Office of Student Financial Assistance (Atwater, 2006).

For Herb F. Hyman, procurement manager with the Town of Davie, Florida, his whistleblowing experience related to the purchasing practices of the town administrator, Christopher J. Kovanes. Hired by the town council as a contract employee, Kovanes was the town's top leader. Thus, Kovanes was Hyman's boss (Atwater, 2006).

Another whistleblower can be found at the office of information technology in Washington DC, involving white-collar corruption in public procurement. In the case of the Acar fraud investigation, Yusuf Acar was unveiled through whistleblowing from the Office of the Chief Technology Officer by a confidential informant, since Sidley (2010: 28) state in their report that it was "the cooperation of a confidential informant that led to the discovery of the fraud."

Miceli et al. (2009) suggest that employees can be encouraged to report wrongdoing both before concerns are expressed and once concerns are expressed. Before concerns are expressed, employees can be encouraged in the development of moral identity and moral agency, in creating a tough anti-retaliation policy that permits disciplining or dismissing employees who retaliate against whistleblowers, and in disseminating the policy through the intranet, in orientation materials, and elsewhere. After concerns are expressed, employees can be encouraged to focus on the wrongdoing alleged in the complaint and not on the complainant, to investigate reports fully and fairly, and to take swift action when the complaint is well-founded.

In a study of corruption in public procurement in the European Union, Wensink and Vet (2013) found that approximately 40 percent of fraudulent activities are detected by a whistleblower alert. They recommend furthering investment in good functioning systems for whistleblowers, including proper protection of whistleblowers. Legislation on whistleblowing as well as protection of whistleblowers represent areas that are not well regulated yet.

Some potential whistleblowers are reluctant to blow the whistle because they adhere to the loyalty–betrayal paradox. They consider whistleblowing an act of treachery against the organization. The loyalty–betrayal paradox leads to a pro-organizational behavior defined by a dedication to the in-group and reflects such values as patriotism, self-sacrifice, and allegiance. In the name of loyalty, individuals will sacrifice themselves to save their group members (Fehr et al., 2015).

DETECTION OF WHITE-COLLAR CRIME

According to Kaplan et al. (2011), employee tips are the most common form of initial fraud detection, suggesting that employees frequently are aware of fraud before others professionally charged to unveil fraud, such as internal and external auditors. The willingness of employees, who learn about fraud, to report this information, varies with several factors. For example, if the executive to whom misconduct should be reported is not trusted, employees will tend not to report. Whistleblowing decisions are dependent on information, trust, security, predictability, self-confidence, job security, and organizational culture in general.

In the database of 405 convicted white-collar criminals in Norway reported by Gottschalk (2017), whistleblowers are not registered as a source of detection. Journalists are at the top of the detection list. It is very likely that many, probably most, of the media work was initially based on tips from insiders. Whistleblowers were probably also the main source of initial information for internal auditors and police investigators. Thus, it might be argued that more than half of all detected white-collar criminals in Norway were revealed by whistleblowers. If we add up journalists (25 percent), internal auditors (11 percent), police investigators (2 percent), and others (22 percent), and assume their main source to be whistleblowers, then 60 percent of all detections of white-collar crime can be attributed to whistleblowers.

FRAUD INVESTIGATIONS

When suspicions of white-collar crime arise in organizations, fraud examiners are often hired by the organization to investigate the matter. A number of reasons often prevent organizations from reporting suspicions to the police or the public. Fraud examiners in financial crime investigations are employed by accounting firms and law firms to conduct reviews in order to reconstruct the past. An example is Sidley (2010), who investigated procurement practices at the Office of the Chief Technology Officer of the District of Columbia.

Reports of investigations by fraud examiners are typically written at the final stage of private inquiries. Reports are handed over to the clients who pay for the work. Reports are seldom disclosed, so that the public never learn about them and are often protected by attorney–client privilege when investigating firms are law firms (Williams, 2005).

An investigation is an investigation, regardless of whether the investigator is employed by a police agency or a private firm. The goal is to uncover the facts in a particular situation. In doing so, the truth about the situation is the ultimate objective. However, an investigation by the police is going to start with a crime, or a suspected crime, and the end goal is to arrest and successfully prosecute the guilty person(s) or, alternatively, dismiss the case because of innocence or lack of evidence. Professional detectives are employed just as much to look for evidence proving innocence as to look for evidence proving guilt. A private investigation is mainly after the facts, with the goal of determining how a negative event occurred, or the goal of determining whether the suspected action occurred at all. The goal might also be to prevent a situation from ever occurring in the first place, or to prevent it happening again.

Private fraud investigators are not in the business of law enforcement. They are not there to obtain private settlements when penal laws are violated. Their task is to reconstruct the past as objectively and completely as possible. Therefore, sources of information are critical to complete the puzzle as professionally as possible. If the puzzle is not complete, private examiners are unable to draw trustworthy conclusions.

Police investigations differ from private investigations because they aim to convict a person of a crime or dismiss a person from the case, while private investigations are used more to evaluate the potential for economic crime to occur and to get rid of the issue internally rather than through the involvement of the police (Schneider, 2006).

The roles of police officers and private investigators are different in the fact that they do not have the same powers. Police officers have powers of arrest, communication control, and surveillance, as well as technology and document seizure. On the other hand, police officers have strict rules that they have to follow within their department. Officers are responsible for following rules and guidelines set before them by the government. Private investigators have more freedom to explore and conduct inquiries into suspected crime and criminals. However, the police officers' advantage is their ability to seize documents and subpoena the guilty party. The police have formal power in terms of law enforcement on behalf of society. While private investigators have less power in their work, they enjoy more freedom in how they do their work.

Objectivity as well as integrity are important in fraud investigations. Objectivity is the undeniable knowledge of facts and capability to extract true knowledge as well as judgment without prejudice, partiality, and prefixed notions (Zagorin, 2001). Objectivity is a state of mind in which biases do not inappropriately affect understanding and assessment (Mutchler, 2003). Integrity is defined as the quality of being honest and morally upright. Integrity implies absence of misconduct. The term integrity derives from the Latin adjective integer, which means to be complete or whole (Killinger, 2010).

INFORMATION SOURCES

Lack of formal powers requires private fraud investigators to rely on information sources that are voluntarily available to them. As whistleblowing may imply going against formal power structures, this kind of behavior may be regarded as deviant and as an aggressive form of communication (Bjørkelo et al., 2011). Because of the special characteristics of a whistleblower and whistleblowing situations, receivers of complaints and reports have two issues to consider when dealing with whistleblowers as an information source. First, not all that is said and not all accusations from a whistleblower are necessarily true. Therefore, information from a whistleblower has to be carefully checked and verified. Second, a whistleblower may be in danger of retaliation, making it a requirement for receivers to protect the whistleblower. Report receivers have to make sure that a whistleblower contributing to an investigation does not experience negative consequences.

To evaluate sources of information and pieces of information, a framework combining sources and pieces can be helpful. The framework can consist of a matrix of, for example, 4 by 4 or 6 by 6. We choose a matrix of 6 by 6 for sources and pieces, and define first a set of six levels for information sources (Police, 2014):

A. *Completely reliable source.* Tested and trusted; no doubt about authenticity, trustworthiness, and competence; has always provided accurate information.
B. *Usually reliable source.* Minimal uncertainty about authenticity, reliability, and expertise; mostly supplied correct information previously.
C. *Quite reliable source.* Some uncertainty about authenticity, trustworthiness, and competence, but has delivered correct information in the past.
D. *Usually not reliable source.* Considerable uncertainty about authenticity, trustworthiness, and competence, but has in certain situations provided accurate information in the past.
E. *Not reliable source.* Absence of authenticity, reliability, and competence; historically supplied information that is not correct; proven unworthy of any confidence.
F. *Reliability cannot be assessed.* Not sufficient basis to evaluate the source's reliability.

It is interesting to note that a not reliable source (E) is considered better than a source where reliability cannot be assessed (F). An explanation for this classification might be that it is better to have some negative insight into a source than no insight into the source at all.

We now define a set of six levels for information pieces (Police, 2014):

1. *Confirmed by other sources.* Verified by other independent sources; logical; corresponds with other information on the same topic.
2. *Probably correct information.* Not confirmed by other independent sources, but seems logical; corresponds largely with other information on the same topic.
3. *Possibly correct information.* Not confirmed by other independent sources, but seems reasonably logical; corresponds to some other information on the same topic; not in conflict with established pattern/ trend.
4. *Questionable information piece.* Not confirmed by other independent sources; possible but not logical; no other information on the same subject; information tends to be in conflict with established pattern/ trend.
5. *Unlikely information piece.* Not confirmed by other independent sources; not logical; conflicts with other information on the same topic; clearly in conflict with established pattern/trend.
6. *Accuracy cannot be assessed.* Not sufficient basis to evaluate the accuracy of the information.

Information sources and information pieces are combined in Table 7.1, where A1 is very good, while F6 is very bad.

CRIME SIGNAL DETECTION THEORY

Signal detection theory may shed some light onto why some actors discover and disclose more white-collar crime than others. Signal detection theory holds that the detection of a stimulus depends on both the intensity of the stimulus and the physical and psychological state of the individual. A detector's ability or likelihood of detecting some stimulus is affected by the intensity of the stimulus (e.g., how loud the whistleblowing is) and the detector's physical and psychological state (e.g., how alert the person is). Perceptual sensitivity depends upon the perceptual ability of the observer to detect a signal or target or to discriminate signal from non-signal events (Szalma and Hancock, 2013).

Furthermore, detecting persons may have varying ability to discern

Table 7.1 Quality of information sources and information pieces

	Confirmed by other sources	Probably correct information	Possibly correct information	Questionable information piece	Unlikely information piece	Accuracy cannot be assessed
Completely reliable source	Very good	A2	A3	A4	A5	A6
Usually reliable source	B1	B2	B3	B4	B5	B6
Quite reliable source	C1	C2	C3	C4	C5	C6
Usually not reliable source	D1	D2	D3	D4	D5	D6
Not reliable source	E1	E2	E3	E4	E5	E6
Reliability cannot be assessed	F1	F2	F3	F4	F5	Very bad

between information-bearing recognition (called pattern) and random patterns that distract from information (called noise).

Under signal detection theory, some researchers found that people more frequently and incorrectly identify negative task-related words as having been presented originally than positive words, even when they were not present. Liu et al. (2014) found that people have lax decision criteria for negative words. In a different study, Huff and Bodner (2013) applied the signal detection approach to determine if changes in correct and false recognition following item-specific versus relational encoding were driven by a decrease in the encoding of memory information or by an increase in monitoring.

According to the theory, there are a number of determinants of how a person will detect a signal. In addition to signal intensity, signal alertness, and pattern recognition, there are other factors such as personal competence (including knowledge, skills, and attitude), experience, and expectations. These factors determine the threshold level. Low signal intensity, low signal alertness, and limited pattern recognition, combined with low competence, lack of experience, and lack of expectations, will lead to a high threshold level, meaning that the individual will not detect white-collar crime.

Signal detection theory implies that persons make decisions under conditions of uncertainty. The theory assumes that the decision-maker is not a passive receiver of information, but an active decision-maker who makes difficult perceptual judgments under conditions of uncertainty. Whether a stimulus is present or absent, whether a stimulus is perceived or not perceived and whether a perceived stimulus is ignored or not, will influence the decision in terms of detecting or not detecting white-collar crime.

Signal detection theory characterizes the activity of an individual's discrimination as well as psychological factors that bias his or her judgment. The theory is concerned with the individual's discriminative capacity, or sensitivity that is independent of the judgmental bias or decision criterion the individual may have had when the discrimination was made.

In Table 7.2, an attempt is made to describe the signal detection features of observers who have noticed and discover white-collar crime. Signal intensity, signal alertness, pattern recognition, and personal experience are derived from signal detection theory as characteristics of detection ability.

We argue that signal intensity for tips to journalists is normally high, as whistleblowers tend to be upset and want to get attention. Furthermore, we suggest that signal alertness is high among journalists, as they are dependent on tips in their daily work to cover news stories. The issue of pattern recognition is not obvious for journalists, since they often present fragments on a publishing basis, rather than a complete and consistent

Table 7.2   Characteristics of stimulus in detection of white-collar crime

Rank	Crime detection source	Signal intensity	Signal alertness	Pattern recognition	Personal experience	Total score
1.	Journalists	High	High	Low	Medium	9
2.	Crime victims	High	Low	High	Low	8
3.	Internal control	Low	Medium	High	Medium	8
4.	Bankruptcy lawyers	Low	Low	High	Medium	7
5.	Tax authorities	Low	Low	Low	Low	4
6.	Commercial bank	Low	High	Low	Low	6
7.	Accounting auditors	Low	Medium	Medium	Low	6
8.	Police investigations	Low	Medium	High	High	9
9.	Stock exchange	Low	Low	Medium	Low	5
10.	Other sources					

story of events. Personal experience will vary among journalists who may or may not have written about white-collar crime before, depending on the extent of specialization among journalists in the newspaper.

The idea of the above table is to apply four characteristics of signal detection theory to the detection of white-collar crime. At this stage, the items and values represent exploratory research that require further study to be trustworthy. Both selection of characteristics as well as judgment along these characteristics for each crime detection source need multiple raters to enable inter-rater reliability to be computed.

However, it is an interesting personal experiment. For example, the police in Norway are a passive receiver of signals. The Norwegian police has no undercover presence in financial markets and has no informants in business corporations. Therefore, the police's opportunity to receive signals is very limited.

Based on a sample of 369 convicted white-collar criminals in Norway from 2009 to 2014, where 97 offenders were detected by journalists and 272 were detected by others, we found some interesting differences between the two groups. In statistical terms, significant differences can be found in terms of the sums of money involved in crime, and personal finances as registered by the internal revenue service.

There seems to be a lot to learn from investigative media and their journalists. Rather than formal procedures often applied on a routine basis by auditors and internal controllers, information sources in terms of persons in networks seem to be a more fruitful approach to the detection of white-collar crime.

8. Corporate social responsibility

Organizational opportunity and deviant behavior are issues that should be of concern for all executives responsible for compliance and corporate social responsibility (CSR). Unfortunately, many organizations think of CSR as a way of doing good deeds for society without changing business practices. Many case studies illustrate that chief executives have not yet understood their responsibility for CSR in general and certainly not for political CSR. Most executives still believe that CSR is concerned with doing good symbolic deeds in local societies by behaving so as to create an image of being philanthropists.

In this chapter, we suggest that the powerful concept of stages of growth is extremely important in management research. Stages of growth models have been used widely in both organizational research and information technology management research. These models describe a wide variety of phenomena. These models assume that predictable patterns (conceptualized in terms of stages) exist. The stages are (1) sequential in nature, (2) occur as a hierarchical progression that is not easily reversed, and (3) involve a broad range of organizational activities and structures.

White-collar crime is committed in an organizational setting. The organization enables crime to occur and to be hidden among legal transactions. While organizations tend to claim that they are victims of white-collar crime, they do in fact represent enablers of financial crime. Therefore, organizations carry responsibility for crime and crime prevention. Crime prevention and detection is part of corporate citizenship, where the organization should avoid causing costs to society in terms of prosecution and punishment of white-collar criminals. When organizations allow white-collar crime to happen, then harm is caused to society. This is the opposite of CSR, where the organization is expected to contribute benefits to society.

The individual profession and position in the organization makes it possible for the white-collar criminal to commit financial crime. Convenience theory and empirical study of white-collar criminals show that it is in the organizational context that white-collar crime is possible and is committed. Organizations should therefore be held responsible for crime occurring among their trusted and privileged executives.

Both public and private businesses have responsibility for preventing others being victimized by their own white-collar criminals. Empirical study indicates that customers, banks, tax collectors, and others are victims of white-collar crime committed in other organizations. Although there are always individuals who carry out the actual crime, it is the business that opened up the possibilities for carrying out crime. By showing confidence and trust, and by providing privileges, power, and influence, with little or no control in place, the business opens up the possibilities for financial crime.

Empirical study shows that employers are the single largest group among white-collar crime victims. Embezzlement, fraud, and other forms of financial crime make it possible for trusted employees to enrich themselves at the expense of the business. The business itself is hurt. At the same time, the business itself is to blame. The business has enabled – and not prevented – the occurrence of white-collar crime.

WHEN EMPLOYERS BECOME CRIME VICTIMS

Leif Marius Schatvet (born 1963) was a chief financial officer (CFO) at Aschehoug publishing house in Oslo, where he embezzled a total of 9 million Norwegian kroner (about 1.4 million US dollars). The publishing house was partly an owner of a bookstore chain from which Aschehoug decided to remove itself. Schatvet was asked to close the relationship with the chain. A number of financial transactions occurred between the publishing house and the bookstore chain that were all handled by Schatvet and controlled by nobody else. He discovered an opportunity to transfer some of the money to his own bank account, which he did. After having transferred 9 million kroner, he was in the process of transferring 1 million more to his private bank account, when he entered a wrong account number for his own bank account. The typing mistake was reported by the bank to one of his subordinates in the accounting department, who blew the whistle on the CFO to the chief executive officer (CEO). The CEO hired professional services firm KPMG to do an internal investigation using fraud examiners. Schatvet said in court that he was short of money because of an expensive divorce and the purchase of a winter cabin in the mountains (Hegnar, 2014).

Are Blomhoff (born 1952) was a priest and the CEO at the Betanien Foundation, a diaconal institution. The foundation runs nursing homes, kindergartens, and other social institutions in Norway. In addition, it is in charge of a nursing home for retired Norwegians in Spain. Blomhoff frequently visited the nursing home in Spain and bought himself an apartment in the neighborhood. He opened a bank account for himself in a local Spanish bank and started to transfer some Betanien money to his private bank account in Spain. The embezzled money paid for his housing expenses as well as wild parties, where he paid local prostitutes to join in. Two junior employees at Betanien tried to blow the whistle on Blomhoff, but nobody on the board of directors believed their accusations of wrong-doings on the part of the priest and chief executive. Therefore, Blomhoff's embezzlement continued for many years. Finally, someone on the board of directors believed the whistleblowers, and the board hired fraud examiners from BDO to investigate the matter. BDO investigators found evidence of several million Norwegian kroner embezzled by Blomhoff, and he was later sentenced to three years in prison by a district court (Drammen tingrett, 2015).

Bente Selvaag (born 1952) was assistant manager at BNP Paribas, where she was in charge of collection cases after the financial crisis in the banking sector in Norway. Some of the collected money was not transferred to the bank, but rather to interim accounts and onwards to her personal accounts. She was able to continue her embezzlement activity for nine years before she was randomly detected. By then the total embezzled amount was 13 million Norwegian kroner (2 million US dollars). Her position made it possible to embezzle, since the bank had not introduced a control system for her function in the bank (Kleppe, 2011).

Jørn Bertheussen (born 1952) was CEO at the grocery and bakery chain Din Baker. He charged expenses to company accounts at Fokus Bank and Voss Bank by means of invoices and payment requests issued by two Swedish companies, Finshyttan Fastighet and Herrgården Finshyttan. Bertheussen owned both of them. According to internal revenue service figures for 2009, Bertheussen had an annual income of 1.8 million Norwegian kroner (about 300,000 US dollars), which is quite an accept-able wage in Norway. His position in the company allowed him to embez-zle, because the owners had not introduced a control mechanism related to the CEO's activities. The board at Din Baker hired private investigators from PwC to examine fraud. Bertheussen was sentenced to four months in prison by a district court in Norway (Asker and Bærum tingrett district court, 2012).

Lars Brorson (born 1973) was CFO at Hadeland and Ringerike Broadband. He was hired into this position, although someone in the parent company had heard of his previous convictions and jail sentences because of fraud. Brorson had complete control of financial transac-tions between sister companies and to and from the parent company. He approved transactions in both the transferring and the receiving units, because there were so many different legal entities in the group. His fraud was revealed when it was detected that he was involved in financial crime outside his regular job as well. Brorson was sentenced to four and a half years in prison by a district court in Norway. At the same time, PwC (2014a, 2014b) were hired by the board at Hadeland and Ringerike Broadband to identify and present how fraud had occurred.

Aschehoug, Betanien, BNP Paribas, Din Baker, and Hadeland and Ringerike Broadband are only five examples of business organizations that have made it possible for trusted individuals to commit white-collar crime to enrich themselves. In the database of 405 convicted white-collar criminals in Norway, 115 persons (28 percent) were able to victimize their own organizations through financial crime.

These 115 persons caused damage to their employers because their employers had enabled them to commit financial crime. At the same time, damage was caused to society because criminals had to be prosecuted and kept in correctional institutions while serving their prison sentences. Should companies be held responsible for damage caused to society? If these companies had installed controls, reduced degrees of freedom, and relied less on trust then fewer potential white-collar criminals would commit financial crime. This is according to convenience theory, which argues that the tendency to criminality is reduced when opportunities decline and detection likelihood increases.

WHEN OTHERS BECOME CRIME VICTIMS

Among 405 white-collar criminals, 115 of them caused financial losses to their own organization, while 290 criminals caused financial damage to external parties. Eighty-four criminals caused economic losses to the society at large, since the internal revenue service did not get tax payments as required. Sixty-eight offenders caused financial losses to customers, 57 offenders caused losses to banks, and 30 criminal shareholders caused financial damage to other shareholders, while the remaining 51 offenders caused financial losses to a variety of victims.

When tax authorities such as the internal revenue service are victimized, society at large becomes a victim. Financial revenue to the state is dedicated to two main objectives. First, there is authority and government such as police, military, and other functions equipped with power on behalf of the state. Next, there is service provision to inhabitants such as medical care, hospitals, and roads. When tax revenues decline, then the state can either increase taxes for taxpayers who pay, or the state can reduce its administration and service. In a taxi fraud case in Norway, the accounting firm of Henry Amundsen produced accounting figures for hundreds of taxi owners who did not have to pay taxes because of the misrepresenta-tion of financial results. Amundsen was sentenced to eight years in prison. Artist Odd Nerdrum sold his paintings abroad, but did not report his income to Norwegian tax authorities. He was sentenced to two years and eight months in prison. Morten Stang Sausage Factory did not report sales of meat for kebabs. Several members of the Stang family were sentenced to prison (Borgarting, 2009).

When customers are victimized, innocent individuals and firms are financially hurt. One example is attorneys who misuse client funds. Some clients place their money in attorney accounts, for example as a security deposit, as a transfer for payments, or as a receipt of payments. Attorney Odd Arild Drevland was convicted of client fraud and sentenced to prison for two and a half years. Another example is container firm Uniteam, run by father and son Harald (born 1942) and Tommy Engh (born 1985). They were sentenced in a court of appeals to three and a half years and three years of prison respectively for fraud against the Norwegian Army. Fraud occurred because the father and son stated incorrect material costs to their customer (Næss and Ravn, 2013).

When banks are affected, owners, depositors, and borrowers are hurt. A bank becomes less profitable when bank fraud occurs, and bank owners (shareholders) lose money. Depositors can be hurt because the bank may decrease the deposit rate. Borrowers can be hurt because the bank may increase the lending rate. A bank is in the business of connecting people with too much money (depositors) with people who have too little money (borrowers). When borrowers commit bank fraud and thus do not pay back their loans, all stakeholders in the bank suffer financial loss. When Finance Credit in Norway went bankrupt, a number of banks lost a total of 1 billion Norwegian kroner (160 million US dollars). Bankruptcy arose long after the firm Finance Credit was broke. Torgeir Stensrud, chair-man of the board, and Trond Kristoffersen, chief executive, had for years presented misleading economic statements to banks, making banks fund more and more debts that did not exist. Stensrud and Kristoffersen were sentenced to seven and nine years in prison respectively (Riisnæs, 2014).

The last group of victims is shareholders. Some shareholders have been able to sell shares at extremely high prices, or buy shares at extremely low prices, because they had information that other shareholders did not possess. It is not illegal to have exclusive information which represents an information asymmetry among shareholders. What is illegal is exclusive information from a particular source. That particular source is internal people in the organization that is owned by the shareholders. If internal people leak stock-price sensitive information to selected people who act in the stock market on the information, both those who leak information and those who trade shares commit financial crime. It is called insider trading, which is illegal in most countries. Insider trading is organizationally anchored when someone on the inside knows something that is profitable for themselves and also profitable for people on the outside. The Acta case is an example of insider trading in Norway (Stavanger tingrett, 2012).

There are considerable differences between these four groups of victims. Tax authorities like the internal revenue service have in no way been involved, and such services have no way of telling whether tax evasion has occurred. The only way they can find out is to actively retrieve and search documents from taxpayers to control taxpayers' statements. Tax authorities do not know whether accounting statements have been manipulated until they eventually discover misconduct through their own investigations. Similarly, tax authorities have no information about an artist selling his or her paintings abroad, unless they are actively investigating the finances of the artist. Tax authorities are not involved in any way unless they start auditing and other forms of investigations.

The second group of victims is customers. They have some opportunity to know what is going on, since they have involved themselves with someone who has turned out to be a criminal. Customers have the possibility of checking the correctness of invoices and other information from the supplier. However, a client of a law firm often has little or no insight into the internal operations of the firm.

The third group of victims is banks. They are involved, and they may be to blame when they become victims of bank fraud. Banks are actively involved in paying out money to borrowers. When the borrowers present fake documents and manipulated statements, it is the responsibility of banks to avoid making payments based on such misleading information. If banks do pay in such situations, then their risk assessment and background checks of potential borrowers have failed. Norwegian banks trusted blindly Stensrud and Kristoffersen at Finance Credit for many years, without installing proper controls. It was an investigative journalist who revealed that Finance Credit was in reality bankrupt several years ago. Similarly, banks trusted blindly the CEO at Sponsor Service, Terje Bogen, who claimed that sponsoring contracts for top athletes would all be signed in the near future. Banks lost 400 million Norwegian kroner because of their trust in Bogen. In these cases of bank fraud, there is organizational failure not only on the part of the fraudsters, but also on the part of the banks. Because banks have improper controls in relation to potential fraudsters, society is frequently required to punish offenders when they are detected. Therefore, banks do not only lose money but also create expenses for society in courts and prisons.

Other shareholders are not responsible for being cheated by insider trading. They had no inside information. If they had possessed inside information, it is not obvious that they would have acted on the information. A company owned by shareholders is like a zero-sum game when the value of the company at a given point in time is constant. When someone is able to acquire a share of the company similar to the share owned by someone else, but at a lower price, then the same value is obtained at a lower cost.

GJENSIDIGE AND THE HELLS ANGELS

The empirical sample in this book is concerned with financial crime in general and with white-collar crime in particular. So far in this chapter, we have discussed the extent to which businesses may themselves be responsible for crime occurrences, although they are initially perceived as victims of crime. It is a matter of CSR, where organizations are accountable and responsible to society for their own negative impacts.

In this section we will visit a completely different kind of crime often labeled organized crime. The example is concerned with the Norwegian insurance company Gjensidige and their responsibility for combatting crime in society whenever there is a chance for the company to do so. It is a matter of CSR as well, where organizations are expected to take responsibility for society and the environment in broad terms. This example is interesting, because the insurance company found themselves in a peculiar situation after a claim settlement.

A woman was killed in an explosion that occurred in the city of Drammen in June 1997. Five men were in 2003 convicted of blowing up the headquarters of Bandidos. Some of the convicts were members of Hells Angels Motorcycle Club (HAMC) Norway. The buildings in Drammen were insured by Gjensidige. The insurance company tried to recover some of its losses by collecting money from Hells Angels members. Gjensidige took a pledge in a clubhouse at Ringsaker outside the city of Hamar, where some of the convicts were part-owners. Gjensidige has renewed its majority pledge every five years, so that the pledge has not become obsolete (Gottschalk, 2013). However, as of 2015, Gjensidige still has this pledge without having taken any action to retrieve the money.

This case study addresses the relevance of CSR to Gjensidige in the context of their pledge in a clubhouse of the HAMC. HAMC is a criminal matrix organization, where the motorcycle club is a legal organization along the vertical axis, while it organizes criminal activities along the horizontal axis. In terms of CSR, the issue is whether and how Gjensidige might use its majority pledge in contributing to societal welfare, compensating for others' negative impacts, and taking responsibility for society and the environment.

This case study links two different contexts. One is about the insurance business in general as it is exposed to a specific kind of negative event. The negative event leads the insurance company unwillingly into the context of law enforcement as a CSR issue. The other, though more marginal, context is concerned with the extent of symbolic CSR to be found in the conduct of MC clubs to enhance their own reputation. The link can be found when a legal enterprise is facing challenges in relation to outlaws and outlaw MC clubs that portray themselves as socially responsible individuals and organizations.

Gjensidige

The insurance company Gjensidige has safeguarded assets ever since the first mutual fire insurers were established in the 1820s. The company offers all kinds of insurance and is divided into three main sectors: private, agriculture, and business. It also offers retail banking products through its subsidiary Gjensidige Bank as well as pensions and savings products. In November 2007, Gjensidige applied for a listing on the Oslo Stock Exchange, and made its debut on the exchange in 2009.

The social mission of the company is to safeguard life, health, and assets for its customers. This is the company's CSR. Loss prevention is an important part of this work, and the company is involved in many projects. This is how the company presents itself on the Internet:

> *Well prepared with loss prevention.* We are involved in the lives of people and enterprises, **before** and **after** claims. Over the course of many years, we have gathered knowledge about what causes losses and how they can be avoided. We give this knowledge back to our customers, the authorities and society at large through advice, collaboration projects and participation in social debate.
>
> *Responsible and good conduct.* Gjensidige plays an important role in society, and we have to manage the responsibility this involves in a good way. We make strict ethical demands of ourselves, our suppliers and our financial investments. We have zero tolerance for corruption and facilitation payments. Our operations cause few greenhouse gas emissions and have little environmental impact on the environment, and we strive to further reduce it. Gjensidige aims to offer a health encouraging working environment.
>
> *Climate advice and surveying.* There is broad agreement among scientists that human activities cause global warming and climate change. For several years, Gjensidige has contributed to research on the consequences of climate change, and there is much to suggest that water damage in Norwegian homes will become more common in future.

According to the annual report of 2013, Gjensidige had solid growth in premiums in all market segments, improved quality in customer portfolios, and efficient operations, all of which formed the basis of a good profit performance in 2013. The letter from the CEO in the annual report reads as follows:

> Gjensidige recorded a profit before tax expense of NOK 4.6 billion for 2013, an underwriting result of NOK 2.0 billion and a combined ratio for the whole general insurance operations of 89.2. This is very satisfying. The banking and pension operations in Norway also developed very positively in 2013 and they are making a bigger and bigger contribution to Gjensidige's results.
>
> The basis for profitable growth and development was strengthened in 2013 through the acquisitions of Gouda Travel Insurance, which operates in the three Scandinavian countries, and Solid Försäkringar's motor and home content insurance portfolio in Sweden. The distribution agreement with Nykredit, which was adjusted during this year, strengthens our position in the Danish private market, and new partnership agreements with the Norwegian Trekking Association and the Norwegian Association of Hunters and Anglers provide new opportunities for business in Norway.

HAMC Norway

A distinction must be made between non-criminalized and criminalized bikers. The latter, outlaw bikers, are typically motorcycle club members referring to themselves as "1 percenters". Among the criminal biker clubs, we find Hells Angels, Outlaws, Bandidos, Pagans, Black Pistons, Mongols, and Coffin Cheaters, the most well-known being the Hells Angels Motorcycle Club (HAMC), which is in charge of many criminal business enterprises all over the world.

Lavigne (1996: 1) described criminal bikers in this way:

> The darkness of crime lies not in its villainy or horror, but in the souls of those who choose to live their lives in the abyss. A man who toils from youth to old age to violate the line that divides civilization from wilderness, who proclaims he is not of society, but an outsider sworn to break its laws and rules, yet who readily seeks refuge in its lenient legal system, embraces its judicial paternalism and gains substance from its moral weakness; whose very existence as an outlaw is defined by society's being, is but a shadow of the real world, bereft of freedom and doomed to tag along in society's wake.

The history of HAMC starts in 1948 and the organization has since grown to encompass several thousand members worldwide (www.wikipedia.org – search Hells Angels):

> The Hells Angels were originally formed in 1948 in Fontana, California through an amalgamation of former members from different motorcycle clubs, such as The Pissed Off Bastards of Bloomington. The Hells Angels website denies the

suggestion that any misfit or malcontent troops are connected with the motor-cycle club. However, the website notes that the name was suggested by Arvid Olsen, an associate of the founders, who had served in the Flying Tigers "Hells Angels" squadron in China during World War II. The name "Hells Angels" was believed to have been inspired by the common historical use, in both World War I and World War II, to name squadrons or other fighting groups by a fierce, death-defying name.

Over the years, studies of HAMC have repeatedly shown that running an outlaw club is costly and that the funds required are earned by organized crime (Quinn and Koch, 2003; Rassel and Komarnicki, 2007). In Scandinavia, a war on organized drug crime broke out in the 1990s that involved the Hells Angels (www.wikipedia.org – search Hells Angels):

> A gang war over drugs and turf between the Hells Angels and the Bandidos, known as the "Great Nordic Biker War", raged from 1994 until 1997 and ran across Norway, Sweden, Denmark and even parts of Finland and Estonia. By the end of the war, machine guns, hand grenades, rocket launchers and car bombs had been used as weapons, resulting in 11 murders, 74 attempted murders, and 96 wounded members of the involved motorcycle clubs. This led to fierce response from law enforcement and legislators, primarily in Denmark. A law was passed that banned motorcycle clubs from owning or renting property for their club activities. The law has subsequently been repealed on constitutional grounds.

The historical background for this case study of the insurance company Gjensidige and HAMC is set against an account of one of the bombs that exploded during the "Great Nordic Biker War" in 1997 (Gottschalk, 2013).

Hells Angels Clubhouse

After the bomb exploded in the city of Drammen outside of Oslo in Norway in 1997, police investigations concluded that it had been placed outside the Bandidos clubhouse by members of HAMC Norway. Several HAMC members were tried, convicted, and sentenced to jail sentences. Furthermore, Gjensidige, which had insured the destroyed buildings, had to pay out close to 100 million US dollars to the owners of the buildings. Following several court sentences of HAMC members, Gjensidige sought repayment from those members. Although the members did not pay, Gjensidige discovered that they owned shares in a clubhouse outside the city of Hamar and acquired a majority pledge in the clubhouse based on the debts of these members. More than a decade later, in 2015, Gjensidige had still not taken any action to retrieve the money, despite holding this pledge.

Gjensidige argues that their role is to retrieve money lost in insurance payments that arose due to the Drammen bomb. They say that forcing Hells Angels out of the clubhouse does not make sense for three main reasons. First, the value of the clubhouse is less than a million dollars, and Gjensidige lost 100 million dollars. Second, the efforts and costs involved in throwing Hells Angels members out will probably exceed the benefits for Gjensidige. Third, it is not the responsibility of a business firm to become involved in law enforcement, even if it is a matter of serious organized crime where the firm might make a difference.

The small town of Ringsaker where the clubhouse is located would very much like to be rid of the Hells Angels and view Gjensidige's pledge as a golden opportunity to displace the criminals. All the politicians in the town have encouraged Gjensidige to deploy their economic and legal force to evict Hells Angels members from the clubhouse and then sell it on the open market. Similarly, local police in Ringsaker would also very much appreciate some help from Gjensidige in order to get rid of the club, the members, and the associated criminal activity in drugs, prostitution, and violence.

In an attempt to localize Gjensidige in terms of CSR in the Hells Angels case, a maturity model presented later in this chapter is applied.

Evaluation of CSR

In this case study, the specific context of Gjensidige is concerned with the firm's contribution to fighting organized crime as carried out by members of the HAMC in Norway. We evaluate what the firm can do and what the firm is willing to do. Gjensidige is willing to renew their majority ownership in the Hells Angels clubhouse. Gjensidige is not willing to expel Hells Angels members from the clubhouse and prevent the house from being sold back to the criminally loaded motorcycle club. Gjensidige considers such an action to be the responsibility of the police and other public authorities.

Based on this situation with Gjensidige, the following evaluation can be justified in terms of the extent to which Gjensidige in the Hells Angels context already has CSR in place:

1. *Being accountable:* Gjensidige takes on business responsibility to society by controlling the ownership of a clubhouse where a number of organized criminals are living as members of the legal HAMC Norway. The firm applies a business perspective, where it keeps the pledge as long as persons have debts to the firm. Conclusion: Yes, Gjensidige is being accountable.

2. *Compensating for one's own negative impacts:* The issue of whether or not Gjensidige is compensating for their own negative impacts, which is a matter of business responsibility to society, is not relevant in our context of HAMC. Conclusion: No, Gjensidige is not compensating.

3. *Compensating for others' negative impacts:* This is an issue of business responsibility for society, where Gjensidige certainly could do more to fight a criminal organization, since the firm has a majority pledge in the clubhouse of HAMC. Conclusion: No, Gjensidige is not compensating.

4. *Contributing to societal welfare:* Again, here Gjensidige could do much more. Many citizens who live in the neighborhood of the clubhouse dislike it, and the city of Hamar is not at all happy to have a local HAMC gang in its region. Societal welfare is not only threatened by organized crime but also by international parties held in the clubhouse, where members tend to recruit young local girls for pleasure. Conclusion: No, Gjensidige is not contributing.

5. *Operations:* The issue of whether Gjensidige is operating their business in an ethically responsible and sustainable way in terms of business responsible conduct is not really relevant for the HAMC context, apart from their professional handling of the majority pledge. Conclusion: No, Gjensidige is not operating ideally.

6. *Broad responsibility:* Gjensidige is not taking responsibility for society and the environment in broad terms. Rather, they argue that their business mission is to insure people to help with loss prevention. But this is how they make money; it has nothing to do with CSR. Conclusion: No, Gjensidige is taking no broad responsibility.

7. *Managing through business its relationships with society:* Yes, this is exactly what Gjensidige does. The firm considers its relationship with society as a business issue. To relate to society has to do with transactions that can be justified by short-term or long-term profitability. Conclusion: Yes, Gjensidige manages business relationships.

The list above is concerned with the current situation. The next list is based on the desired situation. The following evaluation can be justified in terms of the extent to which Gjensidige in the Hells Angels context can have CSR in place in the future. The list represents recommendations for how firms ending up in similar situations can behave to successfully manage their CSR:

1. *Being accountable (business responsibility to society):* Yes, is already in place.

2. *Compensating for one's own negative impacts (business responsibility for society):* No, this aspect is not really relevant for organizations that end up in similar situations with outlaw organizations, even though they want to practice CSR.
3. *Compensating for others' negative impacts (business responsibility for society):* Yes, by reducing the financial muscles of outlaw biker gangs, an insurance firm can compensate for their negative impacts.
4. *Contributing to societal welfare (business responsibility for society):* No, this is not relevant for the circumstance of law enforcement.
5. *Operating their business in an ethically responsible and sustainable way (business responsible conduct):* No, this is not relevant for the circumstance of law enforcement.
6. *Taking responsibility for society and the environment in broad terms:* Yes, this is already in place.
7. *Managing through business its relationships with society:* Yes, this is already in place.

The insurance business is all about helping people and enterprises avoid heavy losses in cases of negative events. The business model is simple: everyone pays a little premium every year, and those hit by an accident receive a larger sum. This is a useful contribution to society, but it has nothing to do with CSR. CSR goes beyond the business itself (Adeyeye, 2011; Basu and Palazzo, 2008; Mostovicz et al., 2009; Zollo et al., 2009). We have tried to illustrate this with the case of Gjensidige. CSR is about what the insurance business does in addition to insuring people and places.

So far in this case study, only CSR for Gjensidige has been discussed. But organizations such as the HAMC Norway should also engage in responsible efforts in support of society, even though some of the members make their living from organized crime. And there are indeed examples of contributions from Hells Angels in Norway. The club has engaged itself in activities for children in general and retarded children in particular. The club has staged events for the public to communicate differences for peaceful coexistence.

Seven criteria were applied to evaluate the extent of CSR by Gjensidige as it relates to their majority pledge in a clubhouse occupied by HAMC Norway. Two criteria seem irrelevant for the specific context of HAMC: compensating for one's own negative impacts and Gjensidige operating their business ethically. Two criteria seem to be met by Gjensidige: being accountable and managing through business its relationships with society.

Three remaining criteria are not being met by Gjensidige: compensating for others' negative impacts, contributing to societal welfare, and taking on a broad responsibility for society.

Asset Recovery in 2015

Gjensidige had a total claim of 300 million Norwegian kroner against members of HAMC Norway after the bombing of Bandidos in 1997. In the spring of 2015, the insurance company was able to retrieve and recover 2 million kroner. At the same time, Gjensidige had once again renewed its claim on the clubhouse. The asset recovery is a sign of increased CSR by Gjensidige (Rostad and Sletmoen, 2015):

> The bombing of the Bandidos clubhouse in Drammen in 1997 led to serious material damage, and a passerby woman was killed. Seven Hells Angels members were sentenced to heavy penalties after the attack. The insurance company Gjensidige filed a claim of NOK 300 million in damages. Now they have succeeded in collecting two million kroner.
>
> – The money has come in through valuable items such as cars and boats and was recovered in the spring. This has happened through a distraint, says Bjarne Rysstad, chief of public information at Gjensidige.
>
> Rysstad and Gjensidige do not expect to get all of the 300 million, but will keep trying. Gjensidige has therefore taken a pledge in a variety of assets among members of Hells Angels to secure the greatest possible part of the claim. Perhaps the most important item is a lien on 55.5 percent of the clubhouse of the Hells Angels in Ringsaker. Part of the strategy to bring in money is to ensure that the money claim does not become obsolete. A forced sale of the clubhouse is one of the alternatives the insurance company is looking into.
>
> – We think long term and look at all the ways we can recover assets. When it comes to the house, a forced sale is not applicable at present, but this is something that could change, says Rysstad.
>
> Professor Petter Gottschalk on BI has written several books on organized crime. In the book "White-collar crime and corporate responsibility" he has devoted over 100 pages to the bombing in Drammen and the economic aftermath.
>
> – For me Hells Angels is a criminal organization, and they admit themselves that they consist of individuals with criminal backgrounds. Therefore, it is positive that Gjensidige has managed to get out parts of the claim. I have long believed that this is an important part of their social responsibility at Gjensidige, Gottschalk says.
>
> He does not exclude that the payment may be part of a strategy in which HA is trying to move away from being the driving force as a criminal organization.
>
> – As far as I know the case, I am surprised over the payment. It poses many questions, and one can speculate on whether this is a deliberate strategy of HA. They have long been working to improve their reputation, and this could be part of a larger mindset.
>
> Spokesman for Hells Angels, Rune Olsgården, says to NRK that he was not aware of payments to Gjensidige, and that the main men from the bombing attack have long been out of the club.

CORRUPTION CASE AT SIEMENS

Hells Angels and Gjensidige is not a white-collar crime case, but it is a case of the role of corporate responsibility in combatting crime. A typical example of white-collar crime and a lack of corporate responsibility, however, is the corruption case at Siemens. The German company faced a series of bribery and money laundering allegations in more than a dozen countries in 2004. In 2006, German police investigators raided Siemens' headquarters in Munich and the homes of leading executives. Police investigations revealed that Siemens had been bribing governmental officials to secure contracts and to gain favorable conditions for more than three decades. Eberl et al. (2015: 1209) argue that most of the executives involved "were clearly aware that they were violating the law, but they acted out of a sense of loyalty to and for the benefit of their company".

The severe violation of integrity at the organizational level at Siemens led to a substantial crisis in terms of the organization's legitimacy and had strong negative effects on stakeholders' trust in the organization. To repair and restore trust in the organization, Siemens established a compliance program to detect corrupt practices, and they implemented corporate governance structures as well as accepted monitoring from external authorities.

Eberl et al. (2015) studied how Siemens tried to repair and restore trust. Their findings suggest that tightening organizational rules is an appropriate signal of trustworthiness for external stakeholders to demonstrate that the organization seriously intends to prevent integrity violations in the future. Their findings also suggest that such rule adjustments were a source of dissatisfaction among employees since the new rules were difficult to implement in practice.

Eberl et al. (2015) argue that these different impacts of organizational rules result from their paradoxical nature. To address this problem, they suggest managing an effective interplay between formal and informal rules.

In their document *Corporate Social Responsibility Policy of Siemens Limited* (Siemens, 2014) and other documents, Siemens emphasizes the fight against corrupton. Siemens supports the International Anti-Corruption Academy, which is dedicated to overcoming current shortcomings in knowledge and practice in the field of compliance and anti-corruption.

WHAT IS CORPORATE RESPONSIBILITY?

This chapter discusses how combatting crime in general, and financial crime and white-collar crime in particular, is an integral part of CSR, especially when crime finds its opportunity structure in the organization. White-collar crime originates and manifests itself in organizations. Organizations must carry responsibility for the negative impacts on society, for example when internal criminals are prosecuted and jailed at the expense of society.

To take on CSR means to pay back to society. Payback is the opposite of creating costs to society. CSR is supposed to be a self-regulatory mechanism whereby a business monitors and ensures its active compliance with the spirit of the law, ethical standards, and national and international norms. CSR is a concept whereby companies integrate social and environmental concerns into their business operations and into the interaction with their stakeholders on a voluntary basis (Ditlev-Simonsen, 2014).

CSR is receiving increased attention. Today, companies are expected to take on responsibilities beyond regulatory compliance and posting profits (Ditlev-Simonsen, 2014: 117): "How companies engage the environment, human rights, ethics, corruption, employee rights, donations, volunteer work, contributions to the community and relationships with suppliers are typically viewed as components of CSR." There are several links between CSR and crime prevention. One link is the company's responsibility toward society if crime occurs, as mentioned above. Another link is the effect of CSR on organizational members. Ditlev-Simonsen (2015) studied this effect in terms of affective commitment among organizational members to active CSR. Her study explored the relationship between employees' CSR perception and employees' affective commitment. Affective commitment is defined as an employee's duty or pledge to the company. Results indicate that CSR perception is a significant predictor of affective commitment, although how employees feel that the company cares about them has a stronger explanatory power on affective commitment.

CSR is about doing good. In the case of Gjensidige and the Hells Angels, seven elements of doing good were mentioned: (1) being accountable: business responsibility to society; (2) compensating for negative impacts: business responsibility for society; (3) compensating for others' negative impacts: business responsibility for society; (4) contributing to societal welfare: business responsibility for society; (5) operating their business in an ethical, responsible, and sustainable way: business responsible conduct; (6) taking responsibility for society and the environment in broad terms; and (7) managing through business its relationships with society.

In total, these elements reflect an organization's active cooperation with values and attitudes in society. For example, anti-corruption has been identified as a core value of corporate responsibility globally. CSR is demonstrated by activities based on assumed obligations to society. Stakeholders' expectations are to be met.

Ditlev-Simonsen and Midttun (2011) raised the question: What motivates managers to pursue corporate responsibility? Branding, stakeholders, and value maximization were found to be key motivators. Branding is concerned with building a positive reputation and brand image, stakeholders is about satisfying different stakeholders, while value maximization is concerned with creating long-term value for shareholders.

CSR is defined as a leadership task. Board members and chief executives in an organization have a particular responsibility to make sure that the organization is in compliance with laws and regulations, and that the organization makes contributions to society wherever relevant. Chief executives should make the organization accountable, compensate for negative impacts, contribute to societal welfare, conduct business ethically, take responsibility for society, and manage the business in relation to society.

But what happens when such trusted persons in important leadership positions in business enterprises and other organizations abuse their positions for illegal gain? That is what white-collar crime is all about, whether it is for personal or company gain. Crime is the complete opposite of CSR. Criminal activity is to abuse a privileged position for a purpose detrimental to CSR. White-collar crime is financial crime by privileged, powerful, and influential people when they occupy positions in business enterprises, public agencies, and political governance.

Osuji (2011) argues that CSR is a relatively underdeveloped concept despite its increasing importance to corporations. One difficulty is the possible inexactness of CSR. Another is the apparent reluctance by regulatory authorities and policy-makers to intervene in the area. Corporate involvement in unethical secrecy in cases of misconduct and crime has emerged as a component of CSR debate and agenda. In recent years, corporate operations and impact in areas such as criminal justice, human rights, and the environment have grown hand in hand with governmental and public concern for firm misconduct, and privatization of law enforcement and criminal justice (Schneider, 2006), particularly in relation to the outsourcing of crime investigations to professional services firms. A critical question is how corporate misconduct and crime and the associated detection by financial crime specialists from professional services firms can be contextualized within the CSR agenda.

Organizations engage in CSR as either an offensive or a defensive strategy. A proactive approach to CSR focuses on the intrinsic value of CSR and sees it as an opportunity to maximize organizational capabilities and identify new avenues for organizational behavior. When CSR is carried out in a defense mode, it mainly serves the purpose of avoiding criticism and other attacks. Although transparency and accountability are expected from all organizations, most of them do everything possible to avoid exposure of their own misconduct and crime. If white-collar crime is detected in an organization, the organization quickly jumps on the rotten apple explanation rather than the rotten barrel explanation.

CSR as a concept has several characteristics: voluntary activities, internalizing as well as managing externalities, multiple stakeholder orientation, alignment of social and economic responsibilities, beyond philanthropy, transparent practice, and accountability in difficult times. The organizational level of CSR focuses on strategy and resource allocation. The individual level of CSR focuses on moral evaluation, sound judgment, and ethical behavior in human action.

STAGES OF GROWTH IN CSR

Researchers have struggled for decades to develop stages of growth models that are both theoretically founded and empirically validated. A number of multistage models have been proposed which assume that predictable patterns exist in the growth of organizations, and that these patterns unfold as discrete time periods best thought of as stages. These models have different distinguishing characteristics. Stages can be driven by the search for new growth opportunities or as a response to internal crises. Some models suggest that an organization progresses through stages while others argue that there may be multiple paths through the stages. Therefore, a stages of growth theory needs to allow for multiple paths through stages as long as they follow a unidirectional pattern.

Maturity models can have varying number of stages, and each stage can be labeled according to the issue at hand. Here we suggest the following four stages of growth for CSR, as illustrated in Figure 8.1:

1. *Business stage of profit maximization for owners within the corporate mission.* At this basic maturity level, the company is only concerned with itself and its owners. In addition, the company seeks to please its customers so that they will continue to buy its goods and services. The sole responsibility corporations have is that of maximizing profits to shareholders while engaging in open and free competition, without deception or fraud. To make decisions that serve other interests at the expense of shareholders would constitute a breach in trust and loyalty. It would be like taking money away from owners and resembles a kind

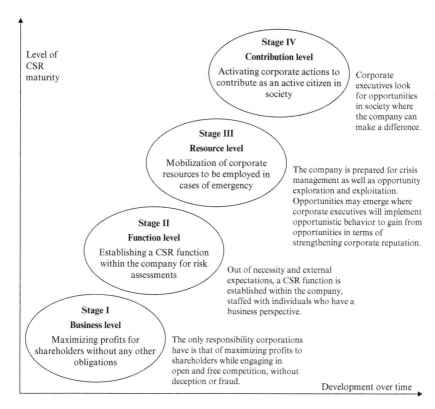

Level of CSR maturity

Stage IV
Contribution level
Activating corporate actions to contribute as an active citizen in society

Corporate executives look for opportunities in society where the company can make a difference.

Stage III
Resource level
Mobilization of corporate resources to be employed in cases of emergency

The company is prepared for crisis management as well as opportunity exploration and exploitation. Opportunities may emerge where corporate executives will implement opportunistic behavior to gain from opportunities in terms of strengthening corporate reputation.

Stage II
Function level
Establishing a CSR function within the company for risk assessments

Out of necessity and external expectations, a CSR function is established within the company, staffed with individuals who have a business perspective.

Stage I
Business level
Maximizing profits for shareholders without any other obligations

The only responsibility corporations have is that of maximizing profits to shareholders while engaging in open and free competition, without deception or fraud.

Development over time

Figure 8.1   Stages of growth model for corporate social responsibility

of theft. According to this perspective, corporate executives do not have the right to behave like modern Robin Hood types, taking money from the rich and giving it to the poor.

2.   *Function stage of establishing a function for corporate social responsibility in the company.* At this second maturity level, business executives have understood that they need to address company relationships with the outside world in a professional manner. Out of necessity and external expectations, a CSR function is established within the company, staffed with individuals who have a business perspective. The function here is to survey the implications of business activities in the external environment; to develop intelligence to learn about external reactions to business practices; and to conduct risk assessments in terms of effects on corporate reputation. CSR can here be defined as a process. The process implies that corporate leaders in the organization reflect over, and discuss, relationships with stakeholders and partners.

The process also implies that corporate leaders identify their own and the organization's roles in relation to societal conditions and societal utility. This kind of reflection and discussion will cause them to endow their roles with relevant content and action. At this stage, executives follow the compliance perspective, where corporations meet the legal and ethical requirements, but do not go beyond that.

3. *Resource stage of resource mobilization for potential threats and opportunities.* At this level, we find a complete, yet passive, form of CSR. It represents a reactive strategy where the company has mobilized resources for cases of emergency. The company is prepared for crisis management, as well as opportunity exploration and exploitation. Opportunities may emerge where corporate executives will implement opportunistic behavior to benefit from opportunities in terms of strengthening corporate reputation. CSR, at this level, is a concept that causes the company to integrate principles of social and environmental responsibility and induces engagement in the company's activities, both internally and externally. Two perspectives emerge from this definition. First, CSR implies a strong link to internal business processes; second, interactions with stakeholders and society at large also require the involvement of stakeholders and society at large in terms of their relationships to the company.

4. *Contribution stage of proactive involvement in society.* At this final maturity level, corporate executives as well as all other organizational members perceive their business as part of a greater cause in society. They adopt a comprehensive and active responsibility in both local and global society, and they look for opportunities in society where the company can make a difference. At this level of CSR, short-term loss to the company can be acceptable when weighed against the long-term good to society. CSR at this level is a long-term commitment to society (Mostovicz et al., 2009). Evidence is emerging that long-term citizen commitment on the part of the company by no means has to harm corporate profitability, in either the short term or the long term.

One example might be the Norwegian insurance company Gjensidige. Gjensidige had a claim in the clubhouse of the Hells Angels (Gottschalk, 2013). Although the claim involved an insignificant amount of money, which was almost impossible to retrieve, the claim has a greater value in that it could nevertheless help both the municipality and the police in fighting organized crime in society.

WHITE-COLLAR CONVENIENCE AND CSR

As emphasized in this book's main topic of convenience in white-collar crime, the judgment of CSR and its relevance must be conducted in a context. The contingent approach to CSR implies that what is needed in one context may neither be needed nor relevant in another context. Thus, the stage model developed in this chapter must be adapted to the relevant context before it can prove useful. The relevant context is white-collar crime.

It might be expected that the extent of white-collar crime will be large at Stage I and small at Stage IV. The argument would be that profit maximization is possible by both legal and illegal means, and profit maximization is all executives care about at Stage I. The argument for Stage IV would be that organizations contributing to the general welfare in society will never have criminals within them.

However, from a theoretical viewpoint, we may find a different pattern depending on the stages of growth. According to convenience theory, convenience occurs in the economical dimiension, in the organizational dimension, and in the behavioral dimension. CSR does not really influence individuals in the behavioral dimension within the organization, and CSR does not really influence internal opportunities for financial crime. In fact, organizations at Stage IV may think so highly of themselves with their high ethical standards and moral values, that they neglect controls and deny suspicions against any key persons in the organization. Knowing that they will not be suspected decreases the perceived likelihood of detection and thereby increases potential criminals' willingness to commit crime. Organizations at Stage 1, on the other hand, may be so well-organized and structured to reach business goals, that deviant behavior is not possible or is quickly detected.

Therefore, to create a link between stages of growth in CSR with prevention and detection of white-collar crime, there is a need to make explicit statements about combatting crime at each stage:

1. *Business stage of profit maximization for owners within the corporate mission.* All means are acceptable to reach the goal of profit maximization, including means that are on the wrong side of the law.
2. *Function stage of establishing a function for corporate social responsibility in the company.* White-collar crime is not an issue for the newly established function.
3. *Resource stage of resource mobilization for potential threats and opportunities.* Potential white-collar crime is perceived as a threat to the reputation of the organization. Resources are employed to reduce

the degrees of freedom of privileged individuals in the organization, and proper controls are installed.
4. *Contribution stage of proactive involvement in society.* If the organization provided an opportunity for financial crime by enabling a white-collar criminal to commit offenses, then the enterprise will cover the costs of all correctional services and compensate for all other costs in society.

GOVERNANCE MODEL FOR CSR

We argue that political CSR can be found at the contribution stage. Executives understand their business as part of a greater cause in society. Since Gjensidige executives seem reluctant to act in the Hells Angels clubhouse case, we argue that Gjensidige is not at Stage IV in the growth model for CSR. Although the claim involves an insignificant amount of money, which is almost impossible to retrieve, the claim has a greater value in that it could help both the municipality and the police in fighting organized crime in society.

Researchers argue that corporations ought to step up to the challenge of political CSR and take on new political responsibilities (Basu and Palazzo, 2008; Palazzo and Scherer, 2006; Scherer et al., 2006). They suggest the concept of corporate political responsibility or political corporate social responsibility (Scherer and Palazzo, 2011: 901): "Political CSR suggests an extended model of governance with business firms contributing to global regulation and providing public goods." A new theory of the firm is called for, since the old way of thinking is outdated (Scherer and Palazzo, 2011: 901): "We suggest that, under the conditions of globalization, the strict division of labour between private business and nation-state governance does not hold any more." In order to clarify what the concept of political CSR means, and in what way it is distinguished from earlier approaches of corporate responsibility, Scherer and Palazzo provide a contrast between political CSR and stakeholder theory. Both of these approaches imply that corporations have commitments toward society, but the scope of these commitments differs. Stakeholder theory suggests that corporations are responsible toward those who are affected by the results of corporate activity, whereas political CSR goes beyond this and argues that corporations have a general commitment to work for the good of society. These extended commitments arise from the global nature of the challenges facing humanity (Scherer and Palazzo, 2011: 910):

> In contrast to stakeholder management which deals with the idea of internalizing the demands, values, and interests of those actors that affect or are affected

by corporate decision making, we argue that political CSR can be understood as a movement of the corporation into the political sphere in order to respond to environmental and social challenges such as human rights, global warming, or deforestation.

Of course, on the basis of the broad understanding of the stakeholder concept, one could argue that there is no practical difference between these two perspectives, since certain decisions by big business might directly or indirectly affect more or less the entire global society. However, the difference lies in the justification. Normative stakeholder theory finds moral commitments in the mutual relationship between corporations and stakeholders, whereas political CSR points to a more general corporate duty arising from the political power of corporations.

Scherer and Palazzo's (2011) normative standpoint regarding the political commitments of corporations is based on a realization of the global challenges we face, and on the more or less pragmatic point that corporations are in the best position to take on these challenges.

However, the ascription of increased political responsibility inevitably points in the direction of a strengthening of political rights. Scherer and Palazzo (2011) are not blind to this problem when they discuss the democratic deficit of the growing engagement of business firms in public policy. Their claim is that globalization is a given and not something we can opt out from, and that this makes a new perspective on CSR necessary and unavoidable (Scherer and Palazzo, 2011: 906): "In order to respond to the globalization phenomenon and the emerging post-national constellation, it is necessary to acknowledge a new political role of business that goes beyond mere compliance with legal standards and conformity with moral rules."

In line with the idea of corporate CSR, corporations are responsible for contributing to social security and crime prevention. Rather than presenting themselves as victims of financial crime, corporations need to step up to their responsibility in terms of:

- *Offenders in crime.* Corporations enable white-collar crime and participate in white-collar crime. They need to take on the responsibility of offenders.
- *Detectors of crime.* Corporations need to introduce efficient prevention mechanisms rather than window-dressing routines such as compliance guidelines.
- *Preventors of crime.* Corporations have to apply their powers to prevent crime in society.

Under the conditions of increasing globalization, governments tend to lose some of their capacity to regulate and control, and private corporations must step in. A renegotiation of the social contract seems to be currently taking place. Society does not primarily exist to enable corporations to make money. Rather, corporations exist to produce goods and services that benefit society. If corporations fail in their obligations to cover needs for goods and services within a responsible framework, then society may change the rules of the game, for example by abolishing capitalism and market places. Corporations are to serve society more than society serves corporations.

Does it make sense to hold a company responsible for cleaning up a river it has not helped to pollute, sheltering the homeless it has not deprived of property, or fighting corruption even when it has not been part of such activity? Political CSR is often discussed in abstract terms with a focus on grand challenges such as climate change and global poverty alleviation. In contrast to such discussion, the case of white-collar crime that we are dealing with in this book is concrete and manageable: The company is in a position to make a difference, but should we expect it to, even if it probably does not pay it to do so?

9. Testing convenience theory

This chapter presents a number of studies to empirically test and validate convenience theory. Colquitt and Zapata-Phelan (2007) define theory testing as the application of existing theory in an empirical study as a means of grounding a specific set of a priori hypotheses. Existing theory is used to formulate hypotheses before testing those hypotheses with observations. Data are then gathered to explicitly test theories.

The test of convenience theory is concentrated on establishing the validity of the theory's core propositions. However, we describe the current research as an empirical study of convenience theory, rather than an empirical test of convenience theory. Ideally, testing convenience theory as an explanation of white-collar crime would imply obtaining empirical evidence from convicted white-collar criminals, which is hard – if not impossible – to obtain. Therefore, this is not empirical theory testing, only theory testing by evidence.

STATISTICAL SAMPLE OF WHITE-COLLAR CRIMINALS

Gottschalk (2017) registered and conducted research on white-collar criminals convicted and sent to prison in Norway from 2009 to 2015. A total of 405 offenders can be found in his database, where the average age is 49 years old, and the average prison sentence is two years and four months. Consistent with the economical dimension in convenience theory, all 405 white-collar criminals had profit as a motive for their crime.

Consistent with the organizational dimension of convenience theory, all 405 white-collar criminals were professionals who occupied trusted positions in enterprises and other kinds of organizations in the private and public sector. A professional is a person who earns his or her living from a specified activity. Examples include procurement managers, finance executives, and property developers. Some white-collar criminals are only loosely connected to the organization as, for example, board members and investors. Some white-collar criminals are self-employed in their own small firms. What they all have in common is that they commit financial crime as an activity in their profession and position associated with a private or public business.

In the database, organizational size is registered both in terms of turnover and in terms of number of employees. The average business where white-collar crime occurred had an annual turnover of 322 million Norwegian kroner (about 50 million US dollars) and 288 persons employed.

The organizational dimension of convenience theory emphasizes that white-collar criminals have extensive freedom without controls to carry out transactions of illegal character that are easily disguised among legal transactions. A sign of freedom and independence is the title of the position occupied. Lawyers, chief executive officers (CEOs), chief financial officers (CFOs), and chairpersons are typical examples. In their professional capacities, these individuals have considerable power and influence that they can abuse.

Also persons further down the hierarchy have substantial power, influence, independence, and freedom, but in limited areas of the business. For example, a property developer or a chief information officer (CIO) enjoys freedom in selecting suppliers of maintenance services and computer equipment to the organization. In their positions, they can easily select vendors that return personal favors without anyone approving or noticing. Another example are finance executives, who handle company bank accounts and can simply transfer money to unauthorized accounts, such as accounts owned by relatives and friends.

Convenience theory emphasizes that crime committed on behalf of the business makes it particularly evident that there is an organizational connection. When a sales manager bribes a customer, it is mainly to achieve sales that probably otherwise would not take place. When the accounting manager manipulates traffic numbers in deserted areas, it is mainly to enable the shipping company to receive more government subsidies for the line. When the CFO manipulates sales figures, it is mainly to reduce company payments of value added tax (VAT) to the government.

Out of 405 white-collar criminals, 68 persons (17 percent) committed financial crime on behalf of the business. The remaining 83 percent did it to enrich themselves. Those who committed corporate crime were on average 53 years old, committed crime for 131 million Norwegian kroner (about 20 million US dollars), and were connected to organizations with 769 employees on average. Those who committed occupational crime were on average 48 years old, committed crime for 27 million Norwegian kroner, and were linked to organizations with 104 employees. The tendency is that corporate crime is committed in larger organizations when compared to occupational crime.

Consistent with the behavioral dimension of convenience theory, most white-collar criminals in the database apply neutralization techniques. An example of frequent media appearance is Christer Tromsdal. He has been convicted several times for white-collar crime, and his latest sentence of six years in prison was from 2015. Table 9.1 shows neutralization techniques applied by Tromsdal, as they appear in numerous media reports and court documents in the most recent decade. "Yes" means that Tromsdal applies this neutralization technique, while "No" means that there is no sign of this neutralization technique in his many interviews in the media (Oslo district court, 2015).

AUTOBIOGRAPHIES BY WHITE-COLLAR CRIMINALS

Later on in this chapter, we will present statistical analyses based on opinions about concepts and relationships in convenience theory. However, case studies are also suited for theory testing. Løkke and Sørensen (2014: 68) argue that a theory as an object of interest can be developed, modified, and tested using case studies and thus serve as both input and output to a study: "Theories-as-objects is the special focus when case studies are used for theory testing, which distinguishes them from other types of case studies." A theory such as convenience theory allows for a focus on key variables – such as neutralization techniques in the behavioral dimension of convenience theory – leading to the required parsimony of analysis. Thus, when the purpose of a case is theory testing, not only in-depth knowledge of the cases and the methods is needed, but also knowledge of the theory involved. Concepts and relationships in the theory are compared to observations in cases.

An excellent source for case studies of white-collar crime are autobiographies by white-collar criminals. Another source is internal investigations, as presented later in this chapter. An autobiography is a written account of the life of a person written by that person. It is a story that the person wrote about himself or herself.

Examples of white-collar criminals who have written books about their own sentences are Bogen (2008), Eriksen (2010), and Fosse (Fosse and Magnusson, 2004) in Norway. A quote from Bogen's (2008: 271) book can illustrate some of his neutralization by denial of responsibility:

> I was never informed or updated of what was recognized, and what was restored, but as CEO I knew of course that we had this practice. In court, it emerged that many of the agreements Økokrim (the prosecutor) claimed I should be judged for, were reversed by the firm's finance department. The accounting executive confirmed then also during her witness statement in court that she had reversed

Table 9.1   Neutralization techniques applied by white-collar criminal
Christer Tromsdal

#	Neutralization technique	Yes/ No	Explanation
1.	Rejects responsibility for the crime and disclaims leadership role in the action.	Yes	He blames others and says he only tried to help some friends: "It is not my responsibility" (Bjørndal and Kleppe, 2013).
2.	Denies injury from the crime and refuses that harm has occurred.	No	There is no sign of this neutralization technique.
3.	Dismisses victims of the crime and rejects that anyone has suffered harm.	No	There is no sign of this neutralization technique. However, he seems to consider himself as the main victim of the crime: "I have let myself be used by others" (Bjørndal and Kleppe, 2013).
4.	Condemns the condemners and is skeptical of those who criticize his action.	Yes	He feels that he has been a victim of a witch-hunt by Økokrim for more than ten years, and he condemns investigators and prosecutors at Økokrim: "I choose to call the whole process for a witch hunt" (Hultgren, 2012); "People say it is the crock that cheated all the old people" (Kleppe, 2015).
5.	Invokes appeal to higher loyalties as a reason for his action.	Yes	He had to do it for his friends and acquaintances: "I have helped friends and acquaintances" (NTB, 2015).
6.	Alleges normality of action and argues that the action is quite common.	Yes	"When someone hears the word 'straw man', it sounds scary, but to me it is like an assistant" (Meldalen, 2015).
7.	Claims entitlement to action because of the situation.	No	There is no sign of this neutralization technique.
8.	Notes legal mistake and considers infringement irrelevant because of error in the law.	Yes	"In my head it is not illegal to do business with others" (Kleppe, 2015).
9.	Feels entitled to make mistakes and argues action is within acceptable mistake quota.	Yes	Since he once was a police informant, he feels entitled to do business his own way: "I was shot at work for Oslo police" (Dahle, 2011).
10.	Presents dilemma tradeoff by weighing various concerns with conclusion of committing the act.	No	There is no sign of this neutralization technique.

the accounting entries under "agreements at work", without this being conferred with me. She, like the auditor, also confirmed that she had very little direct contact with me in these questions. She dealt with many project managers in the company.

Autobiographies by white-collar criminals can be found in other countries as well. In the United States, former New York police commissioner, Bernard B. Kerik, published his autobiography, where there is evidence of denial of responsibility, condemnation of condemners, and claim for normality of action (Kerik, 2015).

We searched for quotes in Kerik's book that seem to resemble attitudes recognized by neutralization techniques. We found varying degrees of supportive statements for the various neutralization techniques.

Kerik sets the neutralization stage as soon as the introduction chapter of his book by statements presenting himself as a victim ("The system beats you down in a way that remains" and "It's about how shortsighted, inefficient, and cruel our criminal justice system is"). He stresses his performance for the nation ("I saved my wounded partner in a gun battle" and "seized tons of cocaine and millions of dollars from the Cali cartel"). He does however take on responsibility for the consequences of his actions ("I am accountable and responsible for how my life has turned out").

Throughout the 288-page book, we find the following supporting quotes for the various neutralization techniques:

1. *Denial of responsibility.* "My accountants made mistakes" (page 11). "I had called my accountant and told him that I wanted to pay the payroll tax" (page 153). "I let him" pay the renovation bill for me (page 157).
2. *Denial of injury.* There is no sign of this neutralization technique, while at the same time there is no confirmation of injury in the book.
3. *Denial of victim.* There is no sign of this neutralization technique, while at the same time there is no confirmation of victim in the book.
4. *Condemnation of the condemners.* "Accusing me of having connections to organized crime" and "I thought were downright preposterous" (page 149). "If this is how the members of the House and Senate want to apply their scrutiny, then more than half of them should step down and go find another job, because they certainly wouldn't make it through the process intact"(page 151). "Prosecutors too often overcriminalize, overreach, and overpunish" (page 195). Kerik goes on condemning government prosecutors: "They can distort and exaggerate their justifications to lock up your property, bank accounts, and other assets. They can drain you and your family of everything you've ever worked for; rip you in the court of public opinion; destroy

your family's financial future; and do everything in their power to prevent you from being able to pay for your defense" (page 232). On page 239, Kerik develops a conspiracy theory involving a number of powerful people named in the book, suggesting that they all took part in "continually bashing Giuliani and me in the press". The conspiracy theory centers on him as a Republican versus others who were Democrats. "Was it general political ill will, or were these men boosting their careers on my conviction?" (page 240).

5. *Appeal to higher loyalties.* There is no sign of this neutralization technique related to his crime. However, there is a strong message about his loyalty to the nation in serving his country.
6. *Normality of action.* "The indictment criminalized minor ethical issues and accounting errors" (page 194). "I understand that 'But everybody's doing it' is rarely a winning argument – even if it is in large part true" (page 201).
7. *Claim to entitlement.* Kerik claims a very stressful work situation for many years.
8. *Legal mistake.* "I was prosecuted criminally for what are essentially civil violations" (page 12). "Everything I was charged with – tax fraud; false statements – could have been handled ethically or civilly, without criminal charges" (page 241). "There are tens of thousands of nonviolent, first-time, white-collar offenders and drug offenders in prison today serving draconian sentences, individuals who could have been punished with alternatives to incarceration, such as fines and restitution, home confinement or house arrest, and community service" (page 243). "I do believe that a fair, objective look reveals my case and prosecution to have been selective and political. I don't feel that it was justice" (page 270).
9. *Acceptable mistake.* "Feds were taking honest mistakes by me and my accountants and alleging they were crimes" (page 194).
10. *Dilemma tradeoff.* "This was one of those ethical moments that any person in public office faces repeatedly", about not stopping the extra renovation work paid by others (page 157).
11. *Victim of crime.* "They would subpoena and harass my friends, family, colleagues, and just about everyone I knew" (page 156). "Investigators ripped my life to shreds, harassing and intimidating my friends, family, and colleagues" (page 158).
12. *Role in society.* "I had defended, worked, fought, and nearly died for our country many times in the past thirty years and was now being jailed" (page 201).

We find support for ten out of twelve neutralization techniques in Kerik's book. It is interesting to note that we only find support for three out of five of the original neutralization techniques developed by Sykes and Matza (1957). This could mean that Sykes and Matza had mainly had violent street crime in mind when they developed their neutralization theory.

Kerik served mainly in public service. His book illustrates his dedication to work for his country, and the final sentence in his book is: "But I still believe in this great country of ours, and I am still searching and fighting for justice" (page 284).

Kerik is dedicated to public service. A theory relevant to shed light on his dedication is public service motivation theory. This theory seeks to explain why individuals choose public service or private service, given the perceived disparities in pay scale, advancement opportunities, and overall work environment (Kjeldsen and Jacobsen, 2013; Perry et al., 2010). The theory suggests that some individuals work in the public sector based on their values. They have a desire to contribute to the well-being of society in general through their work (Nalbandian and Edwards, 1983). The concept of public service motivation is a theorized attribute of government employees that provides them with a desire to serve the public (Perry and Wise, 1990).

Kerik's (2015) book indicates a strong public service motivation through these characteristics. Now, after his rise and fall, he makes the case for reform and calls for wholesale change that will make America "smart on crime" and forestall what he calls "the erosion of the very fabric of our nation". While his book details the fall from grace through the criminal justice system, it also offers a perspective on the American penal system as he details life on the inside with the experience of an acclaimed correction commissioner from the outside. He takes readers deep into what he calls the "wasteland", where inmates are warehoused and treated like animals, abused by those with power and authority, and deprived not only of their freedom but also of respect and basic human dignity. He expresses public service motivation by not mainly complaining about his own treatment, but by focusing on those around him in prison.

Kerik emphasizes his social concern. A theory relevant to shed light on his dedication is social concern and crime theory suggested by Agnew (2014). Social concern involves an inclination that can lead people to pay more attention to others' interests rather than their own. It is the opposite of self-interest as a motivation for behavior. Most people Kerik presents in his book are his social concern.

This case of Kerik above has studied neutralization theory in terms of neutralization techniques applied by a white-collar criminal. We found evidence of ten out of twelve neutralization techniques being applied by Kerik (2015) in his book. He strongly condemns his condemners, he denies responsibility, he claims normality of action, and he argues that prosecutors charged him criminally for what are essentially civil violations.

Autobiographies and memoirs seem to be a suitable source of secondary material to study neutralization techniques applied by criminals. It would be interesting to see analysis of more autobiographies and memoirs in future research.

In terms of theory testing, the above discussion is concentrated on the behavioral dimension of convenience theory, and mainly on neutralization of guilt. Other aspects of convenience theory can be explored by autobiographies as well. Case studies of autobiographies by white-collar criminals can contribute in several ways. Theory testing using case studies evaluates the explanatory power of a theory and its boundaries, thus assessing external validity (Løkke and Sørensen, 2014).

INTERNAL INVESTIGATIONS OF WHITE-COLLAR CRIME

Reports of investigations by fraud examiners are typically written at the final stage of private investigations. Reports are handed over to the clients who pay for the work. Reports are seldom disclosed, so that the public never learn about them. Reports are often protected by the attorney–client privilege when investigating firms are law firms. Therefore, it is quite a challenge to identify and obtain a sample of investigation reports to empirically evaluate and test convenience in white-collar crime. It is not easy to get access to private investigation reports for research.

Gottschalk (2016) documents findings from a sample of reports acquired in the United States as well as a sample of reports acquired in Norway. Well-known examples in the United States of economical convenience include Kenneth Lay and Jeffrey Skilling at Enron.

Examples in the United States of organizational convenience include Yusuf Acar at the Office of the Chief Technology Officer (OCTO) and Harriette Walters at the tax and revenue office, both in Washington DC.

The Acar fraud involved a series of loosely related fraudulent schemes over the course of a three-and-a-half-year span from September 2005 to March 2009. While none of these schemes were particularly complex according to fraud examiners Sidley (2010), they all escaped detection and would likely have remained undiscovered but for the cooperation of an informant. Over time, these schemes grew more brazen, reflecting Acar's growing confidence that there were no mechanisms in place to detect the fraud. The initial plan was a basic corruption scheme with kickbacks from Sushil Bansal. Bansal's company, AITC, had been awarded a contract to provide temporary contractors in the security division. Bansal had tendered a number of candidates, but Acar and his co-workers had rejected them as unqualified. Yusuf Acar had ample organizational opportunity to commit convenient white-collar crime:

- He was in charge of hiring consultants to the security division.
- He was in charge of buying software licenses.
- He was able to monitor emails by others.

OCTO had 231 full-time employees and employed 267 contractors, most of whom were full-time. OCTO had a longstanding contractor culture where contractors drew a salary from a third-party vendor that contracted with the District government. Contractors played a key role in managing numerous, simultaneous, one-time modernization projects.

Some quotes from the internal investigation report by Sidley (2010) illustrate convenience in the organizational dimension:

- "Acar told us that the genesis of the first kickback was a 2005 contract for forensics engineers in the security division. Acar was going to supervise these engineers, and he was among the OCTO employees with input on the hiring decisions" (page 22).
- "Acar would manipulate the requirements listed in the procurement requests to direct hiring decisions towards Bansal's candidates" (page 23).
- "Acar and Bansal concocted a plan whereby bills for individuals who had finished their work at OCTO without exhausting all the allotted hours in the purchase order would continue to be issued for the remaining time in the contract by using fraudulent timesheets" (page 24).
- "This overbilling scheme evolved into a plan in which Acar and Bansal would bill the remaining time in the name of individuals who had never even worked at OCTO" (page 24).
- "Acar and Bansal also collaborated to get the agency to overpay for software purchased by the security division" (page 25).
- "In 2009, Acar began monitoring incoming District emails to OCTO employees to detect any communications from the Office of the Inspector General" (page 26).
- "OCTO's internal controls failed to detect or prevent Acar's various fraudulent activities" (page 27).
- "Many OCTO employees attribute Acar's prolonged success to what they describe as the isolation of the Security Division. Because the Security Division has access to all District email and

telecommunication messages, OCTO treated the Division differently from its other programs" (page 30).

- "For several years before discovery of the fraud, Acar was a key decisionmaker in the hiring of contractors for the security division, which facilitated his kickback scheme. Moreover, on several occasions he served as acting program manager of the department, at which time he was able to make procurement decisions without any careful, third-party scrutiny. Further, as the acting leader of the group, Acar was able to expand the fraud by exercising substantial control over the division's annual budget request. The lack of external scrutiny prevented these decisions from receiving the sort of oversight that might have prevented the fraud" (page 31).

According to the investigation report by Sidley (2010), the internal controls at OCTO played no role in detection of the fraud.

The Walters fraud investigated by WilmerHale and PwC (2008) illustrates convenience in the organizational dimension:

- "Jones deposited the fraudulent payments into accounts controlled by Walters, her family, or her friends" (page 40).
- "In early March 2007, Walters created an $85,000 credit on a property associated with Samuel Earl Pope, Walters' friend" (page 47).
- "Walters apparently provided cover stories to explain her generosity. According to one rumor, she was from a wealthy family and had inherited large sums of money. According to another rumor, she had a wealthy boyfriend or a second job and was good at 'budgeting' her money" (page 60).

Walters' motive was private money spending for herself, her friends, and family. Unfortunately, the investigation by WilmerHale and PwC (2008: 8) "did not attempt to trace the stolen money or to determine how the money was distributed or spent".

WilmerHale and PwC (2008: 2) describe Walters' scheme, which is part of the organizational dimension of white-collar crime:

> Harriette Walters was a long-time employee and starting in 2001, a low-level manager in RPTA. As Walters explained to us, she first became involved in a fraudulent tax refund scheme in the mid-1980s when she learned from a co-worker how to process fake refunds, how to waive penalty and interest charges in exchange for gifts and cash, and how to cash refund checks that were returned to RPTA when the taxpayer recipient had died. According to Walters, she eventually concluded that her co-worker, whom she described as a substance

abuser, was unreliable as a partner in these activities. Walters then embarked on her own embezzlement scheme in the late 1980s, which focused on the issuance of fraudulent real property tax refund checks. From the late 1980s through late 2007, Walters stole more than $48 million from the District, which, according to the *Washington Post*, is the largest known government-related embezzlement scandal in the District's history.

While the economical convenience for Walters was consumption by spending money far in excess of personal income for herself, friends, and family, and the organizational convenience was tax returns and other special transactions that she could manipulate, the behavioral dimension is difficult to understand based on the investigation report by WilmerHale and PwC (2008). She pleaded guilty to federal charges related to theft of over 48 million US dollars of District of Columbia funds.

STUDENT ELICITATION ON WHITE-COLLAR CRIME

The student elicitation in this book documents support for convenience theory. Students supported general statements such as:

- If it is more convenient to achieve a financial goal illegally, then many top executives will do it illegally.
- If it is impossible for top executives to get a bonus legally, then many do it illegally.
- If it is impossible to avoid bankruptcy legally, then many top executives do it illegally.
- If it is impossible for top executives to keep their jobs legally, then many do it illegally.
- If it is impossible to achieve a financial goal legally, then many top executives do it illegally.

Furthermore, all relationships suggested in the convenience model found support in the second student elicitation:

- A heightened pursuit of profit to cover perceived needs increases the organizational opportunities for white-collar crime.
- The more ambitious a financial goal is for the business, the more convenient it is to commit economic crime at work.
- A heightened pursuit of profit to cover perceived needs increases the willingness to commit white-collar crime at work.

- The more ambitious a financial goal is for the business, the more convenient it is to accept one's own criminal behavior.
- Increased opportunity to commit white-collar crime at work strengthens the desire for profit to cover perceived needs.
- The more convenient it is to commit economic crime at work, the more important it is to achieve an ambitious financial goal.
- Increased opportunity to commit white-collar crime at work strengthens the willingness for a deviant behavior that includes criminal acts.
- The easier it is to commit economic crime at work, the more convenient it is to accept one's own criminal behavior.
- Increased willingness to commit white-collar crime at work strengthens the desire for profit to cover perceived needs.
- The easier it is to accept one's own criminal behavior, the more convenient it is to achieve an ambitious financial goal.
- Increased willingness to commit white-collar crime strengthens the opportunity to commit economic crime at work.
- The easier it is to accept one's own criminal behavior, the more convenient it is to commit economic crime at work.

The extent of white-collar crime can be explained by desire in the economical dimension, opportunity in the organizational dimension, and willingness in the behavioral dimension, as illustrated by the research model in Figure 9.1. The research model is expected to predict the extent of white-collar crime based on convenience theory.

The research model in Figure 9.1 stimulates the following research hypotheses:

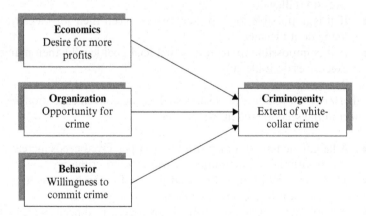

Figure 9.1   Research model to predict the extent of white-collar crime

Hypothesis I: *A stronger desire for more profits will lead to a greater tendency to commit white-collar out of convenience.*

The economical dimension of convenience theory suggests that the desire for profits is caused by perceived needs. It is convenient to satisfy desires through white-collar crime.

Hypothesis II: *A greater organizational opportunity to commit crime will lead to a greater tendency to commit white-collar crime out of convenience.*

The organizational dimension of convenience theory suggests that the profession and privileged position of the potential offender provides an opportunity to commit crime and makes crime a convenient action.

Hypothesis III: *A stronger willingness to commit crime will lead to a greater tendency to commit white-collar crime out of convenience.*

The behavioral dimension of convenience theory suggests that members of the elite are willing to commit white-collar crime.

We operationalize economics as desire for more profits in the following statements (disagree–agree):

1. Top executives are very concerned about profitability.
2. Top executives choose convenient solutions to achieve ambitious financial goals.
3. Top executives choose convenient solutions to satisfy their own financial greed.
4. Top executives choose convenient solutions when they are exposed to financial stress.

We operationalize organization as opportunity for crime in the following statements (disagree–agree):

1. Top executives have ample opportunities to commit financial crime related to their positions.
2. It is convenient for top executives to commit financial crime in their positions.
3. It is convenient for top executives to express that apparently illegal financial actions are legitimate.
4. It is convenient for top executives to conceal illegal financial actions among legal actions.

We operationalize behavior as willingness to commit crime in the following statements (disagree–agree):

1. Top executives are willing to commit financial crime at work.
2. Top executives perceive that financial crime is convenient because they do not look at themselves as criminals.
3. Top executives perceive that financial crime is convenient because they lack self-control.
4. Top executives perceive that financial crime is convenient because they think the end justifies the means.

We operationalize criminogenity – the tendency to commit crime – as the extent of white-collar crime in the following statements (disagree–agree):

1. Top executives often commit financial crime by virtue of their positions.
2. Financial crime is accepted among top executives.
3. Top executives often solve challenges by committing financial crime by virtue of their positions.
4. Top executives have a great tendency to commit financial crime by virtue of their positions.

THEORY BUILDING AND THEORY TESTING

In their classical article on theory building and theory testing, Colquitt and Zapata-Phelan (2007) conceptualize theory building as the introduction of constructs and relationships. Work on convenience theory represents theory building as we introduce the construct of convenience and define relationships between desire for profits, opportunity in the organizational context, and willingness for deviant behavior. The introduction of the new construct of convenience creates a departure from existing work by generating a number of new research directions that can shape future thinking.

Colquitt and Zapata-Phelan (2007) conceptualize theory testing as the application of theory in an empirical study as a means of grounding a specific set of a priori hypotheses. Testing of convenience theory requires digging into underlying processes that explain relationships, touching on neighboring concepts or broader social phenomena, and describing convincing and logically interconnected arguments. Tests described so far do not necessarily satisfy all these requirements.

However, Colquitt and Zapata-Phelan (2007) define different levels of theory testing. Their third point on the theory-testing axes seems to fit our testing so far, where predictions are grounded in past conceptual arguments. We explain why a given relationship should exist by asking a population of students to agree or disagree with each statement. Describing the causal logic behind a given prediction and then gaining support for this description supplies a critical ingredient to theory testing.

Furthermore, Colquitt and Zapata-Phelan (2007) identified five distinct types of research outcomes concerning theories: reporters, testers, qualifiers, builders, and expanders. Our approach seems to fit the description of builders that are relatively high in theory building but relatively low in theory testing. Builders include inductive studies that focus on new constructs, relationships, or processes.

The goal of theory testing is not simply falsification or verification. The goal is to test explanatory power by evaluating the theory in different contexts. Theory testing is a matter of external validity (Løkke and Sørensen, 2014). Miller and Tsang (2010: 144) suggest critical realism as an approach to theory evaluation:

> Critical realism interrelates ontology and epistemology. On the one hand, it posits a realist ontology, that is, the existence of a world independent of the researchers' knowledge of it. On the other hand, critical realism holds to a fallibilist epistemology in which researchers' knowledge of the world is socially produced. These two claims jointly motivate the need for and possibility of critically evaluating theories. As such, they make up the core of the critical realist philosophy of science. Because of the existence of an external referent, knowledge claims may be challenged and their merits assessed logically and empirically.

To successfully test theories, researchers must overcome a number of practical and philosophical obstacles, including complexities and contingencies in social phenomena such as deviant behaviors and human interactions. The openness of social systems versus the bounded theory is yet another challenge, where a theory must be based on a limited number of concepts and mechanisms, while the real world is an almost limitless mix of factors.

Miller and Tsang (2010) propose a series of four complementary steps for testing theories, that we will discuss later in this chapter to evaluate convenience theory. The four steps are: (1) identify the hypothesized mechanisms, (2) test for the presence of the mechanisms in the empirical setting, (3) test isolated causal relations using experimental or quasi-experimental designs, and (4) test the theoretical system using correlational methods.

CONVENIENCE HYPOTHESES FOR RESEARCH

First, each of the four multiple item scales in Figure 9.1 had to be studied in terms of reliability. The Cronbach's alpha turned out to be .619, .809, .617, and .768 respectively for economics, organization, behavior, and crime. While two of them are below the acceptable threshold of $p<.7$, the scales were still applied in this research because of the limited number of respondents.

Table 9.2 indicates that the three independent variables can predict variation in the dependent variable to a large extent. More than half of the variation in crime tendency is predicted by motive, organization, and behavior as indicated by an adjusted R square of .565.

Table 9.3 indicates that the regression model is indeed significant with a high F-value of 14.439.

Table 9.4 shows that only one of the predictors is by itself significant. While neither financial desire nor organizational opportunity are significant predictors of the tendency to commit white-collar crime, behavior is indeed a very significant predictor. With a steep slope of .677 in the relationship,

Table 9.2   Variation in criminogenity explained by three predictors

Model summary				
Model	R	R square	Adjusted R square	Std. error of the estimate
1	.779[a]	.607	.565	.84766

Note: a Predictors: (Constant), behaviorial dimension, economical dimension and organizational dimension.

Table 9.3   Significance of regression model

ANOVA[a]					
Model	Sum of squares	df	Mean square	F	Sig.
1 Regression	31.124	3	10.375	14.439	.000[b]
Residual	20.119	28	.719		
Total	51.242	31			

Notes:
a   Dependent variable: Criminogenity.
b   Predictors: Motive, opportunity, behavior.

Table 9.4   Significance of predictor variables for white-collar crime

	Coefficients[a]					
Model	Unstandardized coefficients		Standardized coefficients		t	Sig.
	B	Std. error	Beta			
1 (Constant)	−1.403	1.082			−1.297	.205
Motive	.206	.182	.139		1.129	.269
Opportunity	.144	.142	.132		1.011	.321
Behavior	.896	.171	.677		5.255	.000

Note: a Dependent variable: Criminogenity.

and a significant relationship at .000, willingness to get involved in deviant behavior is the main explanation for white-collar crime.

Those who believe that top executives often commit financial crime by virtue of their positions, that financial crime is accepted among top executives, that top executives often solve challenges by committing financial crime by virtue of their positions, and that top executives have a great tendency to commit financial crime by virtue of their positions, also believe that top executives have a strong financial desire, organizational opportunity for crime, and willingness to commit crime. In particular, criminogenity is influenced by top executives' willingness to commit financial crime at work, top executives' perception that financial crime is convenient because they do not look at themselves as criminals, top executives' perception that financial crime is convenient because they lack self-control, and top executives' perception that financial crime is convenient because they think the end justifies the means.

IMPROVING SCALE RELIABILITY FOR RESEARCH

A major shortcoming of the research results presented above is the low scale reliability found for both economic motive (.619) and deviant behavior (.617). To improve scale reliability, some items were modified before new survey research was carried out. Specifically, the following items were revised:

- "Top executives are very concerned about profitability." This item in the economics scale is lacking the key word "convenient" and achieved a very high score among respondents. The revised item is:

"Top executives choose to achieve profitability in convenient ways." It is expected that this modification will bring the item more in line with the other three items in the scale in terms of average score. The average scores were all on the agree-side, but the first score was very different from the others: 6.38 versus 4.53, 4.31, and 5.31 on a scale from 1 (disagree) to 7 (agree).

- "Top executives are willing to commit financial crime at work." Respondents disagreed with this statement by providing an average score of 3.84. The revised item was expected to achieve agreement: "Top executives find it convenient to commit crime in stressful situations at work."
- Respondents also disagreed with another statement that achieved an average score of 3.13. This was the statement "Top executives perceive that financial crime is convenient because they lack self-control". The item was revised to: "Top executives perceive financial crime as convenient when they think they do nothing wrong."
- Respondents also disagreed with the statement "Financial crime is accepted among top executives". The statement was expanded into "Financial crime is accepted among top executives in stressful situations".
- "Top executives have ample opportunities to commit financial crime related to their positions" was changed to "Top executives have convenient opportunities to commit financial crime related to their positions" to stress the importance of convenience.

These changes were implemented in a revised questionnaire that was distributed in the bachelor class in the second lecture hour. One hundred and two students were present, and again all of them filled in the questionnaire. Improvement in scale reliabilities was achieved: .807 for strength of financial motive, .685 for organizational opportunity, .702 for willingness to commit crime by deviant behavior, and .801 for the tendency to commit white-collar crime. In the opportunity scale, one item was deleted to improve reliability from .645 to .685. Further improvement was not possible. In the willingness scale, two items were deleted to improve reliability from .656 to .702. Further improvement was not possible.

When desire, opportunity, and willingness are introduced in regression to predict the extent of crime, as illustrated in Figure 9.2, then an adjusted R square of .219 is the result. The regression is significant with an F-value of 9.766 and significance .000.

In the previous regression, willingness in the behavioral dimension was the only significant predictor. In the current survey, opportunity for crime is the only significant predictor of criminality. While desire was

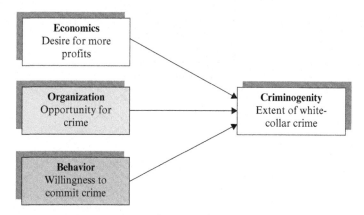

Figure 9.2   Significant predictors of criminality

not significant with a p-value of .651, and willingness was not significant with a p-value of .356, willingness to commit crime is significant with p=.001.

There are no obvious explanations for the different survey results. While the first group of students consisted of a mixture of part-time students and full-time students, the second group consisted only of full-time students. Modification in scales is a second source of explanations.

However, it is most interesting to note that opportunity in the organization to commit crime and willingness to commit crime are significant determinants of the extent of white-collar crime.

CAUSAL HYPOTHESES IN CONVENIENCE THEORY

Miller and Tsang (2010) suggest that rather than verification or falsification, theory testing should contribute to developments and improvements in suggested theories. They affirm the importance of testing efforts for progress in theory development.

So far in this chapter, we have been testing:

1. *Concepts*: Convenience, Desire (for profit to avoid threats and gain from possibilities), Opportunity (to commit financial crime and conceal crime in the organization), Willingness (of individual to commit crime by accepting his or her own deviant behavior), and Criminogenity (as tendency to commit white-collar crime).

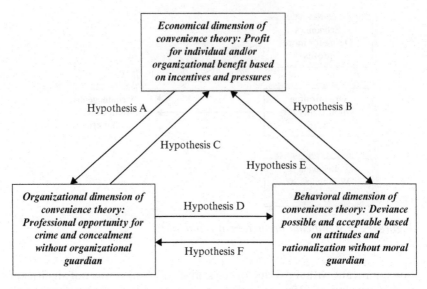

Figure 9.3   Model for hypotheses to study convenience theory

2. *Relationships*: Six causal relationships between economics (desire for more profits), organization (opportunity for crime), and behavior (willingness to commit crime).
3. *Effects*: Three causal relationships from economics (desire for more profits), organization (opportunity for crime), and behavior (willingness to commit crime) on criminogenity (extent of white-collar crime).

So far survey research among financial crime students, case studies of autobiographies by convicted white-collar criminals, and case studies of internal investigation reports by fraud examiners have served as empirical data for convenience theory testing. Findings from internal investigation reports are described more thoroughly in the next chapter.

To develop convenience theory further, there is a need to return to concepts, relationships, and effects. In particular, there is a need to discuss the six causal relationships suggested in Chapter 6 and repeated in Figure 9.3.

Chapter 6 presented survey responses and correlation analysis that supported all the relationships A–F. However, causality is different from correlation. Causality implies that each hypothesis represents a cause-and-effect relationship. A causal mechanism is assumed to account for a hypothesized relation. This requires interpretive work at the interface of theory and the empirical context of interest (Miller and

Tsang, 2010). Such interpretive work is described in the following for each hypothesis, where each hypothesis is reformulated into a causal relationship.

Hypothesis A: *An increase in the desire for profits to handle threats and possibilities causes an increase in the organizational opportunity to commit and conceal white-collar crime.*

Previously, the correlation hypothesis was formulated as: "Increased desire for convenient profit is positively related to increased convenient organizational opportunity to commit financial crime." Student surveys supported causality by agreement to the statements: "A heightened pursuit of profit to cover perceived needs increases the organizational opportunities for white-collar crime" (4.51) and "The more ambitious a financial goal is for the business, the more convenient it is to commit economic crime at work" (4.74). However, there is a need for theoretical reasoning to support this hypothesis. Why does it become easier for an offender to commit white-collar crime at work when the offender has a rising desire for profits? One explanation might be that the eager offender is more capable of searching and finding opportunities. Another explanation might be that the eager offender takes on roles in the organization that increase his or her opportunities to commit and conceal white-collar crime. A third explanation might be that extremely profit-oriented individuals are more capable of creating space for themselves in the organizational context.

Piquero and Benson (2004) found that an extreme desire for profits based on personal or occupational crisis often occurs when offenders are in their forties, when they are at their career peak with ample opportunities for deviant behavior. The presence of a favorable combination of circumstances renders a possible criminal course of action relevant (Aguilera and Vadera, 2008). A variety of pressures, or strains, increase the likelihood of finding ways to engage in crime (Holtfreter, 2015). Cressey's (1972) fraud triangle supports links between incentives and pressures, opportunities, and attitudes and rationalization. Similarly, Dodge's (2009) analysis reflects tough rivalry that makes executives in the organization commit crime to attain goals.

Chasing profits leaves people more creative in finding ways to make more legal as well as illegal profits for themselves as well as the organization, and people become more creative in concealing crime in various ways (Füss and Hecker, 2008).

Hypothesis B: *An increase in the desire for profits to handle threats and possibilities causes an increase in the personal willingness to commit and conceal white-collar crime.*

Previously, the correlation hypothesis was formulated as: "Desire for profits and success makes it attractive for individuals to commit white-col- lar crime." Student surveys supported causality by agreement to the state- ments: "A heightened pursuit of profit to cover perceived needs increases the willingness to commit white-collar crime at work" (5.11) and "The more ambitious a financial goal is for the business, the more convenient it is to accept one's own criminal behavior" (4.68). The causal relationship between desire and willingness seems intuitively very obvious. If I really want something, then I am willing to do whatever it takes. Normal self- control is challenged (Gottfredson and Hirschi, 1990), and neutralization is more actively applied by the offender.

The attractiveness of profits influences the willingness to commit crime in Clarke's (1999) reasoning about hot products, where hot targets influ- ence the tendency for deviant behavior. As argued by Agnew (2014), crime is often the most expedient way to get what you want. The American dream is caused by an overemphasis on success in visible assets (Schoepfer and Piquero, 2006), thereby increasing individual crime willingness by a concurrent emphasis on what means are acceptable for reaching desired goals (Pratt and Cullen, 2005). The American dream emphasizes eco- nomic success, while at the same time society is perceived to be restricting individuals' access to legitimate opportunities for upward socioeconomic mobility, which, in turn, can result in high levels of criminogenic anomie in society (Pratt and Cullen, 2005). The opposite of the American dream is the fear of falling, where crime willingness increases in order to main- tain privileged positions (Piquero, 2012). Inequality of opportunity causes a strain on goals and creates a motive for white-collar crime (Wood and Alleyne, 2010). Crime is a possible avenue for action, which might be per- ceived as a means to escape from or reduce strain (Froggio and Agnew, 2007). The strain of pursuing goals within diverse possibility structures may lead to adaptations such as crime, delinquency, and other deviant behaviors (Hoffmann, 2002). Delinquency results when individuals are unable to achieve their goals through legitimate channels (Agnew, 2012). In an empirical study by Langton and Piquero (2007), they found that the strain perspective is useful for predicting a select group of white-collar offenses. According to Ngo and Paternoster (2016), angry responses to strain seem to increase the likelihood of illegitimate coping.

Hypothesis C: *An increase in the organizational opportunity to commit and conceal white-collar crime causes an increase in the desire for profits to handle threats and possibilities.*

Previously, the correlation hypothesis was formulated like A, as: "Increased desire for convenient profit is positively related to increased convenient organizational opportunity to commit financial crime." Student surveys supported causality through agreement to the statements: "Increased opportunity to commit white-collar crime at work strengthens the desire for profit to cover perceived needs" (4.53) and "The more convenient it is to commit economic crime at work, the more important it is to achieve an ambitious financial goal" (4.15). Many convicted white-collar criminals seem to support this causal relation. They first discovered how easy it was to commit crime and seemingly get away with it without cost. Based on the perception of convenient opportunities in the organization to commit white-collar crime, many offenders became more interested in reaching business and personal objectives. Some of them discovered how easy it was to get new contracts for the business and to get new summerhouses and boats for themselves by deviant behavior at work that initially was noticed by nobody. The desire for profits both professionally and personally increases as opportunities become evident at work for potential offenders.

The absence of capable guardians makes it more attractive to pursue illegal avenues for desired profits (Cohen and Felson, 1979). Pontell et al. (2014) found that the absence of prosecution after the disclosure of crime because the organization is considered too powerful to fail, makes illegal profits more attractive. An opportunity is attractive as a way to respond to needs (Bucy et al., 2008).

Hypothesis D*: An increase in the organizational opportunity to commit and conceal white-collar crime causes an increase in the personal willingness to commit and conceal white-collar crime.*

Previously, the correlation hypothesis was formulated as: "Increased convenient organizational opportunity to commit financial crime is positively related to increased convenient deviant criminal behavior." Student surveys supported causality through agreement to the statements: "Increased opportunity to commit white-collar crime at work strengthens the willingness for a deviant behavior that includes criminal acts" and "The easier it is to commit economic crime at work, the more convenient it is to accept one's own criminal behavior". People avoid complicated tasks, and they are not willing to commit crime if it is too complicated and perceived subjective detection risk is too high. On the other hand, if the task is simple, then it is more convenient, and it is easier to commit crime within reasonable self-control (Gottfredson and Hirschi, 1990) and by application of neutralization techniques (Sykes and Matza, 1957). A neutralization phrase applied by some convicts is that the organization had no guardian and therefore can blame itself for financial crime. Executive misconduct increases as there are no visible consequences (Valukas, 2010). Dion (2009) argues that organizational culture makes it possible to adopt organizational purposes and objectives, which are basically deviant in comparison with social norms yet in line with the competition. Deviant purposes can be chosen when business corporations are trapped by doubtful, immoral, or disloyal means that are used by competitors. Benson and Simpson (2015) found that the more lawful and legitimate access to the premises and systems where crime can be committed the more convenient white-collar crime might be to potential offenders. When the organization is characterized by a criminal mindset, crime is not perceived as a deviant behavior (O'Connor, 2005). In a principal–agent perspective, the agent will be open to more opportunistic behavior when the principal is unable to control the agent (Chrisman et al., 2007; Li and Ouyang, 2007; Williams, 2008). Lack of social control (Hoffmann, 2002) and social disorganization (Wood and Alleyne, 2010) also stimulate opportunistic criminal behavior.

Shadnam and Lawrence (2011) found that in organizations with low morale, the propensity for unethical behavior will be greater, which can create favorable conditions and willingness for economic crime.

Hypothesis E: An increase in the personal willingness to commit and conceal white-collar crime causes an increase in the desire for profits to handle threats and possibilities.

Previously, the correlation hypothesis was formulated as: "Desire for profits and success makes it attractive for individuals to commit white-collar crime." Student surveys supported causality by agreement to the statements: "Increased willingness to commit white-collar crime at work strengthens the desire for profit to cover perceived needs" (4.81) and "The easier it is to accept one's own criminal behavior, the more convenient it is to achieve an ambitious financial goal" (4.78). The personal tendency to commit crime varies in the elite. Criminogenity – the extent of willingness – is related to acceptance of and lack of perception of personal deviant behavior. The hypothesis suggests that individuals willing to commit financial crime will have a stronger desire for profits. This causal relationship is intuitively not obvious. Why should individuals who enjoy crime be greedier than others who do not enjoy crime? The willingness can stem from excitement and thrill, rather than greed. It can stem from curiosity and challenge, to see if it is possible to get away with corruption, embezzlement, or fraud. Therefore, it is indeed difficult to argue theoretically for hypothesis E.

Benson (2013) found that narcissistic self-confidence and insensitivity to others may lead to drive and ambition. Benson and Simpson (2015) found that white-collar criminals seldom think of injury or victims.

Hypothesis F: *An increase in the personal willingness to commit and conceal white-collar crime causes an increase in the organizational opportunity to commit and conceal white-collar crime.*

Previously, the correlation hypothesis was formulated as: "Increased convenient organizational opportunity to commit financial crime is positively related to increased convenient deviant criminal behavior." Student surveys supported causality through agreement to the statements: "Increased willingness to commit white-collar crime strengthens the opportunity to commit economic crime at work" (5.18) and "The easier it is to accept one's own criminal behavior, the more convenient it is to commit economic crime at work" (5.65). The two average scores from respondents indicate the strongest support for this causal relationship. One explanation might be that the willing offender is more capable of searching and finding opportunities. Another explanation might be that the willing offender takes on roles in the organization that increase his or her opportunities to commit and conceal white-collar crime. A third explanation might be that extremely willing individuals are more capable of creating space for themselves in the organizational context.

In an empirical study of white-collar crime by Bucy et al. (2008), they found that typical white-collar criminals are willing to take risks. A willing individual is not necessarily bad or lazy. On the contrary, the person can be seen as smart and rational (Sundström and Radon, 2015). Willingness is related to the concept of convenience orientation, which is the degree of interest in spending as little time and effort as possible to achieve an objective (Mai and Olsen, 2016). A convenience-oriented person is one who seeks to accomplish a task in the shortest time with the least expenditure of human energy and pain (Berry et al., 2002). When a dilemma arises for potential offenders, they make a reasonable tradeoff where willingness increases with neutralization (Siponen and Vance, 2010; Sykes and Matza, 1957). Willingness increases when criminal behavior learning occurs in association with those who find such criminal behavior favorable (Sutherland, 1949), and who let others learn about organizational opportunities for crime (Benson and Simpson, 2015). Benson (2013) found that social changes for the individual influence various types of white-collar crime.

The desire to spend as little time, effort, and pain as possible on a task as defined by convenience orientation make the potential offender search for convenient solutions in the organizational setting (Mai and Olsen, 2016).

Some members of the elite feel that they are not provided the ability to achieve their ambitious goals. They blame the system rather than themselves for their lack of success, and they compensate through white-collar crime in the system (Wood and Alleyne, 2010). Therefore, increased willingness leads to greater organizational opportunity. Elnan (2016) found that criminals are often more innovative than most people.

EVALUATING CONVENIENCE THEORY BY TESTING

There is a need for further empirical research to evaluate and test convenience theory. As argued by Miller and Tsang (2010), science is a personal and social process, and nothing in the methods of science guarantees success in arriving at the truth. While reality exists independent of a researcher's knowledge, a researcher's knowledge of reality is socially constructed. They argue that a critical realist perspective affirms the possibility of truthful knowing but acknowledges that human limitations undermine claims to indubitable or objective knowledge. Within critical realism, to theorize is to propose mechanisms that explain events.

Miller and Tsang (2010) argue that the empirical domain is made up of events experienced through direct and indirect observation, such as detection through survey or interview instruments. Critical realists seek to test explanations, not just correlations between observable antecedents and consequences. As illustrated in this chapter, we are able to find support both for correlation and causality, where it was possible to substantiate convenience theory's causal explanations based on referenced research literature.

We have identified the causal mechanisms believed to account for the hypothesized relations in convenience theory. We have contextualized specification of the explanatory properties and processes that underlie hypothesized causal relations. We have selected those mechanisms that we believe operate in our particular research setting.

More than one mechanism may be relevant to a given causal relation. This was illustrated by the regression model where the tendency to commit white-collar crime could be explained by motive, opportunity, and willingness.

Furthermore, Miller and Tsang (2010) suggest that mechanisms may have complementary or conflicting implications for a hypothesized relation. To illustrate this point, they mention the varied and conflicting ways top management team diversity affects firm performance. So far in our evaluation of convenience theory, we have found no conflicting implications from the mechanisms.

Tests for the presence of mechanisms can involve looking for implications of the mechanisms. For example, in our study of autobiographies we find a number of strong neutralization techniques among convicted white-collar criminals. These neutralization techniques do not necessarily lead to increased willingness to commit crime. Rather, they may lead to increased perception of lawful behavior even in situations where law-breaking takes place.

Even if a particular mechanism is not directly observable, the more observable effects that logically are attributable to the mechanism, the more compelling is the case for its presence. For example, in the relation between economical and organizational dimensions of convenience theory, detected white-collar crime is observable, and the benefits from crime are observable as well. In this case, at least two observable indicators provide indirect support for the presence of an unobserved mechanism.

An offender's reasons as well as willingness operate as causes, which in turn are responsible for producing crime in the organizational setting. Such intentional human behavior provides an opportunity for testing the mechanisms of a theory. Miller and Tsang (2010) suggest that the assumption about intentions relies upon either truthful disclosure by the individual involved, generalizations about similarly situated others, or projections of the researcher's own intentions onto the studied subjects. While very few – if any – white-collar criminals will admit to intentional crime, they may admit to actions that are labeled crime.

In order to infer reasons and evaluate subjects' espoused reasons, Miller and Tsang (2010) argue that we draw heuristically upon our own self-understanding for insights into others' unobservable intentions. Our common humanity and experiences, rather than a posture of objectivity, inform the act of inferring intentions from others' actions. When we study white-collar offenders, they are similar to non-offenders in almost all aspects. Our approach is not to say that they are bad and we are good, hence we cannot understand them. On the contrary, we might have ended up like them in similar circumstances. Given a strong desire to avoid pain and threats, given an acceptable deviance from normal behavior, and given an organizational setting without guardians, then it is not obvious that we would not have done it. Therefore, we can inform the act of inferring intentions from others' criminal actions.

Miller and Tsang (2010) contend that behavioral assumptions are fundamental to the explanations of behavioral theories, yet they are often overlooked in empirical evaluations. Important behavioral assumptions about white-collar criminals are concerned with ambitions, goals, networks, positions, and trust.

Miller and Tsang (2010) suggest that when available evidence affirms the presence of theoretical mechanisms, we should move to testing their causal effects. Prior to attempting to verify or falsify an entire theoretical system in an open context, they advocate testing binary or more complex subsets of relations under controlled circumstances. They mention approaches such as laboratory experiments, behavioral simulations, and quasi-experiments. Student questionnaires applied in survey research in class as presented earlier in this book may be defined as laboratory experiments where they responded to binary and more complex subsets of relations in convenience theory.

For example, respondents disagreed with the statement that "if it is more convenient to achieve a financial goal legally, then many top executives nevertheless do it illegally" (2.96). We interpret this result to mean that members of the elite are not interested in crime or motivated toward crime as such. Top executives do not commit crime just for the sake of being criminals. This is in line with our intuitive assumption about people in general.

Furthermore, respondents disagreed with the general statement that "top executives are willing to commit financial crime at work" (3.84). The revised item was expected to achieve agreement, "Top executives find it convenient to commit crime in a stressful situation at work", which it did (4.30). When we draw upon our own self-understanding for insights into others' unobservable intentions, we tend to agree with the latter mechanism, but not with the initial mechanism.

In their next theory evaluation step, Miller and Tsang (2010: 150) suggest that if empirical data corroborate a theory's mechanisms and their effects, then the next critical issue is to examine the implications of its mechanisms jointly: "This step moves the analysis from isolated mechanisms to the entire theoretical system, thereby adding complexity to the evaluative procedure. At this stage, we are interested in whether all of the theory's mechanisms are necessary and whether they are jointly sufficient to explain the outcome." The outcome in convenience theory can either be defined in a digital form, that is, whether or not a crime is committed; or it can be defined in a discrete form, that is, defined as a change in the tendency to commit crime in terms of criminogenity. In the discrete form, convenience theory argues that a stronger motive, a more willing person, and greater organizational opportunity will stimulate the tendency to commit crime. In the digital form, convenience theory does not suggest a tipping point where a particular strength of motive, a particular degree of willingness, and a particular extent of opportunity will lead to white-collar crime.

Maybe the digital form could be explored by multiple case studies, where some cases led to crime while others did not. However, the challenge would be to identify similar cases where case differences could be isolated from the analysis. For example, some businesses operating in corrupt countries get involved in bribing, while other businesses do not. This kind of comparison is extremely difficult to carry out, since social systems are always open, while a theoretical system such as convenience theory is closed. The empirical contexts of individuals and organizations are always open and not closed. Miller and Tsang (2010: 150) contend that critical realism is highly pluralist in terms of empirical research methods: "Because different methods focus on different aspects of reality, combining several methods together in a research program yields a rich understanding of the phenomenon of interest."

So far we have applied student surveys, autobiography analysis, and internal investigation reports, the last of which are more thoroughly described in the next chapter. An additional method at this stage might be the study of convicted white-collar criminals who have confessed crime. Confession in court signals that the offender has some insights into his or her own deviant behavior. Confession is not necessarily motivated by the potential for sentence reduction. Confession can be motivated by the desire to settle past offenses. Interviews with this group of offenders might potentially provide joint empirical insights into all the dimensions of convenience theory, as suggested by Miller and Tsang (2010).

Miller and Tsang (2010) distinguish between extensive and intensive designs for empirical research at this stage. Extensive research attempts to test empirical generalities across cases and typically employs quantitative methods. Intensive research tries to uncover the explanatory mechanisms relevant in particular cases, and is often associated with qualitative modes of analysis. Mixed designs attempt to combine both extensive and intensive designs, thereby utilizing their complementary strengths and weaknesses.

OPEN SYSTEM TEST OF CONVENIENCE THEORY

Open systems do not necessarily undermine empirical regularities, and the occurrence of such regularities can provide insights into the operative mechanisms. Miller and Tsang (2010) suggest that working from a critical realist perspective, a researcher uses regression analysis to demonstrate the effects of theorized causal mechanisms after controlling for other mechanisms that also could affect the outcome. In our previous regression model, we only applied mechanisms defined in convenience theory to predict the tendency to commit white-collar crime: motive, willingness, and opportunity. We have to ask ourselves: What other factors may influence the tendency to commit white-collar crime?

Identifying factors that are not implicitly part of the three dimensions can be challenging. For example, a number of personal and situational characteristics – such as age and family – influence willingness in the behavioral dimension. A number of work-related characteristics such as business size and corporate culture influence opportunity in the organizational dimension. A number of psychological characteristics – such as self-perception and labeling by others – influence financial desire in the economical dimension of convenience theory.

An alternative approach more suited for our theory is to identify factors at different levels and explore whether or not outside factors have the same impact as mechanisms included in convenience theory. The open social system consists of factors at the individual, organizational, and societal levels. In convenience theory, only individual (motive and willingness) and organizational (opportunity and concealment) factors are included. We have to ask ourselves: What factors in society may influence the tendency to commit white-collar crime?

Based on this question, we conducted an open system test of convenience theory. Again, we asked students in the financial crime class to answer questions and this time questions concerning influences on criminogenity from factors inside convenience theory (individual and organizational) as well as factors outside convenience theory (national).

Respondents were asked to what extent a number of factors influence a person's tendency to commit white-collar crime. At the individual and organizational levels, factors were as before from convenience theory. At the national level, respondents were asked on a scale from little extent to great extent about the influence from the following factors:

- Magnitude of unemployment in the country.
- Size of gross national product in the country.
- Extent of equality before the law in the country.
- Extent of gender equality in the country.
- Extent of wage differences in the country.
- Extent of democracy in the country.
- Tax burdens in the country.
- Level of society morale in the country.

We define these factors as external to convenience theory, while we define individual and organizational factors as internal to convenience theory. We developed two scales for the two sets of factors and computed reliability for each scale before calculating t-statistics for difference between the scales. We expected both scales to be reliable in terms of Cronbach's alpha (alpha>.700), and we expected the t-statistic to be significant (p<.010).

If, however, there is no significant difference between the two scales, then this test undermines hypothesized relations in convenience theory. If the individual- and organizational-level scale is not significantly different from the national-level scale, then it is not obvious anymore that

Table 9.5 Items for open system test of convenience theory

#	Item	System	Score	Std. dev.
1.	Personal willingness to commit white-collar crime	Convenience	5.96	0.953
2.	Personal desire for financial profit	Convenience	5.84	1.075
3.	Personal extent of self-control	Convenience	5.41	1.075
4.	Personal fear for financial problems	Convenience	5.38	1.019
5.	Organizational opportunity to conceal financial crime	Convenience	5.38	1.121
6.	Tax burdens in the country	Society	5.00	1.265
7.	Organizational opportunity to commit financial crime	Convenience	4.71	1.187
8.	Level of society morale in the country	Society	4.39	1.410
9.	Extent of equality before the law in society	Society	4.35	1.322
10.	Extent of wage differences in the country	Society	4.30	1.426
11.	Magnitude of unemployment	Society	4.02	1.711
12.	Extent of democracy in the country	Society	3.87	1.630
13.	Size of gross national product in the country	Society	3.63	1.579
14.	Extent of gender equality in the country	Society	3.23	1.144

the extent of white-collar crime is mainly determined by financial desire, crime willingness, and crime opportunity. As suggested by Miller and Tsang (2010), this kind of result may require adjustments in theoretical arguments to fit the findings. Specifically, it would require that a fourth dimension is included in convenience theory, which is concerned with the environment in society.

A total of 56 responses were obtained in class, and Table 9.5 lists results. The Likert scale ranges from 1 (little extent) to 7 (great extent) as a response to the question: To what extent do you think the following factors influence a person's tendency to commit white-collar crime? While the 14 statements were distributed randomly in the questionnaire, Table 9.5 lists them according to the respective scores.

Out of 14 statements, 6 statements are concerned with issues in convenience theory, while 8 statements are related to issues in society as a whole. The 8 statements about society are not included in convenience theory as explanations of white-collar crime.

Respondents' average responses indicate that issues in convenience theory are more important in determining white-collar crime than issues in society. The five most important issues are all convenience items. We find a society item at number 6, which is concerned with tax burdens in society. It is surprising that tax burden is ahead of organizational opportunity in the table. Otherwise, the table confirms the importance of individual and organizational issues rather than societal issues when explaining the extent of white-collar crime.

In terms of standard deviations in responses as listed in the last column, respondents agree strongly about the importance of personal willingness to commit white-collar crime. Respondents disagree strongly about the importance of magnitude of unemployment in society.

Next, to test the difference between factors external to convenience theory versus factors internal to convenience theory, we first identified the reliability of each scale before a t-test was performed. Reliability for the society scale with eight items was indeed acceptable, with a Cronbach's alpha of 0.827. Reliability for the convenience scale, however, was unacceptable, with a Cronbach's alpha of 0.574. The low reliability might be explained by the more or less random selection of statements related to convenience theory. Therefore, we selected one single item that most strikingly represents convenience theory. We selected item 5, which is organizational opportunity to conceal financial crime.

To conduct a proper t-test, the scale for society with eight items was first computed. While the mean value for the society scale is 4.09, the mean value for item 5 is 5.38. The t-test for significance of difference between the two results in a t-value of 6.106 and p=0.000.

The above analysis is an example of an extensive research design for theory testing. Statistical analysis supported the view in convenience theory that the extent of white-collar crime is determined by factors at the individual and organizational level, rather than at the national level.

Miller and Tsang (2010: 152) suggest that intensive designs complement extensive designs for theory evaluation by addressing the differences across cases that one would expect if empirical outcomes result from conjunctions of multiple mechanisms in open systems:

> The purpose behind intensive designs is to identify and describe the generative mechanisms operating in particular cases, which is often not feasible for extensive designs. An intensive design emphasizes the collection of detailed data within one or more cases. The data are often qualitative, as are the analytic methods. Established methods for case study, ethnographic, grounded theory, and action research guide intensive design.

We will argue that our case studies of autobiographies by convicted white-collar criminals in fact were carried out in line with the intensive design.

We were able to find a variety of statements produced by offenders that illustrated the application of neutralization techniques in the behavioral dimension of convenience theory. Miller and Tsang (2010) suggest that contrasting cases can provide evidence regarding how mechanisms operate under different conditions.

10. Sample of US investigation reports

Many internal investigation reports are kept secret. Reports are the property of clients who often do not want to damage their reputation or leak business secrets. In 2015, it was possible to identify and obtain a total of 13 publicly available investigation reports. These 13 investigations are presented in this chapter.

CASE 1: ACAR INVESTIGATED BY SIDLEY

On March 12, 2009, Yusuf Acar, a mid-level manager at the District of Columbia's office of the chief technology officer (CTO), was arrested and charged with bribery, conspiracy, money laundering, and conflict of interest related to procurement improprieties. A few weeks later, on April 9, the council of the district authorized an investigation into the nature and causes of the Acar fraud. The committee retained Sidley (2010) to conduct the investigation.

The Sidley (2010) investigation had three questions in its mandate. First, how did the fraud occur? Second, how did it go undetected for nearly four years? Third, what vulnerabilities existed in the procurement process that facilitated this fraud, and how can those vulnerabilities best be addressed to reduce the risk of recurrence of this type of fraudulent activity in the future?

The investigation consisted of data collection, data analysis, and witness interviews. Investigators studied district procurement policies, transaction data involving vendors receiving the most contracts, local supply schedules, and employees who made procurement requests or oversaw contract fulfillment. Investigators interviewed more than 30 individuals, including current and former technology employees (Sidley, 2010).

The Federal Bureau of Investigation (FBI) published on its website (http://www.fbi.gov/washingtondc/press-releases/2010/wfo081210a.htm):

WASHINGTON – Yusuf Acar, the former acting Chief of Security Officer for the District of Columbia's Office of the Chief Technology Officer (OCTO), was sentenced today to two concurrent terms of 27 months in prison for his role in a bribery and kickback scheme. The sentence, in U.S. District Court for the District of Columbia, was announced by U.S. Attorney Ronald C. Machen Jr., Shawn Henry, Assistant Director in Charge of the FBI's Washington Field Office, and Charles J. Willoughby, inspector general for the District of Columbia.

Acar, 41, of Washington, D.C., pled guilty on December 18, 2009 before the Honorable Henry H. Kennedy, Jr. to a two-count information that charged him with bribery and engaging in monetary transactions in property derived from specified unlawful activity.

During his guilty plea, Acar admitted that, between September 2005 and March 12, 2009, he accepted bribes on at least 59 occasions from Sushil Bansal, who owned a company called Advanced Integrated Technologies Corporation (AITC). Bansal paid Acar a total of $558,978.50 in bribe payments during this time. Acar also admitted to engaging in 17 transactions, each over $10,000, that involved the bribe money and which utilized financial institutions.

In addition to the 27-month prison term, Judge Kennedy ordered Acar to pay $558,978.50 in restitution. He will be on supervised release for three years after serving his sentence.

"The residents of the District of Columbia deserve an ethical government with ethical employees, and have the right to know that their money is being spent honestly and for the public good," said U.S. Attorney Machen. "The prison sentence in this case should send a strong message to any public official who may be tempted to accept a bribe or kickback that we will not tolerate corruption."

Acar has been held without bond since March 2009.

Bansal, 43, of Dunn Loring, Virginia, pled guilty in April 2010 to federal charges, as did his company. He was sentenced August 6, 2010 to two concurrent 20-month prison terms. He and his company were ordered to pay $844,765.50 in restitution to the District of Columbia government. He will be on three years of supervised release once he gets out of prison.

Earlier today, a second OCTO employee was sentenced to prison for his role in the scheme. Farrukh Awan, 38, of South Riding, Virginia, was sentenced to 14 months in prison and ordered to pay $156,807 in restitution. He also must forfeit $46,647.50 as part of the sentence. He will be placed on three years of supervised release once his prison sentence is completed. Awan pleaded guilty in November 2009 to conspiracy to commit wire fraud.

In announcing the sentence, U.S. Attorney Machen, FBI Assistant Director in Charge Henry, and D.C. Inspector General Willoughby commended the outstanding investigative work of the Special Agents from the FBI's Washington Field Office, and Special Agent Teddy Clark and the late Special Agent Lloyd Hodge of the D.C. Office of the Inspector General. They also acknowledged the efforts of U.S. Attorney's Office paralegals Diane Hayes, Tasha Harris and Maggie McCabe, former legal assistant Lisa Robinson, as well as Assistant U.S. Attorneys Thomas Hibarger and Glenn Leon, who prosecuted this case.

CASE 2: COATESVILLE INVESTIGATED BY BDO

Auditing firm BDO was hired to investigate the Coatesville area school district in Pennsylvania. Pratt at BDO (2014) wrote the report. In addition, investigative reports about the school district were written by Haverstick et al. (2014a, 2014b) at law firm Conrad O'Brien as well as by the Chester Grand Jury (2014), who investigated possible criminal charges. Issues included fiscal mismanagement, lack of accountability, abuse of power, and the misappropriation, including theft, of school district funds.

For the initial report by Haverstick et al. (2014a), investigators interviewed 93 current and former employees of the Coatesville Area School District (CASD), and the report makes a point of specifying that all of their interviews were completely voluntary. Investigators also interviewed individuals from vendors and contractors of CASD whose work crossed paths with the investigation. The Haverstick et al. (2014a) report states that there were a number of individuals that they wished to speak with, but were refused or, in one case, blocked from speaking with by the board of school directors. Particularly interesting is that in the supplemental report by Haverstick et al. (2014b), investigators state that they feel that the individual that they were blocked from interviewing was important enough that they were willing to do so without charging CASD for their time.

The forensic audit was performed by BDO at the request of Conrad O'Brien law firm (Haverstick et al., 2014a). The BDO investigator spoke with a number of district employees and made use of the school district's financial statements and accounting records. BDO (2014: 8) described the scope of the report for CASD as follows:

> The scope of our report is specifically limited to the application of forensic accounting procedures and an analysis of the issues identified by CASD and its outside legal counsel. The issues identified include certain transactions involving former Superintendent Richard Como and former Athletic Director James Donato, specifically related to CASD Athletic Department revenue, Athletic Department expenses, and other particular issues. These other issues analyzed during our engagement include overall budgeting and financial reporting, purchasing, budget transfers, transfers between funds, bank account reconciliations, financial controls over Student Activities' Funds and the sale of delinquent tax liens.

The individuals that the reports primarily focus on are Richard Como, the superintendent of CASD; James Donato, the athletic director for CASD; and James Ellison, the Coatesville area school district solicitor. Other individuals that played a significant role in the events that triggered the investigation and the findings of the investigation included Abdallah Hawa, the CASD director of technology; and Teresa Powell, the CASD director of middle school education. Members of the board of school directors and others also played important roles.

The misconduct was initially detected based on a cell phone. In the late spring or early summer of 2013, Donato requested a new cell phone from Hawa, the district director of technology. Hawa obtained the new cell phone and transferred Donato's information to the new device. Donato's old phone was put into storage to be reissued to another employee. On August 15, 2013 Hawa pulled the phone with the intention of wiping it so that it could be reissued, and discovered that there were "numerous racist, sexist and bigoted messages" on the phone, "primarily between Mr. Donato and Mr. Como" (Haverstick et al., 2014a). Given the individuals that were involved, Hawa chose to go to Powell, specifically because he felt that she was not beholden to Como.

The major issue in the reports by Haverstick et al. (2014a, 2014b) is the financial irregularities surrounding both Donato and Como. Irregularities were found in sales of football game tickets as admission revenues had dropped sharply. The estimated total discrepancy in admission revenues during Donato's tenure was 60,000 US dollars.

The major issue in the report by BDO (2014) was unusual and improper expenses of almost 20,000 US dollars. Some of this money was claimed to be paid for fundraisers, but there were no corresponding deposits made that were identified as money raised for these fundraisers.

In total, Haverstick et al. (2014a, 2014b) and BDO (2014) discovered a discrepancy of 80,000 US dollars. Both Como and Donato resigned from their posts, but they faced no criminal charges.

While the investigators identified several rotten apples in the form of the former superintendent, Richard Como, and former athletic director, James Donato, they also identified the factors that allowed the rot to become as extensive as it did in the CASD, which was the poor management provided by the board of school directors. As superintendent, Como centralized hiring to the extent that he had almost complete control over who was hired, allowing him to hire individuals with connections to either himself or the board of school directors. This could happen regardless of their qualifications, usually without the input from and at times over any objections of the faculty and staff that were the supervisors of those who Como hired. Como was able to keep faculty and staff in fear for their jobs if they objected, in part because the board of school directors failed to provide adequate oversight.

CASE 3: ENRON INVESTIGATED BY POWERS

The special investigative committee of the board of directors of Enron corporation submitted a report of investigation in 2002 (Powers et al., 2002). The mandate for the investigation was to address transactions between Enron and investment partnerships created and managed by Andrew S. Fastow, Enron's former chief financial officer (CFO), and other Enron employees who worked for Fastow.

There were some practical limitations on the information available to the committee in preparing their report. They had no power to compel third parties to submit to interviews, produce documents, or otherwise provide information. Certain former Enron employees who played substantial roles in one or more of the transactions under investigation – including Fastow, Michael J. Kopper, and Ben F. Glisan, Jr. – declined interview either entirely or with respect to most issues. The investigators had only limited access to certain work papers of Arthur Andersen, Enron's outside auditors, and no access to materials in the possession of the Fastow partnerships or their limited partners. Information from these key people sources could affect the investigation's conclusions.

Kenneth Lay, the chief executive officer (CEO) of Enron, approved the arrangements under which Enron permitted Fastow to engage in related-party transactions with Enron. Jeffrey Skilling was the chief operating officer (COO) at Enron, Richard Causey was chief accounting officer, and Richard Buy was senior risk officer.

Kenneth Lay died in 2006 before his final sentencing. Andrew Fastow served a six-year prison sentence. Jeffrey Skilling received a sentence of 24 years in prison.

Sixteen Enron executives pleaded guilty for financial crime committed at the expense of the company and were sentenced to jail. The private investigation also turned up that Arthur Andersen received 25 million US dollars in audit fees and 27 million US dollars in consulting fees, which totaled 27 percent of all fees from clients of Arthur Andersen, so there was motive for a scandal within the audit company as well. Investigators found that Arthur Andersen failed to take note how many deficiencies there were in Enron's public disclosure statements. Eventually, prosecutors found Arthur Andersen guilty of obstruction of justice for deleting emails of company files and shredding numerous documents from the scandal. The company surrendered its Certified Public Accountant (CPA) license on August 31, 2002, which left 85,000 employees without jobs.

Due to the seriousness of the Enron scandal, the Sarbanes-Oxley Act became a reality on July 30, 2002. This act aimed to fix the major problems that became apparent in the Enron scandal such as developing standards for the preparation of audit reports, relinquishment of executive bonuses in cases of financial restatement, and increased penalties for destroying records in a federal investigation.

The Powers et al. (2002) investigation does not constitute an independent examination, as all members of the committee came from within Enron, either from the board of directors or from other executive positions in the company. This is a crucial fact, because it can lead to biased results, which are included in the private investigation report at the end. With all members being from within the company, they could have a different objective or feel like they have an obligation to not make it look like Enron or the board were the cause of the company's bankruptcy. There were no external private investigators involved throughout the investigation process. Without any external investigators, the chances of having a biased and less valid report increases.

Why did the board of directors not hire any external investigators to gather knowledge on what had occurred? A plausible explanation for this is that the board was trying to keep certain information hidden and not have that information revealed to anyone external to the company. Usually, when conducting a private investigation, the client will hire someone who digs deep and gathers sufficient information to draw conclusions. An indication of hidden information was the board's restriction on the documents the investigation committee could use. They had limited access to information regarding Enron, and what the company did during the time Fastow utilized his partnerships. Investigators did not succeed in obtaining access to most of the documents relating to Arthur Andersen. With the lack of access to a substantial amount of the required information, the investigation's credibility drops severely.

The first two people that the investigators attempted to interview were Andrew Fastow and Michael Kopper. These two men were mostly responsible for causing Enron to go bankrupt. Both men refused interviews with the investigation committee. The committee also went to third parties to conduct interviews. All third-party entities that the investigators approached refused to participate in interviews or offer any facts or knowledge about their involvement with Enron. They did not want to get involved in the investigation because they did not want anything coming out that could negatively affect them. In the end, the investigators were not able to conduct any interviews to gather information. They were not able to convince anyone to attend an interview or to get any outside help in making Fastow or

Kopper to partake in interviews. Without any interviews being successfully conducted, the investigation lacked substantial information, resulting in gaps in the report.

In the end, the investigators did not conduct a satisfactory or beneficial internal investigation. From their results, attained by searching through documents, nothing new about what exactly happened seems to have emerged. This may be because the investigation occurred after Enron filed for bankruptcy. The major reason why the investigation was a failure seems to be that the investigative committee was not capable of reconstructing the past.

In the end, the costs outweighed the benefits for this investigation. Investigators spent months going through files and documents just to find out who was involved and how much money they got out of the scheme. This time-consuming process seems to have been a large expense for Enron's board of directors, with little or no gain in the knowledge from the results of the investigation. When considering the investigation as an investment in knowledge creation, it was a bad investment.

Perhaps a summary of media accounts of the Enron scandal, as presented by Williams (2008), would be more valuable. He drew from an analysis of over 300 newspaper articles to study the diagnosis of the scandal. His study coded newspaper reports based on the following questions: (1) what are the identified causes and consequences of the scandal; (2) to what extent are they attributed to individual versus systemic factors; (3) what types of policy and regulatory responses are advocated and why; and (4) how are markets, regulation, and terms such as market integrity and investor confidence represented.

The media is a representational medium as well as an interpretive and sense-making device. Williams (2008) found that some newspapers commented on the Enron case as stemming from a handful of bad apples, while other newspapers viewed the scandal as a systemic expression of institutionalized wrongdoing and crime facilitated by an inadequate regulatory machinery. All media reports described financial markets as autonomous entities that have a tendency to ignore the law.

CASE 4:   GENERAL MOTORS INVESTIGATED BY VALUKAS

General Motors' CEO Mary Barra and the GM board directed Anton R. Valukas and Jenner to investigate the circumstances that led to the recall of the Cobalt and other cars because of a flawed ignition switch. They were to investigate what happened and why it happened. Jenner was also asked to focus on the knowledge of specific senior executives and board members. Attorney Valukas (2014), from law firm Jenner & Block, headed the private internal investigation at GM.

Valukas (2014) addresses in the report the role of senior leadership and the board in the scandal. Investigators reviewed a large number of documents collected from numerous custodians, including any potentially relevant emails that the senior leaders sent or received at pertinent times. They interviewed GM employees in the top leaders' respective chains of reporting who might have discussed Cobalt-related issues with them, and they interviewed and examined senior executives.

All the evidence that the investigators reviewed corroborated the conclusion that none of the senior executives had knowledge of the problems with the Cobalt ignition switch or non-deployment of airbags in the Cobalt until December 2013 at the earliest.

Before becoming the CEO at GM in January 2014, Mary Barra had served for the preceding three years as the senior vice president for global product development. Barra became well acquainted with the recall process when an issue involving the Chevrolet Volt's lithium battery arose in 2011. Based on that experience and others she believed that recall issues were addressed with appropriate urgency, and that the recall decision-making process worked well (Valukas, 2014).

Investigators provided opportunities for witnesses to contradict this. For example, Raymond DeGorgio, an engineer who allegedly approved the faulty switch and later replaced it with a better one without notifying anyone, just refuted the allegations and stated during the interview that he knew nothing. While reading the report (especially the ignition switch portion), one finds that the report from the very beginning points to one suspect, DeGorgio. The testimonies from Delphi mechatronics directly incriminate him for his negligence and persistence in using flawed switches. After publication of the report, engineer DeGorgio, alongside many other engineers, was terminated from his position.

The costs of the investigation are not disclosed, but they were probably substantial. The company achieved some benefits from their investment in the investigation. First, it provided a signal to the public and government authorities that GM was still a socially responsible organization. Second, it helped the organization to identify the misconduct behind the issue and to clean up the confusion in the organization. Third, it helped GM to identify the weak spots within the organization. Finally, it helped the CEO at GM to emerge as a leader when issues of leadership were at stake.

CASE 5: LEHMAN BROTHERS INVESTIGATED BY VALUKAS

Attorney Anton R. Valukas at law firm Jenner & Block was hired to investigate the collapse of Lehman Brothers. The bank went bankrupt in 2008. Valukas (2010) concluded in the private investigation report that Lehman failed because it was unable to retain the confidence of its lenders and counterparties, and because it did not have sufficient liquidity to meet its current obligations. Lehman was unable to maintain confidence because a series of business decisions had left it with a heavy concentration of illiquid assets with deteriorating values, such as residential and commercial real estate. Confidence was further eroded when it became public that attempts to form strategic partnerships to bolster its stability had failed.

The investigation report begins with a discussion of the business decisions that Lehman made well before the bankruptcy and the risk management issues raised by those business decisions. Ultimately, investigators conclude that while certain risk decisions by Lehman can be described in retrospect as poor judgment, they were within the business judgment rule and do not give rise to colorable claims. But those judgments, and the facts related to them, provide important context for the other subjects on which investigators found colorable claims. For example, after saddling itself with an enormous volume of illiquid assets that it could not readily sell, Lehman increasingly turned to deviant acts to manage its balance sheet and reduce its reported net leverage (Valukas, 2010).

The time allotted to the examiner, Anton R. Valukas, was reduced compared to other large investigations due to the rapidity necessary in a bankruptcy proceeding. The examiner began his investigation by requesting access to Lehman Brothers' records, both online files and physical files stored within their office. Once his request had been granted he used key search terms to sort through approximately 350 billion pages of online data sheets and client information sheets (Valukas, 2010).

Valukas then requested hard copy files from other companies whose records corresponded with Lehman Brothers. Valukas looked specifically at companies such as JP Morgan, Ernst & Young, and S&P among records from sources such as the Federal Reserve. Over 5 million records from these sources were maintained in an online database cataloging them by company and then by relevance (Valukas, 2010).

The examiner was able to gain access to 90 of Lehman Brothers' operating, financial, valuation, accounting, trading, and other data systems. Much of the software was unorganized and outdated, which only slowed down the process. Valukas enlisted the help of numerous attorneys in scouring through the endless databases and documents, searching for the use of key terms and essential events which could point to misconduct (Valukas, 2010).

Valukas then continued his investigation by speaking with examiners from other large bankruptcy cases such as WorldCom, Refco, and SemCrude in order to obtain advice from them as to the best practices for producing a successful investigation report. Valukas used some of the above-mentioned attorneys and examiners in the next step of his investigation, the interview stage. Valukas used a set of informal interviews, with two attorneys present during each, to take precise notes and make sure all laws were followed (Valukas, 2010).

The main goals of the interviews were to gain a better perspective on where everyone's opinion stood on the filing for bankruptcy, why they thought Lehman Brothers failed, and other essential questions that could lead to evidence of misconduct or point to new information. The examiner gave the person to be interviewed advanced notification of the topics to be discussed and the documents they would be asked to interpret. Valukas received great cooperation from all the 250 people he and the attorneys interviewed (Valukas, 2010).

Valukas (2010) concluded his investigation as follows:

1. The examiner does not find colorable claims that Lehman's senior officers breached their fiduciary duty of care by failing to observe Lehman's risk management policies and procedures.
2. The examiner does not find colorable claims that Lehman's senior officers breached their fiduciary duty to inform the board of directors concerning the level of risk Lehman had assumed.
3. The examiner does not find colorable claims that Lehman's directors breached their fiduciary duty by failing to monitor Lehman's risk-taking activities.

Valukas (2010) planned the investigation strategy with the goal of finding the presence of white-collar criminal activity; however, he found no evidence of such crime.

When investigators were unable to find evidence of any misdeed in relation to Repo 105 transactions that had taken place, the investigation abruptly finished because investigators were seemingly unable to adjust their viewpoint to look at other forms of transactions that had taken place.

As for the aspect of lack of contradiction, this is when investigators avoid giving suspects and witnesses a chance to contradict what is said about them in the report. It seems that investigators did not give any employees at Lehman Brothers an opportunity to look over what was written about them before they published the report.

The blame game is a potentially important aspect of an investigation report, where investigators complete the report by placing the blame on an individual/ individuals the client who ordered the investigation would prefer to see blamed for it. Valukas was commissioned by the Securities and Exchange Commission (SEC) to conduct this investigation. From the beginning of suspicions that Lehman Brothers' collapse was due to misconduct by the board of business executives, the SEC was probably intent on blaming the board of executives for the bank for pocketing what money was left over from collapsing stocks and market values. Valukas was probably influenced by their goal of detecting misconduct and therefore focused much of the investigation on those esteemed members of the company.

The main goal of an investigation report is not to jump to conclusions about who committed what and then accuse them of such acts, but instead to simply reconstruct the past. Valukas succeeded in reconstructing how Lehman Brothers collapsed following a precise timeline. Valukas followed the company from the beginning of the trouble in late 2008 when the housing market crashed, to when the bank put into place a more aggressive business strategy, to when they began losing increasingly large amounts of investors' money, to when they began conducting Repo 105 transactions in order to cover up the exact amount of money they were losing, to the end when the company was forced to file for the largest bankruptcy proceeding ever recorded to date in the United States.

If considered as an investment, the investigation was probably not profitable. The investigation into Lehman Brothers was lengthy and costly. Assuming that the investigation had costs of a million dollars, it is hard to identify equivalent or larger benefits. Valukas produced such a hefty bill due to his hiring of attorneys and assistants, his own hourly rate, his use of expensive technology and software to extract information from the offices of Lehman Brothers, and his travel costs in and around New York City. Due to the high cost of this investigation and the fact that no white-collar criminal was identified and then convicted, it seems that this investigation was not worth it. The report may not have benefited Lehman Brothers, the SEC, or the public.

The role of CFO Erin Callan is discussed in the investigation report on page 930:

> In her interview with the examiner, Callan recalled very little about Lehman's Repo 105 program. Callan said she had little to no independent recollection of Lehman's use of Repo 105 transactions, but that her memory had been refreshed to a limited extent by documents the examiner provided her in advance of her interview.

In 2016, six years after she was interviewed by fraud examiners for the Valukas (2010) report, Erin Callan published her own memoir entitled *Full Circle: A Memoir of Leaning in too Far and the Journey Back.* An interesting issue is whether her book adds new insight into possible misconduct and crime related to the collapse of the bank. She had been working for the bank since 1995. She recalls in her book (Montella, 2016: 142):

> One thing I do remember is the sense that I had a shocking lack of control over the state of Lehman Brothers and its financial health. Maybe that seems like it would be obvious, but it felt very strange and alarming to me. I was used to running businesses where the decisions I was making every day had real consequences. The market environment itself was always a wild card in terms of how quickly the profitability of those decisions could be realized, but I had the ability to create a respected, highly competent business under any circumstances [. . .]
>
> I came to understand how the mere existence of a concentrated portfolio of mortgage assets on our balance sheet was a big problem, regardless of any quality or hedging arguments that might be made.
>
> By late January of 2008, when I was fully committed to the view that some assets should be sold regardless of our opinion of their future profitability, then my complete lack of control and influence came home to roost. It was one thing to live with legacy decisions that had defined the position of the firm, but it was another to not be able to convince Dick and Joe that we had to move quickly to reduce our positions, even if that meant selling at a loss. Since they had been part of those initial decisions, they were vested, not willing to abandon ship with the same urgency.

Richard "Dick" Fuld was the CEO at Lehman Brothers, while Joseph "Joe" Gregory was the president and COO when the bank collapsed.

Erin Callan was the CFO of Lehman Brothers and a member of its executive committee during the height of the financial crisis in 2007. Prior to holding the CFO position, she held various business head positions over a dozen years throughout the bank. She was a corporate tax lawyer at Simpson Thacher & Bartlett, a New York-based law firm, for five years before joining Lehman in 1995. She graduated from Harvard University and then from New York University (NYU) law school.

In 1844, 23-year-old Henry Lehman, the son of a Jewish cattle merchant, migrated to the United States. With his brothers Emanuel and Mayer, he created the firm Lehman Brothers. The last Lehman to be in charge of the bank was Robert Lehman, who died in 1969 after 44 years as the patriarch of the firm, leaving no member of the Lehman family actively involved with the partnership.

The bank filed for bankruptcy in 2008. Lehman had by then borrowed significant amounts to fund its investing, a process known as leveraging or gearing. A significant portion of this investment was in housing-related assets, making it vulnerable to a downturn in that market. One measure of this risk-taking was its leverage ratio, a measure of the ratio of assets to owners' equity, which increased from approximately 24 to 1 in 2003 to 31 to 1 by 2007. While generating tremendous profits during the boom, this vulnerable position meant that just a marginal decline in the value of its assets would entirely eliminate its book value of equity. It only took about ten days before the Lehman bankruptcy came knocking at Erin Callan's door. On Friday, September 26, 2008, two FBI agents came to personally hand her the subpoena.

While in her book Elin Callan criticizes bosses and illustrates her struggles through the bank's collapse, her former boss, ex-Lehman CEO Dick Fuld, spoke at a New York banking industry conference and continued to present his defense of his tenure at the top of the now defunct bank. Unlike Callan, Fuld seemed intent in May 2015 to argue the case that Lehman was not a bankrupt company in 2008.

CASE 6:　MOTOROLA INVESTIGATED BY SEC

The division of enforcement at the Securities and Exchange Commission (SEC) conducted an investigation into whether Motorola, Inc. violated the federal securities laws when one of its senior officials selectively disclosed information about the company's quarterly sales and orders during private telephone calls with sell-side analysts in March 2001. During those calls, Motorola's director of investor relations told analysts that first quarter sales and orders were down by at least 25 percent. Previously, in a February 23, 2001 press release and a public conference call, Motorola had said only that sales and orders were experiencing "significant weakness", and that Motorola was likely to miss its earnings estimates (SEC, 2002).

SEC (2002) found that the conduct in question was inconsistent with the disclosure mandate, which generally prohibits issuers from communicating material, nonpublic information to securities professionals without simultaneous public disclosure of the same information. When an issuer endeavors to make a public disclosure of material information, but later learns that it did not, in fact, fully communicate the intended message, and determines that further disclosure is needed, the proper course of action is not to selectively disclose the corrected message in private communications with industry professionals, but rather to make additional public disclosure.

According to the enforcement manual at SEC (2013), an investigation is an inquiry into potential violations of the federal securities laws. The purpose is to protect investors and the markets by investigating potential violations of the laws and litigating the SEC's enforcement actions. Values integral to that mission include integrity, fairness, passion, and teamwork.

The main suspect in the investigation was the director of investor relations. He is blamed in the report and is presented as a rotten apple. Motorola as a company seems to avoid the rotten barrel label in the report. Blaming the director of investor relations without even interviewing the person, is a shortcoming of the investigation. The report suggests that the director misinformed the public, then cleared it up with analysts, but neglected to inform the public again with a public release. Such allegations should have caused investigators to interview the director to get the other side of the story.

CASE 7: PADAKHEP INVESTIGATED BY INSPECTOR GENERAL

Padakhep Manabik Unnayan Kendra (PMUK) is a non-governmental organization in Bangladesh. PMUK received 5.2 million US dollars from Save the Children for HIV/AIDS work among children in Bangladesh. An investigation by the office of the Inspector General (2012) resulted from irregularities found in multiple audits performed by the principal donor, Save the Children USA (SCUSA). The investigation confirmed that there were acts of misappropriation and a fraud scheme from 2004 to 2009, as identified through the audits. A loss of grant funds in the amount of 1,894,426 US dollars was disbursed to PMUK.

PMUK engaged in a scheme to divert the grant funds disbursed to them as a sub-recipient under the HIV/AIDS program. They concealed the diversion through fabricated documents for submission to SCUSA, including "a set of manufactured books and records to justify withdrawals that never actually took place, and then withdrew funds separately" (Inspector General, 2012: 3):

> The fictitious books and records included: (i) fabricated and falsified bank statements; (ii) accounting journals maintained for recording the false program expenditures and activities in detail; (iii) falsified bids and invoices for purchases of services and goods by third party vendors that did not in fact occur; and (iv) copies of checks allegedly issued to vendors that were never actually issued or presented for payment.

The documents were all created to justify the expenditures for a legitimate program purpose, but it never occurred. PMUK withdrew funds and diverted them to unknown locations. While the diversion of the program funds was well-concealed through a scheme of creating documentation that appeared on the face of it generally complete and mutually consistent, upon closer examination, indicators of fraud were evident (Inspector General, 2012: 4):

> For example, typographical and arithmetic errors appeared on the forged bank statements provided by PMUK. In addition, vendors who allegedly provided goods and services under the program confirmed in several instances that the bids and invoices bearing their companies' names were not authentic, that the vendors never provided the services/goods, and that these entities never actually received the money.

The investigation unit of the Office of the Inspector General is responsible for conducting investigations of fraud, abuse, misappropriation, corruption, and mismanagement that may occur when grants are given for various purposes. Investigations aim to uncover the specific nature and extent of fraud and abuse of funds, to identify the staff or private entities implicated in the schemes, and to determine the amount of funds misappropriated. The office is an administrative body with no law enforcement powers (Inspector General, 2012).

While PMUK was not able to justify the proper use of funds, investigators were not able to find out where PMUK placed the money and were unable to locate the misappropriated sums. The fabricated and falsified bank statements were evidence of fraud, but investigators failed in reconstructing the past in terms of financial transactions.

It seems that investigators entered the country of Bangladesh with disregard for the country's culture. The investigators should have understood the culture better instead of showing up at the NCC Bank requesting access to documents. The investigators went in confrontationally and accused the locals of embezzlement, intimidating them. It probably caught PMUK and bank staff off guard because the investigators may have been viewed as outsiders, and locals were not sure how to handle such external critics from the United States.

Investigators requested access to bank statements on May 26, 2011 and did not receive them until June 19, 2011. For about three weeks, investigators were being played around in Bangladesh because they may have been seen as foreign and intimidating people. It is understandable that Bangladesh executives were hesitant in giving up documents to foreign investigators. They did not want to self-incriminate themselves to someone unfamiliar. The investigators should probably not have barged into Bangladesh without understanding their culture and may have gained the trust of Bangladesh executives better if they had identified some allies in their struggle to reconstruct the past.

CASE 8:   PEREGRINE INVESTIGATED BY BERKELEY

The investigative team at Berkeley Research Group was tasked with conducting a review of the National Futures Association's audit regulatory framework after the failed audit of Peregrine Financial Group (Berkeley, 2013). It was not the team's mandate to determine how former Peregrine Financial Group CEO Russell Wasendorf conducted the fraud that caused the failure of Peregrine, and the team did not conduct an exhaustive analysis into how he perpetrated the fraud.

The investigation found that National Future Association (NFA) auditors conducted a total of 27 audits of Peregrine from 1995 to 2012. The investigation further found that these audits were, for the most part, routine audits designed to review Peregrine's operations and systems and not specifically directed at a particular tip or complaint alleging that Wasendorf was conducting a fraud. Investigators inquired whether there were any complaints indicating that Wasendorf was conducting a fraud and found none. Investigators also found that Wasendorf was able to conceal the fraud meticulously by providing numerous convincingly forged documents to NFA auditors (Berkeley, 2013).

Investigators found that, overall, the NFA audits were conducted in a competent and proper fashion, and the auditors dutifully implemented the appropriate modules that were required in the annual audits. However, they found that certain areas, such as internal controls, Wasendorf's capital contributions, and Pelegrine's accounts, were not examined closely in the audits (Berkeley, 2013).

CASE 9: PHILADELPHIA POLICE INVESTIGATED BY THE PENNSYLVANIA CRIME COMMISSION

The Pennsylvania Crime Commission investigated police corruption and the quality of law enforcement in Philadelphia. The investigation was based on allegations of corruption within the Philadelphia Police Department. Thirty investigators were involved in the investigation. A plan was devised to spend two months on the street developing crime profiles of ongoing police corruption linked to liquor outlets, gambling locations, prostitution activities, narcotics trade, stolen cars, and other crime opportunities (Pennsylvania Crime Commission, 1974).

Investigators were arrested, interrogated, and beaten in police custody. Investigation problems climaxed when it was discovered that some of their rooms in a hotel had been wiretapped. The facts and circumstances surrounding the subsequent charges and countercharges, the resignation of the Attorney General, and the dismissal of the Commissioner of State Police, as well as the state's unsuccessful attempts to bring criminal charges against many of the individuals believed to be involved in the wiretapping, received widespread publicity in the news media (Pennsylvania Crime Commission, 1974).

The commissioner found evidence to suggest that police officers were taking possessions and money while investigating burglaries, while serving warrants, or when an individual was under arrest or being detained so that they could not protect their belongings. The commissioner received sworn testimony from police witnesses that such instances had occurred. Similar to the stealing of possessions, the commission also found proof that police officers were taking advantage of poorly monitored police impound lots by stripping the cars in the lot in order to sell the parts, and then receiving a reward from insurance companies later on when they "recovered" the stolen car parts. The investigation into the stripping of cars began when a claims manager reported that cars that went in to a particular impound lot always had parts stolen and that the police would then be paid for recovered parts. The commission team then set up surveillance and subpoenaed five major insurance companies; however, the companies denied ever paying the police for such services.

Within the police department itself, corruption was also found as the commission uncovered mishandled pensions. In some cases good pensions only went to those who were well connected, while in other cases an individual received a disability pension but then took on a new job doing work incompatible with the injury they had supposedly received. In a different case the commission caught an officer on videotape participating in a bribe. But when the officer refused to cooperate with the investigation, he was allowed to resign after arrest and still collect a pension even though he was caught performing an illegal activity.

The commissioner had many suggestions as to how the various forms of crime, including financial crime, being committed by the Philadelphia police could be handled. In order to stop the police from accepting money in exchange for illegal gambling facilities being protected from raids or shut down, the commissioner suggested that gambling laws needed to be rewritten, the police needed to be properly trained as to how to handle illegal gambling crime, and an outside investigation unit, which did not use police department staff, needed to be established that would handle all things related to gambling and integrity. The commissioner also stated that vice departments needed to be more realistic about the types of crime they could prevent and what policies they were incapable of enforcing so that officers did not end up feeling bogged down and that their efforts were not making a difference. Along with the new unit, the commission also stated that it was necessary to change the department's attitude toward corruption so that it was no longer viewed as something everyone did. Leadership needed to accept the fact that corruption was an issue within their department rather than turning a blind eye, more senior staff needed to be held responsible for those underneath them, and officers in the Academy needed to be warned about corruption hazards and trained in how to avoid those scenarios. In order to make sure that this newfound honesty and integrity would remain intact, the commissioner suggested that the Internal Affairs Bureau be strengthened. The commission recognized the potential for an internal system to greatly decrease crime so long as it was strengthened and utilized with clear and specific guidelines. It was also suggested that a Special Deputy Attorney General, a special prosecutor, and a prosecuting committee be put into place to prosecute police corruption specifically.

There was a rotten barrel problem in the Philadelphia Police Department; however, the commissioner insisted upon it being a rotten apples issue instead. The commissioner made it clear at the start of his report that he did not want the report to reflect negatively on the entire Philadelphia Police Department or the individuals who were working hard to do good despite the negative image the others were painting for all Philadelphia police officers, but rather that there were a large handful of individuals creating the problem and affecting everyone else in the department. The commissioner also noted the hardships of doing the investigation, including being under constant public scrutiny over the years of the investigation. The investigation team also lacked the staff needed to effectively investigate the large-scale corruption and had to deal with a Supreme Court Case filed by the police department questioning the constitutionality of the investigation. It was also noted in the report that the investigation received limited support in looking into the police department and that multiple agents of the investigation had cars illegally searched, were unlawfully detained, and were subject to other sorts of harassing behaviors by the Philadelphia police during the three-month period of the investigation.

Investigators collected evidence by getting informants to tape record conversations with the police discussing the corruption. They also had sworn testimonies verifying the facts further. They got these informants and sworn testimonies by letting an individual see the facts they had piled up against them proving that they were involved in the corruption scheme and would give them the opportunity to cooperate with the investigation and give names and other details of the crime to avoid prosecution. The commissioner ran into problems here due to the police code of silence that made many choose to take their chances with the system rather than tell on the other officers.

CASE 10:   SANDSTORM (BCCI) INVESTIGATED BY PWC

The Bank of Credit and Commerce International (BCCI) was investigated by PwC (1991). The Bank of England was the client for the investigation. The investigation report was concerned with irregularities and related matters which came to the investigators' attention during the course of their work. Investigators reviewed correspondence and other files, and conducted interviews with former management.

According to Block (2001), the Sandstorm case was one of the financial crime activities of the BCCI. The bank was founded in 1972 by Agha Hasan Abedi, a Pakistani financier. The bank came under the scrutiny of numerous financial regulators and intelligence agencies in the 1980s due to concerns that it was poorly regulated. Subsequent investigations revealed that it was involved in massive money laundering.

One of these was the Sandstorm case. Sandstorm was a code name for BCCI (Wikipedia, downloaded March 28, 2015):

> In March 1991, the Bank of England asked Price Waterhouse to carry out an inquiry. On 24 June 1991, using the code name "Sandstorm" for BCCI, Price Waterhouse submitted the Sandstorm report showing that BCCI had engaged in "widespread fraud and manipulation" that made it difficult, if not impossible, to reconstruct BCCI's financial history.
>
> The Sandstorm report, parts of which were leaked to the *Sunday Times*, included details of how the Abu Nidal terrorist group had manipulated details and through using fake identities had opened accounts at BCCI's Sloane Street branch, near Harrods in London. Britain's internal security service, MI5, had signed up two sources inside the branch to hand over copies of all documents relating to Abu Nidal's accounts. One source was the Syrian-born branch manager, Ghassan Qassem, the second a young British employee.
>
> The Abu Nidal link man for the BCCI accounts was a man based in Iraq named Samir Najmeddin or Najmedeen. Throughout the 80s, BCCI had set up millions of dollars in credit for Najmeddin, largely for arms deals with Iraq. Qassem later swore in an affidavit that Najmeddin was often accompanied by an American, whom Qassem subsequently identified as the financier March Rich. Rich was later indicted in the U.S. for tax evasion and racketeering in an apparently unrelated case and fled the country.
>
> Qassem also told reporters that he had once escorted Abu Nidal, who was allegedly using the name Shakir Farhan, around town to buy a tie, without realizing who he was. This revelation led in 1991 to one of the London *Evening Standard*'s best-known front-page headlines: "I took Abu Nidal shopping".

Investigators from PwC (1991) emphasized that much of the information in their report was based on records which had previously been concealed from them. The documents only came to light as a result of investigators' insistence on the files being unsealed, such records having been in the personal possession of top executives in the bank.

According to the Bank of England, the PwC (1991) report was the basis for the closure of BCCI in July 1991. The report was prepared for the Bank of England, though it was never finalized (http://visar.csustan.edu/aaba/BCCISandstorm Release.html). Some 1.4 million depositors lost 11 billion US dollars.

While Agha Hasan Abedi was the founder of the bank, Zafar Iqbal was the chief executive and also the general manager of treasury of Grand Cayman. Ziauddin Akbar was the bank treasury official, and Swaleh Naqvi was a bank executive and deputy to bank founder Abedi. These are some of the names presented in the investigation report by PwC (1991).

PwC (1991) writes that Abedi had "a grandiose vision of the bank, and the global role it should play". His deputy Naqvi "manipulated transactions". When Akbar resigned, he left a record of his activities with Naqvi who brought under his own control the amounts which had been financed by unorthodox means. Naqvi had a number of core documents in his personal possession when PwC (1991) started its investigation. Investigators found evidence of CEO Iqbal's approval of certain questionable transactions booked through the accounts of the crown prince of Abu Dhabi.

The PwC (1991) investigation was focused on illegal money transfers that caused the bank to collapse. Transfers occurred from a bank in India to various entities. The report deals with the implications of those money transfers and looks into which of the bylaws had been violated during the money transfers. The report is aimed at reaffirming the illegal money transfers made by Bank of India to different entities due to which the bank faced heavy losses.

PwC (1991) were unable to find out where the stolen money went. The team assigned to the investigation attained circumstantial evidence that the involved brokers did not always trade with the treasury and may have been involved with the manipulation of profits. The Special Duties Department was identified as being involved in the fabrication of offshore accounts.

CASE 11: WALTERS INVESTIGATED BY WILMERHALE AND PWC

Harriette Walters served as a tax assessments manager for the District of Columbia. She was convicted of being the central participant in the largest fraud scheme ever perpetrated by a government official in the district. In September 2008, Walters pleaded guilty to federal charges related to the theft of over $48 million of district funds. Counsel from Wilmer Cutler Pickering Hale and Dorr and forensic accounting advisors from PricewaterhouseCoopers were hired to investigate how Walters was able to embezzle 48 million US dollars of funds from the District of Columbia (WilmerHale and PwC, 2008).

Walters masterminded a nearly two-decade-long scheme in which she processed fraudulent real property tax refunds and arranged for the proceeds of those funds to be deposited into bank accounts controlled by her and her friends and family. For example, she cashed refund checks that were returned when the taxpayer recipient had died. She also fabricated several tax refund checks. It appeared that Walters had figured out that she had the last eyes on the tax refund check and operated with little monitoring (Stewart and Nakamura, 2007).

Because of the lack of monitoring, four managers were held responsible for failing to catch the fraud. The four managers resigned: deputy CFO Sherryl Hobbs Newman, her deputy director Matthew Braman, the director of real property tax administration Martin A. Skolnik, and the chief assessor Thomas Branham (Stewart and Nakamura, 2007).

The investigation by WilmerHale and PwC (2008) had the mandate of determining how Walters was able to embezzle over nearly 20 years and recommending changes in controls, work environment, and oversight structures that could help prevent future fraudulent schemes. The investigation was not to attempt to trace the stolen money or determine how the money was distributed or spent. Nor did the mandate seek to determine the guilt or innocence of any participants in Walters' scheme. Federal authorities had addressed those issues.

The WilmerHale and PwC (2008) investigation involved three phases: (1) document and data collection; (2) document and data review and analysis; and (3) witness interviews. The investigators reviewed and analyzed more than 680,000 electronic and hard copy documents. They reviewed emails and other electronic documents associated with 87 current and former employees.

The second phase of the investigation involved a review of the collected documents and an analysis of the data included in the documents. WilmerHale and PwC reviewed documentation for manual real property tax refunds, including all refunds dating back to 1998, no matter the amount. One thousand six hundred documents required more in-depth review because (1) the identity of the refund recipient was fraudulent – the voucher packets reflecting the refund were issued to a legitimate business or entity, but the check was addressed to a "care of" address related to several of Walters' payees; (2) there was a lack of authorizing signatures; and (3) either the documentation did not correspond to the property or taxpayer listed as the recipient of the refund or it was missing. In addition, WilmerHale and PwC closely scrutinized the following types of real property transactions:

- Refunds over 10,000 US dollars
- Refunds that were to be held for taxpayer pickup and those issued to taxpayers that did not appear to own property in the district
- Refunds ordered by the court for which an original court order with a raised seal did not accompany the refund documentation.

Following the review of the refunds, WilmerHale and PwC analyzed the data in various tax systems, where they identified "refunds with characteristics consistent with refunds previously identified as fraudulent in court documents filed by the US Attorney's Office". The analysis also identified suspicious refunds where hard copy documentation was unavailable, unclear, or incomplete. The analysis of the Financial Management System (FMS) revealed several refunds to entities or individuals involved in Walters' scheme; unfortunately hard copy records were unavailable. FMS was a system that required refunds to be processed manually. It was replaced in October 1998 with the System of Accounting and Reporting (SOAR), which also required manual processing of refunds.

A similar analysis of data in SOAR was conducted. Real property tax refund payments in the general ledger, which was housed in SOAR, were isolated and searched for refunds characteristic of fraud (i.e., known entities involved in the fraud scheme, refunds sent to "care of" addresses or coded "hold for pickup" and so on). Lastly, WilmerHale and PwC analyzed documentation for real property tax refunds processed through the Integrated Tax System, in order "to identify patterns of data and activity indicative of Walters' scheme". The system was an automated system introduced in 2005. It was composed of several applications which supported the district's various tax types (i.e., personal income, business and real property tax). This system interacted with some of the district's relevant computer systems, but not all. There was no direct interface between the system and SOAR, which meant entries from the system had to be manually entered into SOAR. The private investigation team discovered that Walters "manipulated the system to process fraudulent refunds at least twice".

In addition, WilmerHale and PwC requested copies of canceled checks associated with the refunds previously identified during the review and those associated with all other real property tax refunds of 100,000 US dollars or more. Reviewing the canceled checks allowed WilmerHale and PwC to determine whether the refunds were legitimate or illegitimate and to identify checks that "had been deposited at bank branches where known fraudulent refunds had been processed based on account information on the back of checks". They also compared endorsements to confirm or identify additional fraudulent refunds.

Finally, the private investigation team compared refunds in the SOAR general ledger with those from other databases. WilmerHale and PwC identified refunds that did not coincide with actual properties or property owners contained in the various systems. Furthermore, they "obtain[ed] additional information regarding the fraudulent nature of certain previously identified suspicious payments". This concluded the document review and data analysis.

The final phase of the investigation process was witness interviews, which supplemented the previous reviews and analyses. WilmerHale and PwC conducted interviews of over 70 individuals including current and former employees, representatives of the Office of the District of Columbia Auditor, the Office of the Inspector General, the Office of Risk Management, the district's current and former independent auditors, and other third parties.

Upon completing the investigation, WilmerHale and PwC concluded that Walters perpetrated her lengthy fraud scheme due to a failure of controls, a dysfunctional work environment, and a lack of oversight. The reliability of the real property tax refunds process could not be ensured because no policies or procedures could be found which formally documented how real property tax refunds should be processed. If policies and procedures did exist, managers and employees did not follow them consistently. Managers did not test the refund process or take basic steps to examine real property tax refunds. In fact, when Walters began her scheme, her managers in the Real Property Tax Administration (RPTA) signed off on these refund vouchers without reviewing the attached documentation for legitimacy. "Worse, Walters' direct supervisor in 2003 evidently made clear in words or deeds that she no longer wished to sign off on real property tax refund vouchers at all." This failure of managers to exercise responsibility allowed Walters to process all real property tax refunds without review and approval from upper management. In addition, there was a lack of automated controls.

WilmerHale and PwC (2008) formulated the following recommendations:

- *Controls improvements.* Walters' scheme went undetected for such a long time in part because of the lack of sufficient controls, the failure of existing controls to operate effectively, and the lack of management oversight of those controls.
- *Systems improvements.* The vast majority of Walters' fraudulent refunds were processed manually.
- *Work environment improvements.* A culture of compliance was lacking in the organization.

When evaluating this investigation, it can be assumed that the starting point for the examination was good. The FBI had already identified the who, what (i.e., fraud), and how (processing fraudulent real property tax refunds) for the crime. Evidence had already been collected, and Walters had already been arrested. At this point, Walters already knew she had been caught. According to her attorney, Walters wanted to cooperate and tell the truth. She told investigators loopholes in software allowed her to carry out her scheme, and lax internal controls allowed her to go undetected. Walters revealed her role in the scam, how she did it, how it could have been prevented, and who did not pay attention to their job.

The investigating team focused on the mandate: How did the fraud occur? Why did the scheme go undetected for so long? What changes can be made to reduce the risk of any recurrence of similar fraudulent activity?

The investigative process seems professional. For example, the report makes clear what the investigation was and was not: the investigation was not to determine guilt or innocence, but to audit the administration of real property tax refunds. They do not only blame Walters (rotten apple) but also management (rotten barrel). Evidence and interviews back up report statements. Investigators cooperated with criminal investigations. For example, they obliged a request to hold off on witness interviews; they invited attorneys to sit in on the interviews they conducted; they informed individuals they interviewed of their rights (i.e., if truth would incriminate, no answer); and they hired independent attorneys to represent certain interviewees. Interviews were optional, and many refused. The investigators could probably have made it more attractive for people to participate in interviews.

In addition to Walters, ten more individuals pled guilty in connection with her scheme. None were district employees – they were a bank manager, relatives, and friends. The CFO for the District of Columbia asked several high-ranking managers to resign for their failure to prevent or detect Walters' scheme. More than 30 individuals lost their jobs due to the fraud scheme. Ten million dollars was recovered by law enforcement officials; Walters' assets were seized and sold (i.e., house, car, and handbags); managers and employees were replaced; and new guidelines were introduced.

CASE 12:   WILDENTHAL INVESTIGATED BY BREEN AND GUBERMAN

Private investigators Breen and Guberman (2012) conducted an internal investigation at the University of Texas. They wrote a special investigative report regarding allegations of impropriety by Dr. C. Kern Wildenthal relating to travel and entertainment expenses paid for by the University of Texas Southwestern Medical Center. Wildenthal was first unveiled by a newspaper. From the beginning of 2008, *Dallas Morning News* reporters had been investigating if he had spent university funds for his personal travel and entertainment. He was interviewed in the newspaper on three separate occasions: in October 2008, December 2009, and November 2011.

The university reacted after the third news story and hired law firm Paul Hastings to conduct an investigation regarding whether Wildenthal had engaged in misconduct. Breen and Guberman (2012) gathered, reviewed, and analyzed a number of documents, such as all donations approved by Wildenthal, all requests for reimbursements, and all written correspondence involving Wildenthal. Investigators interviewed Wildenthal and 11 witnesses, including Cyndi Bassel (external affairs), Charles Chaffin (audit executive), and Francis Frederick (general counsel).

The investigation report presented the following findings and conclusions to the University of Texas Southwestern Medical Center (UTSW):

1. Dr. Wildenthal exercised questionable judgment in making discretionary decisions on spending within UTSW's broad mandate.
2. UT System and UTSW had policies and procedures in place governing the approval, documentation, reporting, and auditing of Dr. Wildenthal's travel and entertainment expenses.
3. UT System's policies and procedures governing Dr. Wildenthal's spending were adequate but not enforced at UTSW. Most significantly, Dr. Wildenthal's spending was not in all instances sufficiently documented to show the predominant business purpose and benefit to UTSW, and as a result it was not subjected to meaningful review.
4. UT System and UTSW audits during Dr. Wildenthal's presidency failed to alert officials at UT System or UTSW that there were risks related to Dr. Wildenthal's spending and expense documentation.
5. UTSW's manner of accounting for and acknowledging Dr. Wildenthal's donations was inadequate, at times resulting in inaccurate gift letters being issued to him.
6. UT System's policies and procedures governing the acceptance of anonymous donations were adequate but not followed at UTSW.

The Breen and Guberman (2012) investigation cost nearly half a million US dollars. Wildenthal's one million salary was cut, and he resigned from the position of special assistant to the president. An auditing firm was hired to review Wildenthal's travel expenses to calculate how much he owed the medical center for spending public money on personal travel. However, nobody ever prosecuted Wildenthal, and in 2014 the University of Texas named its newest biomedical research tower after Dr. Kern Wildenthal.

The investigators interviewed Dr. Wildenthal and 11 employees over the phone and not in person. Interviewing witnesses by phone is an interviewing technique with limitations.

The late response by the university to media stories probably affected the investigation. It provided ample opportunity for a suspect to hide and cover actions by changing official records and documents.

CASE 13: WORLDCOM INVESTIGATED BY WILMER AND PWC

Wilmer and PwC (2003) were hired to investigate accounting irregularities at WorldCom, including those that led to WorldCom's announcements that it intended to restate its financial statements for the years 1999 through 2002, and certain actions by the board of directors and its members, including the authorization of large loans and guarantees by WorldCom to Bernard Ebbers, the CEO. The scope of the authority granted to investigators was very broad, making it necessary for them to refine and focus their undertaking.

One of the most infamous white-collar criminals ever is Bernard Ebbers, former CEO of WorldCom (Wagner, 2011: 978):

> To answer why Bernard Ebbers did this, one must take a look at his personal finances. Bernard Ebbers was extremely wealthy by the time WorldCom began to experience difficulties in 2000. Unfortunately for Ebbers (and ultimately for WorldCom shareholders), his desires exceeded his income. Ebbers' purchases included an enormous ranch, timber lands, and a yacht-building company, and his loans totaled over $400 million. To secure these loans, he used millions of shares of WorldCom stock as collateral. Any time the price of WorldCom stock went down he needed more cash or assets to maintain his collateral. At one of WorldCom's financial meetings, Ebbers told his employees that his "lifeblood was in the stock of the company" and that if the price fell below approximately $12 per share, he would be wiped out financially by margin calls. Bernard Ebbers could not allow WorldCom's stock price to fall even if it was realistically inevitable that this would eventually occur. As Judge Winter stated, "[t]he methods used were specifically intended to create a false picture of profitability even for professional analysts that, in Ebbers' case, was motivated by his personal financial circumstances".

WorldCom was a global communications company offering Internet, voice, and data services for business. Key executives convicted and sent to prison were CEO Bernie Ebbers, CFO Scott Sullivan, and controller David Myers. The private investigation was completed in 2003, and Bernard Ebbers was convicted in 2005.

Ebbers, Sullivan, and Myers declined to participate in interviews with investigators in 2003. Investigators found no evidence that members of the board of directors, other than Ebbers and Sullivan, were aware of the improper accounting practices at the time they occurred. The board received regular financial and operational presentations that included a level of detail consistent with what investigators believe most proper and typical boards received at that time.

Cynthia Cooper blew the whistle on the 9 billion US dollar corporate financial scandal involving WorldCom, which eventually led to the imprisonment of five of the company's executives. Cooper had never intended to go public, but a member of Congress released her internal audit memos to the press. She was named as a *Time*'s person of the year in 2002, along with Coleen Rowley, the FBI whistleblower from Minneapolis, and Sherron Watkins, the Enron whistleblower (www.whistle blowerdirectory.com).

Conclusion

Based on previous research (Gottschalk, 2016, 2017), this book has made a novel contribution to the development of convenience theory as a framework to understand white-collar crime. The framework integrates a number of well-known theories from criminology and other fields to explain white-collar offenses in terms of economical motive, organizational opportunity, and deviant behavior.

Convenience theory was empirically discussed by presenting the eight most serious white-collar criminals in Norway. Traces and evidence of convenience was found in all the cases.

Of particular interest in this book were chief executive officers as white-collar criminals. They are alone at their level in the hierarchical structure, where they enjoy much power and are subject to little control.

Both theory development and theory testing have been presented and discussed in this book. In terms of theory testing, we have applied a number of approaches that all indicate the external validity of convenience theory. In particular, organizational opportunity and deviant behavior find strong support in both theoretical studies and empirical studies as explanations for white-collar crime occurrences.

Case studies in the form of autobiographies written by convicted white-collar criminals indicate a strong presence of neutralization techniques in the behavioral dimension of convenience theory. Internal investigation reports by fraud examiners indicate a strong presence of organizational opportunities to commit white-collar crime. Survey research among financial crime students in a business school indicates a strong belief that chief executives sometimes have the motive to commit financial crime in times of crisis, in times of great challenges, and in times of greed. Chief executives tend to accept their own deviant behavior when there are ample organizational opportunities to commit white-collar crime.

The only feasible avenue to combat white-collar crime is to make it less convenient. Increased subjective detection risk makes crime less convenient. More severe consequences for detected offenses make crime less convenient. Reduced organizational opportunity to commit offenses makes crime less convenient.

References

Abadinsky, Howard (2007), *Organized Crime*, 8th edition, Belmont, CA: Thomson Wadsworth.

Adeyeye, A. (2011), 'Universal standards in CSR: Are we prepared?', *Corporate Governance*, **11** (1), 107–119.

Adler, P.S. and S.W. Kwon (2002), 'Social capital: Prospects for a new concept', *Academy of Management Review*, **27** (1), 17–40.

Agnew, Robert (2005), *Pressured into Crime: An Overview of General Strain Theory*, Oxford: Oxford University Press.

Agnew, Robert (2012), 'Reflection on "A revised strain theory of delinquency"', *Social Forces*, **91** (1), 33–38.

Agnew, Robert (2014), 'Social concern and crime: Moving beyond the assumption of simple self-interest', *Criminology*, **52** (1), 1–32.

Aguilera, R.V. and A.K. Vadera (2008), 'The dark side of authority: Antecedents, mechanisms, and outcomes of organizational corruption', *Journal of Business Ethics*, **77**, 431–449.

Ahrne, G. and N. Brunsson (2011), 'Organization outside organizations: The significance of partial organization', *Organization*, **18** (1), 83–104.

Alibux, A.N.R.N. (2015), 'Criminogenic conditions, bribery and the economic crisis in the EU: A macro level analysis', *European Journal of Criminology*, **12** (1), 1–21.

Arjoon, S. (2008), 'Slippery when wet: The real risk in business', *Journal of Markets and Morality*, **11** (1), Spring, 77–91.

Arnold, U., J. Neubauer and T. Schoenherr (2012), 'Explicating factors for companies' inclination towards corruption in operations and supply chain management: An exploratory study in Germany', *International Journal of Production Economics*, **138** (1), 136–147.

Ashforth, B.E., D.A. Gioia, S.L. Robinson and L.K. Trevino (2008), 'Re-reviewing organizational corruption', *Academy of Management Review*, **33** (3), 670–684.

Asker and Bærum district court (2012), Case 12-066481MED-AHER/2, *Asker og Bærum tingrett*, May 30, 2012.

Atwater, K. (2006), 'Whistleblowers enforce procurement ethics', *American City and County*, http://americancityandcounty.com/mag/whistleblowers-enforce-procurement-ethics, published October 23.

Baird, J.E. and R.C. Zelin (2009), 'An examination of the impact of obedience pressure on perceptions of fraudulent acts and the likelihood of committing occupational fraud', *Journal of Forensic Studies in Accounting and Business*, **1** (1), 1–14.

Barry, B. and C.U. Stephens (1998), 'Objections to an objectivist approach to integrity', *Academy of Management Review*, **23** (1), 162–169.

Basu, K. and G. Palazzo (2008), 'Corporate social responsibility: A process model of sensemaking', *Academy of Management Review*, **33** (1), 122–136.

BDO (2014), *Investigative Report to the Coatesville Area School District*, http://casd.schoolwires.net/cms/lib8/PA01916452/Centricity/Domain/513/Forensic%20Audit.pdf, 54 pages.

Bendiktsson, M.O. (2010), 'The deviant organization and the bad apple CEO: Ideology and accountability in media coverage of corporate scandals', *Social Forces*, **88** (5), 2189–2216.

Benson, M.E. (2013), 'Editor's Introduction – White-collar crime: Bringing the offender back in', *Journal of Contemporary Criminal Justice*, **29** (3), 324–330.

Benson, M.L. and S.S. Simpson (2015), *Understanding White-Collar Crime: An Opportunity Perspective*, New York: Routledge.

Berkeley (2013), *Report of Investigation – Analysis of the National Futures Association's Audits of Peregrine Financial Group Inc.*, Berkeley Research Group, http://www.nfa.futures.org/news/BRG/report_of_investigation.pdf, published January 29, downloaded 10 January, 2016, 160 pages.

Berry, L.L., K. Seiders and D. Grewal (2002), 'Understanding service convenience', *Journal of Marketing*, **66**, 1–17.

Bigley, G.A. and M.F. Wiersma (2002), 'New CEOs and corporate strategic refocusing: How experience as heir apparent influences the use of power', *Administrative Science Quarterly*, **47**, 707–727.

Bjørkelo, B., S. Einarsen, M.B. Nielsen and S.B. Matthiesen (2011), 'Silence is golden? Characteristics and experiences of self-reported whistleblowers', *European Journal of Work and Organizational Psychology*, **20** (2), 206–238.

Bjørkelo, Brita and Stig Berge Matthiesen (2011), 'Preventing and dealing with retaliation against whistleblowers', in David Lewis and Wim Vandekerckhove (eds), *Whistleblowing and Democratic Values*, London: International Whistleblowing Research Network, 127–149.

Bjørndal, B. and M.K. Kleppe (2013), 'Mulig jeg har vært dumsnill (I may have been dum nice)', daily Norwegian business newspaper *Dagens Næringsliv*, http://www.dn.no/nyheter/politikkSamfunn/2013/10/21/-mulig-jeg-har-vaert-dumsnill, published October 21, downloaded 10 January, 2016.

Blickle, G., A. Schlegel, P. Fassbender and U. Klein (2006), 'Some personality correlates of business white-collar crime', *Applied Psychology: An International Review*, **55** (2), 220–233.

Block, Alan A. (2001), *The Organized Criminal Activities of the Bank of Credit and Commerce International: Essays and Documentation*, Dordrecht, the Netherlands: Kluwer Academic Publishers.

Bogen, Terje (2008), *Hvor var du, historien om mitt liv (Where Were You, the Story of My Life)*, Oslo, Norway: Schibsted Publishing.

Bookman, Zachary (2008), 'Convergences and omissions in reporting corporate and white collar crime', *DePaul Business and Commercial Law Journal*, **6**, 347–392.

Borgarting (2009), Court of appeals case LB-2008-90794-1, *Borgarting lagmannsrett (Borgarting Court of Appeals)*, April 27, 2009.

Bosse, D.A. and R.A. Phillips (2016), 'Agency theory and bounded self-interest', *Academy of Management Review*, **41** (2), 276–297.

Bradshaw, E.A. (2015), '"Obviously, we're all oil industry": The crimino-genic structure of the offshore oil industry', *Theoretical Criminology*, **19** (3), 376–395.

Breen, K.M. and P.A. Guberman (2012), *Special Investigative Report Regarding Allegations of Impropriety by Dr. C. Kern Wildenthal Relating to Travel And Entertainment Expenses Paid for by University of Texas Soutwestern Medical Center*, Paul Hastings LLP, University of Texas, http://www.lrl.state.tx.us/scanned/archive/2012/18224.pdf, downloaded 10 January, 2016, 365 pages (main report 46 pages).

Brightman, Hank J. (2009), *Today's White-Collar Crime: Legal, Investigative, and Theoretical Perspectives*, New York: Routledge.

Bucy, P.H., E.P. Formby, M.S. Raspanti and K.E. Rooney (2008), 'Why do they do it?: The motives, mores, and character of white collar criminals', *St. John's Law Review*, **82**, 401–571.

Chang, J.J., H.C. Lu and M. Chen (2005), 'Organized crime or individual crime? Endogeneous size of a criminal organization and the optimal law enforcement', *Economic Inquiry*, **43** (3), 661–675.

Chen, J. and S. Nadkarni (2017), 'It's about time! CEOs' temporal dispositions, temporal leadership, and corporate entrepreneurship', *Administrative Science Quarterly*, **62** (1), 31–66.

Chester Grand Jury (2014), *Chester County 18th Investigating Grand Jury's Report re: Coatesville Area School District*, Court of Common Pleas of Chester County, http://casd.schoolwires.net/cms/lib8/PA01916452/Cent ricity/Domain/513/Grand%20Jury%20Report%20CASD.pdf, 114 pages.

Chrisman, J.J., J.H. Chua, F.W. Kellermanns and E.P.C. Chang (2007), 'Are family managers agents or stewards? An exploratory study in privately held family firms', *Journal of Business Research*, **60** (10), 1030–1038.

Clarke, Ronald V. (1999), 'Hot products: Understanding, anticipating and reducing demand for stolen goods', Police Research Series, Paper 112, Policing and Reducing Crime Unit, Home Office, UK: London, www. popcenter.org, downloaded 10 January, 2016.

Cohen, L.E. and M. Felson (1979), 'Social change and crime rate trends: A routine activity approach', *American Sociological Review*, **44**, 588–608.

Collier, J.E. and S.E. Kimes (2012), 'Only if it is convenient: Understanding how convenience influences self-service technology evaluation', *Journal of Service Research*, **16** (1), 39–51.

Colquitt, J.A. and C.P. Zapata-Phelan (2007), 'Trends in theory building and theory testing: A five-decade study of the *Academy of Management Journal*', *Academy of Management Journal*, **50** (6): 1281–1303.

Comey, J.B. (2009), 'Go directly to prison: White collar sentencing after the Sarbanes-Oxley act', *Harvard Law Review*, **122**, 1728–1749.

Corcoran, K.E., D. Pettinicchio and B. Robbins (2012), 'Religion and the acceptability of white-collar crime: A cross-national analysis', *Journal of the Scientific Study of Religion*, **51** (3), 542–567.

Corley, K.G. and D.A. Gioia (2011), 'Building theory about theory building: What constitutes a theoretical contribution?', *Academy of Management Review*, **36** (1), 12–32.

Craig, J.M. and N.L. Piquero (2016), 'The effects of low self-control and desire-for-control on white-collar offending: A replication', *Deviant Behavior*, **37** (11), 1308–1324.

Cressey, David (1972), *Criminal Organization: Its Elementary Forms*, New York: Harper & Row.

Dahle, D.Y. (2011), 'Christer Tromsdal var politiagent (Christer Tromsdal was police agent)', daily Norwegian newspaper *Aftenposten*, http://www. aftenposten.no/nyheter/iriks/Christer-Tromsdal-var-politiagent-6369334. html, published October 19, downloaded 10 January, 2016.

Dearden, T.E. (2016), 'Trust: The unwritten cost of white-collar crime', *Journal of Financial Crime*, **23** (1), 87–101.

Delegationen (2008), *Vad koster felen? Omfattning av felaktiga utbetalingar från trygghetssystemen (What Does the Mistake Cost? Estimation of Wrongful Payments from the Security System)*, Delegationen mot felak- tiga utbetalningar, Stockholm, Sweden.

Desai, V.M. (2016), 'Under the radar: Regulatory collaborations and their selective use to facilitate organizational compliance', *Academy of Management Journal*, **59** (2), 636–657.

Dhami, M.K. (2007), 'White-collar prisoners' perceptions of audience reaction', *Deviant Behavior*, **28**, 57–77.

Dibbern, J., J. Winkler and A. Heinzl (2008), 'Explaining variations in client extra costs between software projects offshored to India', *MIS Quarterly*, **32** (3), 333–366.

DiMaggio, P.J. (1995), 'Comments on "What theory is not"', *Administrative Science Quarterly*, **40**, 391–397.

Dion, M. (2008), 'Ethical leadership and crime prevention in the organizational setting', *Journal of Financial Crime*, **15** (3), 308–319.

Dion, M. (2009), 'Corporate crime and the dysfunction of value networks', *Journal of Financial Crime*, **16** (4), 436–445.

Ditlev-Simonsen, C.D. (2014), 'Are non-financial (CSR) reports trustworthy? A study of the extent to which non-financial reports reflect the media perception of the company's behaviour', *Issues in Social and Environmental Accounting*, **8** (2), 116–133.

Ditlev-Simonsen, C.D. (2015), 'The relationship between Norwegian and Swedish employees' perception of corporate social responsibility and affective commitment', *Business and Society*, **54** (2), 229–253.

Ditlev-Simonsen, C.D. and A. Midttun (2011), 'What motivates managers to pursue corporate responsibility? A survey among key stakeholders', *Corporate Social Responsibility and Environmental Management*, **18**, 25–38.

Dodge, M. (2009), *Women and White-Collar Crime*, Upper Saddle River, NJ: Prentice Hall.

Drammen tingrett (2015), Case 15-002674ENE-DRAM, *Drammen tingrett (Drammen district court)*, February 2, 2015.

Eberl, P., D. Geiger and M.S. Assländer (2015), 'Repairing trust in an organization after integrity violations: The ambivalence of organizational rule adjustments', *Organization Studies*, **36** (9), 1205–1235.

Eberly, M.B., E.C. Holley, M.D. Johnson and T.R. Mitchell (2011), 'Beyond internal and external: A dyadic theory of relational attributions', *Academy of Management Review*, **36** (4), 731–753.

Eisenhardt, K.M. (1985), 'Control: Organizational and economic approaches', *Management Science*, **31** (2), 134–149.

Elnan, T.S. (2016), 'Kriminelle er ofte mer innovative enn folk flest (Criminals are often more innovative than most people)', daily Norwegian newspaper *Aftenposten*, part 2, Thursday, April 14, pages 4–5.

Engdahl, O. (2015), 'White-collar crime and first-time adult-onset offending: Explorations in the concept of negative life events as turning points', *International Journal of Law, Crime and Justice*, **43** (1), 1–16.

Eriksen, Terje Strand (2010), *Arven etter Ole Christian Bach – et justismord (The Legacy of Ole Christian Bach – A Miscarriage of Justice)*, Oslo, Norway: Norgesforlaget publishing.

Fanelli, A. and V.F. Misangyi (2006), 'Bringing out charisma: CEO charisma and external stakeholders', *Academy of Management Review*, **31** (4), 1049–1061.

Farquhar, J.D. and J. Rowley (2009), 'Convenience: A services perspective', *Marketing Theory*, **9** (4), 425–438.

Fehr, R., K.C. Yam and C. Dang (2015), 'Moralized leadership: The construction and consequences of ethical leader perceptions', *Academy of Management Review*, **40** (2), 182–209.

Felson, Marcus and Rachel L. Boba (2010), 'White-Collar crime', in *Crime and Everyday Life*, 4th edition, Thousand Oaks, CA: Sage Publications, 115–128.

Fosse, Gunn and Gunnar Magnusson (2004), *Mayday Mayday! – Kapteinene først i livbåtene! (Mayday Mayday! –The Captains First in the Lifeboats!)*, Oslo, Norway: Kolofon Publishing.

Froggio, G. and R. Agnew (2007), 'The relationship between crime and "objective" versus "subjective" strains', *Journal of Criminal Justice*, **35**, 81–87.

Füss, R. and A. Hecker (2008), 'Profiling white-collar crime: Evidence from German-speaking countries', *Corporate Ownership and Control*, **5** (4), 149–161.

Galvin, B.M., D. Lange and B.E. Ashforth (2015), 'Narcissistic organizational identification: Seeing oneself as central to the organization's identity', *Academy of Management Review*, **40** (2), 163–181.

Garoupa, N. (2007), 'Optimal law enforcement and criminal organization', *Journal of Economic Behaviour and Organization*, **63**, 461–474.

Gibney, P. (2006), 'The double bind theory: Still crazy-making after all these years', *Psychotherapy in Australia*, **12** (3), 48–55.

Gilligan, G. (2009), 'PEEPing at PEPs', *Journal of Financial Crime*, **16** (2), 137–143.

Glasø, L. and S. Einarsen (2008), 'Emotion regulation in leader–follower relationships', *European Journal of Work and Organizational Psychology*, **17** (4), 482–500.

Glasø, L., S. Einarsen, S.B. Matthiesen and A. Skogstad (2010), 'The dark side of leaders: A representative study of interpersonal problems among leaders', *Scandinavian Journal of Organizational Psychology*, **2** (2), 3–14.

Glasø, L., K. Ekerholt, S. Barman and S. Einarsen (2006), 'The instrumentality of emotion in leader–subordinate relationships', *International Journal of Work Organisation and Emotion*, **1** (3), 255–276.

Goldstraw-White, Janice (2012), *White-Collar Crime: Accounts of Offending Behaviour*, London: Palgrave Macmillan.

Gottfredson, Michael R. and Travis Hirschi (1990), *A General Theory of Crime*, Stanford, CA: Stanford University Press.

Gottschalk, P. (2013), 'Limits to corporate social responsibility: The case of Gjensidige insurance company and Hells Angels Motorcycle Club', *Corporate Reputation Review*, **16** (3), 177–186.

Gottschalk, Petter (2016), *Explaining White-Collar Crime: The Concept of Convenience in Financial Crime Investigations*, London: Palgrave Macmillan.

Gottschalk, Petter (2017), *Understanding White-Collar Crime: A Convenience Perspective*, Boca Raton, FL: CRC Press.

Gross, E. (1978), 'Organizational crime: A theoretical perspective', *Studies in Symbolic Interaction*, **1**, 55–85.

Haines, F. (2014), 'Corporate fraud as misplaced confidence? Exploring ambiguity in the accuracy of accounts and the materiality of money', *Theoretical Criminology*, **18** (1), 20–37.

Hamilton, Stewart and Alicia Micklethwait (2006), *Greed and Corporate Failure: The Lessons from Recent Disasters*, Basingstoke, UK: Palgrave Macmillan.

Hansen, L.L. (2009), 'Corporate financial crime: Social diagnosis and treatment', *Journal of Financial Crime*, **16** (1), 28–40.

Hatch, Mary Jo (1997), *Organizational Theory: Modern, Symbolic, and Postmodern Perspectives*, Oxford: Oxford University Press.

Haverstick, M.H., M.E. Seiberling, T.M. Stengel, A.R. Madden and S.T. Damiani (2014a), *Investigative Report to the Board of School Directors for the Coatesville Area School District*, Conrad O'Brien PC, http:// casd.schoolwires.net/cms/lib8/PA01916452/Centricity/Domain/513/Conr ad%20OBrien%20Investigative%20Report.pdf, 194 pages.

Haverstick, M.H., M.E. Seiberling, T.M. Stengel, A.R. Madden and S.T. Damiani (2014b), *Supplement to Investigative Report to the Board of School Directors for the Coatesville Area School District*, Conrad O'Brien PC, http://casd.schoolwires.net/cms/lib8/PA01916452/Centricity/Domai n/513/Supplement to the Conrad OBrien Investigative Report.pdf, 66 pages.

Heath, J. (2008), 'Business ethics and moral motivation: A criminological perspective', *Journal of Business Ethics*, **83**, 595–614.

Hefendehl, R. (2010), 'Addressing white collar crime on a domestic level', *Journal of International Criminal Justice*, **8**, 769–782.

Hegnar, T. (2014), 'Sviket mot Aschehoug (The betrayal of Aschehoug)', daily Norwegian business newspaper *Finansavisen*, Tuesday, January 14, page 2.

Henisz, W.J. and O.E. Williamson (1999), 'Comparative economic organization – within and between countries', *Business and Politics*, **1** (3), 261–277.

Hennestad, B.W. (1990), 'The symbolic impact of double bind leadership: Double bind and the dynamics of organizational culture', *Journal of Management Studies*, **27** (3), 265–280.

Heyman, J. and J. Sailors (2016), 'A respondent-friendly method of ranking long lists', *International Journal of Market Research*, **58** (5), 693–710.

Hirschi, T. and M. Gottfredson (1987), 'Causes of white-collar crime', *Criminology*, **25** (4), 949–974.

Hoel, H., L. Glasø, J. Hetland, C.L. Cooper and S. Einarsen (2010), 'Leadership styles as predictors of self-reported and observed workplace bullying', *British Journal of Management*, **21**, 453–468.

Hoffmann, J.P. (2002), 'A contextual analysis of differential association, social control, and strain theories of delinquency', *Social Forces*, **81** (3), 753–785.

Hollow, M. (2014), 'Money, morals and motives', *Journal of Financial Crime*, **21** (2), 174–190.

Holtfreter, K. (2015), 'General theory, gender-specific theory, and white-collar crime', *Journal of Financial Crime*, **22** (4), 422–431.

Huff, M.J. and G.E. Bodner (2013), 'When does memory monitoring succeed versus fail? Comparing item-specific and relational encoding in the DRM paradigm', *Journal of Experimental Psychology: Learning, Memory, and Cognition*, **39** (4), 1246–1256.

Huisman, W. and J. Erp (2013), 'Opportunities for environmental crime', *British Journal of Criminology*, **53**, 1178–1200.

Hultgren, G. (2012), 'Seks års fengsel for Christer Tromsdal (Six years prison for Christer Tromsdal)', daily Norwegian newspaper *Dagbladet*, http://www.dagbladet.no/2012/11/02/nyheter/christer_tromsdal/krim/24159912/, published November 2, downloaded 10 January, 2016.

Inspector General (2012), *Final Investigation Report of Sub-recipient Padakhep Manabik Unnayan Kendra (PMUK) – Bangladesh*, The Office of the Inspector General, Report No. GF-IG-11-025, www.theglobalfund.org/.../OIG_GFOIG11025InvestigationBangladesh_Report_en.pdf, downloaded 10 January, 2016, 32 pages.

Itzkovich, Y. and S. Heilbrunn (2016), 'The role of co-workers' solidarity as an antecedent of incivility and deviant behavior in organizations', *Deviant Behavior*, **37** (8), 861–876.

Jensen, M.C. and W.H. Meckling (1976), 'Theory of the firm: Managerial behavior, agency costs and ownership structures', *Journal of Financial Economics*, **3** (4), 305–360.

Johnson, Roberta Ann (2005), 'Whistleblowing and the police', *Rutgers University Journal of Law and Urban Planning*, **3** (1), 74–83.

Johnson, S.D. and E.R. Groff (2014), 'Strengthening theoretical testing in criminology using agent-based modeling', *Journal of Research in Crime and Delinquency*, **51** (4), 509–525.

Jones, S., D.R. Lyman and A.R. Piquero (2015), 'Substance use, personality, and inhibitors: Testing Hirschi's predictions about the reconceptualization of self-control', *Crime and Delinquency*, **61** (4), 538–558.

Jonnergård, K., A. Stafsudd and U. Elg (2010), 'Performance evaluations as gender barriers in professional organizations: A study of auditing firms', *Gender, Work and Organization*, **17** (6), 721–747.

Judge, T.A., R.F. Piccolo and T. Kosalka (2009), 'The bright and dark sides of leader traits: A review and theoretical extension of the leader trait paradigm', *Leadership Quarterly*, **20**, 855–875.

Kamerdze, S., T. Loughran, R. Paternoster and T. Sohoni (2014), 'The role of affect in intended rule breaking: Extending the rational choice perspective', *Journal of Research in Crime and Delinquency*, **51** (5), 620–654.

Kaplan, S., K.R. Pope and J.A. Samuels (2011), 'An examination of the effect of inquiry and auditor type on reporting intentions for fraud', *Auditing: A Journal of Practice and Theory*, **30** (4), 29–49.

Kempa, M. (2010), 'Combating white-collar crime in Canada: Serving victim needs and market integrity', *Journal of Financial Crime*, **17** (2), 251–264.

Kerik, Bernard B. (2015), *From Jailer to Jailed: My Journey from Correction and Police Commissioner to Inmate #84888-054*, New York: Threshold Editions.

Killinger, Barbara (2010), *Integrity: Doing the Right Thing for the Right Reason*, Montreal, Canada: McGill-Queen's University Press.

Kjeldsen, A.M. and C.B. Jacobsen (2013), 'Public service motivation and employment sector: Attraction or socialization?', *Journal of Public Administration Research and Theory*, **23** (4), 899–926.

Kleppe, M.K. (2011), 'Banktopp dømt til tre års fengsel (Bank executive convicted to three years imprisonment)', daily Norwegian business newspaper *Finansavisen*, Thursday, December 22, pages 6–7.

Kleppe, M.K. (2015), 'Tromsdal: Der er han skurken som lurte de gamle menneskene (There is the crock who cheated the old people)', daily Norwegian business newspaper *Dagens Næringsliv*, http://www.dn.no/nyheter/2015/01/08/1336/Kriminalitet/tromsdal-der-er-han-skurken-som-lurte-de-gamle-mcnneskene, published January 8, downloaded 10 January, 2016.

Kommunerevisjonen (2006), *Granskingsrapport 2 Undervisningsbygg Oslo KF (Investigation Report on City School Maintenance Service)*, Municipality auditors, Report 27/2006, 36 pages.

Koppen, M.V., C.J. Poot and A.A.J. Blokland (2010), 'Comparing criminal careers of organized crime offenders and general offenders', *European Journal of Criminology*, **7** (5), 356–374.

Lancaster, K. (2017), 'Confidentiality, anonymity and power relations in elite interviewing: Conducting quality policy research in a politicized domain', *International Journal of Social Research Methodology*, **20** (1): 93–103.

Langton, L. and N.L. Piquero (2007), 'Can general strain theory explain white-collar crime? A preliminary investigation of the relationship between strain and select white-collar offenses', *Journal of Criminal Justice*, **35**, 1–15.

Lavigne, Yves (1996), *Hells Angels: Into the Abyss*, New York: Harper Paperbacks.

Leonard, W.N. and M.G. Weber (1970), 'Automakers and dealers: A study of criminogenic market forces', *Law and Society Review*, **4** (3), 407–424.

Li, S. and M. Ouyang (2007), 'A dynamic model to explain the bribery behavior of firms', *International Journal of Management*, **24** (3), 605–618.

Listwan, S.J., N.L. Piquero and P.V. Voorhis (2010), 'Recidivism among a white-collar sample: Does personality matter?', *Australian and New Zealand Journal of Criminology*, **43** (1), 156–174.

Liu, Guofang, Ziqiang Xin and Chongde Lin (2014), 'Lax decision criteria lead to negativity bias: Evidence from the emotional Stroop task', *Psychological Reports: Relationship and Communications*, **114** (3), 896–912.

Locke, S.L. and G.C. Blomquist (2016), 'The cost of convenience: Estimating the impact of communication antennas on residential property values', *Land Economics*, **92** (1), 131–147.

Løkke, A.K. and P.D. Sørensen (2014), 'Theory testing using case studies', *Electronic Journal of Business Research Methods*, **12** (1), 66–74.

Lopez-Rodriguez, S. (2009), 'Environmental engagement, organizational capability and firm performance', *Corporate Governance*, **9** (4), 400–408.

Lyman, Michael D. and Gary W. Potter (2007), *Organized Crime*, 4th edition, Upper Saddle River, NJ: Prentice Hall.

Mai, H.T.X. and S.O. Olsen (2016), 'Consumer participation in self-production: The role of control mechanisms, convenience orientation, and moral obligation', *Journal of Marketing Theory and Practice*, **24** (2), 209–223.

Maslow, A.H. (1943), 'A theory of human motivation', *Psychological Review*, **50**, 370–396.

Mathieu, C. (2013), 'Personality and job satisfaction: The role of narcissism', *Personality and Individual Differences*, **55** (6), 650–654.

McDonnell, M.H. and T. Werner (2016), 'Blacklisted businesses: Social activitsts' challenges and the disruption of corporate political activity', *Administrative Science Quarterly*, **61** (4), 584–620.

McKay, R., C. Stevens and J. Fratzi (2010), 'A 12-step process of white-collar crime', *International Journal of Business Governance and Ethics*, **5** (1), 14–25.

McKendall, M.A. and J.A. Wagner (1997), 'Motive, opportunity, choice, and corporate illegality', *Organization Science*, **8**, 624–647.

Meldalen, S.G. (2015), 'Når noen hører ordet "stråmann", høres det skummelt ut (When someone hears the word "straw man", it sounds scary)', daily Norwegian newspaper *Dagbladet*, http://www.dagbladet. no/2015/01/08/nyheter/innenriks/christer_tromsdal/bedrageri/37075845/, published January 8, downloaded 10 January, 2016.

Menon, S. and T.G. Siew (2012), 'Key challenges in tackling economic and cybercrimes: Creating a multilateral platform for international co-operation', *Journal of Money Laundering Control*, **15** (3), 243–256.

Meyer, Mary A. and Jane M. Booker (2001), *Eliciting and Analyzing Expert Judgment: A Practical Guide*, ASA-SIAM Series on Statistics and Applied Probability, Philadelphia, PA: Society for Industrial and Applied Mathematics (SIAM).

Miceli, M.P., J.P. Near and T.M. Dworkin (2009), 'A word to the wise: How managers and policy-makers can encourage employees to report wrongdoing', *Journal of Business Ethics*, **86**, 379–396.

Michel, P. (2008), 'Financial crimes: The constant challenge of seeking effective prevention solutions', *Journal of Financial Crime*, **15** (4), 383–397.

Miller, K.D. and E.W.K. Tsang (2010), 'Testing management theories: Critical realist philosophy and research methods', *Strategic Management Journal*, **32**, 139–158.

Montella, Erin Callan (2016), *Full Circle: A Memoir of Leaning in too Far and the Journey Back*, Sanibel, FL: Triple M Press.

Mostovicz, I., N. Kakabadse and A. Kakabadse (2009), 'CSR: The role of leadership in driving ethical outcomes', *Corporate Governance*, **9** (4), 448–460.

Mutchler, J.F. (2003), 'Independence and objectivity: A framework for research opportunities in internal auditing', in *Research Opportunities in Internal Auditing*, Altamonte Springs, FL: Institute of Internal Auditors Research Foundation, 231–268.

Næss, A. and L.K. Ravn (2013), 'Livsverket selges fra fengselet (Lifework sold from prison)', daily Norwegian business newspaper *Dagens Næringsliv*, Friday, October 18, pages 4–5.

Nalbandian, J. and J.T. Edwards (1983), 'The professional values of public administrators: A comparison with lawyers, social workers, and business administrators', *Review of Public Personnel Administration*, **4**, 114–127.

Naylor, R.T. (2003), 'Towards a general theory of profit-driven crimes', *British Journal of Criminology*, **43**, 81–101.

Ngo, F.T. and R. Paternoster (2016), 'Toward an understanding of the emotional and behavioral reactions to stalking: A partial test of general strain theory', *Crime and Delinquency*, **62** (6), 703–727.

Nolasco, C.A.R.I., M.S. Vaughn and R.V. Carmen (2013), 'Revisiting the choice model of Ponzi and Pyramid schemes: Analysis of case law', *Crime, Law and Social Change*, **60**, 375–400.

NTB (2015), 'Økokrim ber om seks års fengsel for Tromsdal (Økokrim asks for six years prison for Tromsdal)', daily Norwegian newspaper *Klassekampen*, http://www.klassekampen.no/article/20150320/NTBO/92 8007743, published March 20, downloaded March 20, 2015.

O'Connor, T.R. (2005), 'Police deviance and ethics', in *Part of Web Cited, MegaLinks in Criminal Justice*, http://faculty.ncwc.edu/toconnor/205/205lect11.htm, downloaded February 19, 2009.

Onna, J.H.R., V.R. Geest, W. Huisman and J.M. Denkers (2014), 'Criminal trajectories of white-collar offenders', *Journal of Research in Crime and Delinquency*, **51**, 759–784.

Oslo district court (2015), Case 14-035631MED-OTIR/05, *Oslo tingrett*, June 19, 2015.

Osuji, O. (2011), 'Fluidity of regulation–CSR nexus: The multinational corporate corruption example', *Journal of Business Ethics*, **103** (1), 31–57.

Ouimet, G. (2009), 'Psychology of white-collar criminal: In search of personality', *Psychologie Du Travail Et Des Organisations*, **15** (3), 297–320.

Ouimet, G. (2010), 'Dynamics of narcissistic leadership in organizations', *Journal of Managerial Psychology*, **25** (7), 713–726.

Palazzo, G. and A.G. Scherer (2006), 'Corporate legitimacy as deliberation: A communicative framework', *Journal of Business Ethics*, **66** (1), 71–88.

Pangrazio, L. (2017), 'Exploring provocation as a research method in the social sciences', *International Journal of Social Research Methodology*, **20** (2), 225–236.

Passas, N. (2007), *Corruption in the Procurement Process/Outsourcing Government Functions: Issues, Case Studies, Implications*, Report to the Institute for Fraud Prevention, shortened version by W. Black, www.theifp.org, downloaded 10 January, 2016, 33 pages.

Pennsylvania Crime Commission (1974), *Report on Police Corruption and the Quality of Law Enforcement in Philadelphia*, The Pennsylvania Crime Commission, March, https://www.ncjrs.gov/App/publications/abstract.aspx?ID=25640, downloaded 10 January, 2016, 456 pages.

Pentland, B.T., T. Hærem and D. Hillison (2010), 'Comparing organizational routines as recurrent patterns of action', *Organization Studies*, **31** (7), 917–940.

Perry, J., A. Hondeghem and L. Wise (2010), 'Revisiting the motivational bases of public service', *Public Administration Review*, **70** (5), 681–690.

Perry, J.L. and L.R. Wise (1990), 'The motivational bases of public service', *Public Administration Review*, **50** (3), 367–373.

Pickett, K.H. Spencer and Jennifer M. Pickett (2002), *Financial Crime Investigation and Control*, New York: John Wiley & Sons.

Pillay, S. and R. Kluvers (2014), 'An institutional theory perspective on corruption: The case of a developing democracy', *Financial Accountability and Management*, **30** (1), 95–119.

Piquero, N.L. (2012), 'The only thing we have to fear is fear itself: Investigating the relationship between fear of falling and white collar crime', *Crime and Delinquency*, **58** (3), 362–379.

Piquero, N.L. and M.L. Benson (2004), 'White collar crime and criminal careers: Specifying a trajectory of punctuated situational offending', *Journal of Contemporary Criminal Justice*, **20**, 148–165.

Piquero, N.L., A. Schoepfer and L. Langton (2010), 'Completely out of control or the desire to be in complete control? How low self-control and the desire for control relate to corporate offending', *Crime and Delinquency*, **56** (4), 627–647.

Podgor, E.S. (2007), 'The challenge of white collar sentencing', *Journal of Criminal Law and Criminology*, **97** (3), 1–10.

Police (2014), *Etterretningsdoktrine for politiet (Intelligence Doctrince for the Police)*, Norwegian Police Directorate, Oslo, Norway, www.politi.no, downloaded 10 January, 2016.

Pontell, H.N., W.K. Black and G. Geis (2014), 'Too big to fail, too powerful to jail? On the absence of criminal prosecutions after the 2008 financial meltdown', *Crime, Law and Social Change*, **61** (1), 1–13.

Powers, W.C., R.S. Troubh and H.S. Winokur (2002), *Report of Investigation by the Special Investigative Committee of the Board of Directors of Enron Corporation*, http://news.findlaw.com/wsj/docs/enron/sicreport/, published February 1, 218 pages.

Pratt, T.C. and F.T. Cullen (2005), 'Assessing macro-level predictors and theories of crime: A meta-analysis', *Crime and Justice*, **32**, 373–450.

Proba (2013), *Trygdesvindel i Norge: En kartlegging av fem stønadsordninger (Social Security Fraud in Norway: A Survey of Five Support Areas)*, Proba samfunnsanalyse, Oslo, Norway.

Punch, M. (2003), 'Rotten orchards: "Pestilence", police misconduct and system failure', *Policing and Society*, **13** (2), 171–196.

Puranam, P., O. Alexy and M. Reitzig (2014), 'What's "new" about new forms of organizing?', *Academy of Management Review*, **39** (2), 162–180.

PwC (1991), *Report on Sandstrom SA under section 41 of the Banking Act 1987*, PricewaterhouseCoopers, http://file.wikileaks.info/leak/sandstorm-bcci-report-1881.pdf, 22 + 28 = 50 pages.

PwC (2014a), *Hadeland Energi AS, Rapport – gransking (Hadeland Energi AS, Report of Investigation)*, PricewaterhouseCoopers, June 23, 25 pages.

PwC (2014b), *Hadeland og Ringerike Bredbånd AS, Rapport – gransking (Hadeland and Ringerike Bredbånd AS, Report of Investigation)*, PricewaterhouseCoopers, June 10, 32 pages.

Quinn, J. and D.S. Koch (2003), 'The nature of criminality within one-percent motorcycle clubs', *Deviant Behavior*, **24** (3), 281–305.

Ragatz, L.L., W. Fremouw and E. Baker (2012), 'The psychological profile of white-collar offenders: Demographics, criminal thinking, psychopathic traits, and psychopathology', *Criminal Justice and Behavior*, **39** (7), 978–997.

Rassel, J. and J. Komarnicki (2007), 'Gangs ranked: Crazy Dragons head list of Alberta crime threats', *Calgary Herald*, Saturday, July 21.

Reed, G.E. and P.C. Yeager (1996), 'Organizational offending and neoclassical criminology: Challenging the reach of a general theory of crime', *Criminology*, **34** (3), 357–382.

Riisnæs, I.G. (2014), 'Hverken skyldig eller frikjent (Neither guilty nor acquitted)', daily Norwegian business newspaper *Dagens Næringsliv*, www.dn.no, published November 7, downloaded 10 January, 2016.

Rostad, K. and A.S. Sletmoen (2015), 'Har fått inn to millioner av Hells Angels (Has retrieved two million from Hells Angels)', website of the Norwegian public broadcasting corporation *NRK Hedmark og Oppland*, http://www.nrk.no/ho/har-fatt-inn-to-millioner-av-hells-angels-1.12515257, published August 25, downloaded 10 January, 2016.

Rostami, A., C. Melde and S. Holgersson (2015), 'The myth of success: The emergence and maintenance of a specialized gang unit in Stockholm, Sweden', *International Journal of Comparative and Applied Criminal Justice*, **39** (3), 199–217.

Salter, C.R., M. Green, M. Ree, M. Carmody-Bubb and P.A. Duncan (2009), 'A study of follower's personality, implicit leadership perceptions, and leadership ratings', *Journal of Leadership Studies*, **2** (4), 48–60.

Scherer, A. and G. Palazzo (2011), 'The new political role of business in a globalized world: A review of a new perspective on CSR and its implications for the firm, governance, and democracy', *Journal of Management Studies*, **48** (4), 899–931.

Scherer, A., G. Palazzo and D. Baumann (2006), 'Global rules and private actors: Toward a new role of the transnational corporation in global governance', *Business Ethics Quarterly*, **16** (4), 505–532.

Schneider, S. (2006), 'Privatizing economic crime enforcement: Exploring the role of private sector investigative agencies in combating money laundering', *Policing and Society*, **16** (3), 285–312.

Schoepfer, A. and N.L. Piquero (2006), 'Exploring white-collar crime and the American dream: A partial test of institutional anomie theory', *Journal of Criminal Justice*, **34**, 227–235.

SEC (2002), *Report of Investigation Pursuant to Section 21 (a) of the Securities Exchange Act of 1934: Motorola, Inc.*, US Securities and Exchange

Commission,   http://www.sec.gov/litigation/investreport/34-46898.htm, downloaded 10 January, 2016.

SEC (2013), *Enforcement Manual*, Securities and Exchange Commission, Division of Enforcement, http://www.sec.gov/divisions/enforce/enforce mentmanual.pdf, downloaded 10 January, 2016, 141 pages.

Seiders, K., G.B. Voss, A.L. Godfrey and D. Grewal (2007), 'SERVCON: Development and validation of a multidimensional service convenience scale', *Journal of the Academy of Marketing Science*, **35**, 144–156.

Shadnam, M. and T.B. Lawrence (2011), 'Understanding widespread misconduct in organizations: An institutional theory of moral collapse', *Business Ethics Quarterly*, **21** (3), 379–407.

Shen, W. (2003), 'The dynamics of the CEO–board relationship: An evolutionary perspective', *Academy of Management Review*, **28** (3), 466–476.

Shvarts, A. (2001), 'The Russian mafia: Do rational choice models apply?', *Michigan Sociological Review*, **15**, 29–63.

Sidley (2010), *Report of Investigation Regarding Procurement Practices at the Office of the Chief Technology Officer of the District of Columbia*, Sidley Austin LLP, July 14, DRAFT, http://assets.bizjournals.com/cms_ media/washington/pdf/Sidley%20Report.pdf, downloaded July 5, 2012, 60 pages.

Siemens (2014), *Corporate Social Responsibility Policy of Siemens Limited*, http://www.siemens.co.in/pool/about_us/sustainability/siemens-limited-india-corporate-social-responsibility-policy-december-2014.pdf, downloaded July 4, 2016, 10 pages.

Siponen, M. and A. Vance (2010), 'Neutralization: New Insights into the problem of employee information security policy violations', *MIS Quarterly*, **34** (3), 487–502.

Slottje, Pauline, Jeroin P. Sluijs and Anne B. Knol (2008), *Expert Elicitation: Methodological Suggestions for Its Use in Environmental Health Impact Assessments*, RIVM Letter report, National Institute for Public Health and the Environment, the Netherlands.

Smith, R. (2009), 'Understanding entrepreneurial behavior in organized criminals', *Journal of Enterprising Communities: People and Places in the Global Economy*, **3** (3), 256–268.

Stadler, W.A., M.L. Benson and E.T. Cullen (2013), 'Revisiting the special sensitivity hypothesis: The prison experience of white-collar inmates', *Justice Quarterly*, **30** (6), 1090–1114.

Stavanger tingrett (2012), Court case 11-128794MED-STAV, *Stavanger tingrett* (Stavanger district court), November 15.

Steffensmeier, D. and E. Allan (1996), 'Gender and crime: Toward a gendered theory of female offending', *Annual Review of Sociology*, **22**, 459–487.

Stewart, N. and D. Nakamura (2007), '2 more D.C. tax workers removed', *Washington Post*, www.washingtonpost.com, published Saturday, November 10, downloaded September 30, 2012.

Sundström, M. and A. Radon (2015), 'Utilizing the concept of convenience as a business opportunity in emerging markets', *Organizations and Markets in Emerging Economies*, **6** (2), 7–21.

Sutherland, E.H. (1939), 'White-collar criminality', *American Sociological Review*, **5**, 1–12.

Sutherland, Edwin H. (1949), *White-Collar Crime*, New York: Holt, Rinehart and Winston Publishing.

Sutherland, Edwin H. (1983), *White Collar Crime: The Uncut Version*, New Haven, CT: Yale University Press.

Sutton, R.I. and B.M. Staw (1995), 'What theory is not', *Administrative Science Quarterly*, **40**, 371–384.

Swart, J. and N. Kinnie (2003), 'Sharing knowledge in knowledge-intensive firms', *Human Resource Management Journal*, **13** (2), 60–75.

Sykes, G. and D. Matza (1957), 'Techniques of neutralization: A theory of delinquency', *American Sociological Review*, **22** (6), 664–670.

Szalma, J.L. and P.A. Hancock (2013), 'A signal improvement to signal detection analysis: Fuzzy SDT on the ROCs', *Journal of Experimental Psychology: Human Perception and Performance*, **39** (6), 1741–1762.

Tiwana, A. and M. Keil (2009), 'Control in internal and outsourced software projects', *Journal of Management Information Systems*, **26** (3), 9–44.

Trahan, A. (2011), 'Filling in the gaps in culture-based theories of organizational crime', *Journal of Theoretical and Philosophical Criminology*, **3** (1), 89–109.

Trahan, A., J. Marquart and J. Mullings (2005), 'Fraud and the American dream: Toward an understanding of fraud victimization', *Deviant Behavior*, **26** (6), 601–620.

Vadera, A.K. and R.V. Aguilera (2015), 'The evolution of vocabularies and its relation to investigation of white-collar crimes: An institutional work perspective', *Journal of Business Ethics*, **128**, 21–38.

Vadera, A.K., R.V. Aguilera and B.B. Caza (2009), 'Making sense of whistleblowing's antecedents: Learning from research on identity and ethics programs', *Business Ethics Quarterly*, **19** (4), 553–586.

Valkenhoef, G. and T. Tervonen (2016), 'Entropy-optimal weight constraint elicitation with additive multi-attribute utility models', *Omega*, **64**, 1–12.

Valukas, A.R. (2010), *In Regard Lehman Brothers Holdings Inc. to United States Bankruptcy Court in Southern District of New York*, Jenner & Block, March 11, http://www.nysb.uscourts.gov/sites/default/files/opinions/188162_61_opinion.pdf, downloaded 10 January, 2016, 239 pages.

Valukas, A.R. (2014), *Report to Board of Directors of General Motors Company Regarding Ignition Switch Recalls*, Jenner & Block, May 29, http://www.beasleyallen.com/webfiles/valukas-report-on-gm-redacted.pdf, downloaded 10 January, 2016, 325 pages.

Wagner, R.E. (2011), 'Gordon Gekko to the rescue? Insider trading as a tool to combat accounting fraud', *University of Cincinnati Law Review*, **79**, 973–1017.

Ward, J.T., J.H. Boman and S. Jones (2015), 'Hirschi's redefined self-control: Assessing the implications of the merger between social- and self-control theories', *Crime and Delinquency*, **61** (9), 1206–1233.

Weick, K.E. (1995), 'What theory is not, theorizing is', *Administrative Science Quarterly*, **40**, 385–390.

Welsh, D.T., L.D. Oronez, D.G. Snyder and M.S. Christian (2014), 'The slippery slope: How small ethical transgressions pave the way for larger future transgressions', *Journal of Applied Psychology*, **100** (1), 114–127.

Wensink, W. and J.M. Vet (2013), *Identifying and Reducing Corruption in Public Procurement in the EU*, PwC, Ecorys, and Utrecht University, PwC EU Services, Belgium, ec.europa.eu/. . ./identifying_reducing_corruption_in_public_proc.

Whetten, D.A. (1989), 'What constitutes a theoretical contribution?', *Academy of Management Review*, **14** (4), 490–495.

Williams, J.W. (2005), 'Governability matters: The private policing of economic crime and the challenge of democratic governance', *Policing and Society*, **15** (2), 187–211.

Williams, J.W. (2008), 'The lessons of Enron: Media accounts, corporate crimes, and financial markets', *Theoretical Criminology*, **12** (4), 471–499.

Williamson, O.E. (1979), 'Transaction-cost economics: The governance of contractual relations', *Journal of Law and Economics*, **22** (2), 233–261.

Williamson, O.E. (1981), 'The modern corporation: Origins, evolution, attributes', *Journal of Economic Literature*, **19** (4), 1537–1568.

Williamson, O.E. (2000), 'The new institutional economics: Taking stock, looking ahead', *Journal of Economic Literature*, **38** (3), 595–613.

Wilmer and PwC (2003), *Report of Investigation by the Special Investigative Committee of the Board of Directors of WorldCom Inc.*, Wilmer, Cutler & Pickering (Counsel) and PricewaterhouseCoopers LLP (Accounting Advisors), http://www.sec.gov/Archives/edgar/data/723527/000093176303001862/dex991.htm, downloaded February 8, 2015, 345 pages.

WilmerHale and PwC (2008), *Report of Investigation Submitted by the Council of the District of Columbia*, Wilmer Cutler Pickering Hale and Dorr LLP (Counsel) and PricewaterhouseCoopers LLP (Forensic Accounting Advisors), http://www.dcwatch.com/govern/otr081215.pdf, downloaded February 8, 2015, 126 pages.

Wood, J. and E. Alleyne (2010), 'Street gang theory and research: Where are we now and where do we go from here?', *Aggression and Violent Behavior*, **15**, 100–111.

Wright, Alan (2006), *Organised Crime*, Devon, UK: Willan Publishing.

Zagorin, P. (2001), 'Francis Bacon's concept of objectivity and the idols of the mind', *British Journal of Historical Science*, **34** (4), 379–393.

Zipparo, L. (1999), 'Factors which deter public officials from reporting corruption', *Crime, Law and Social Change*, **30** (3), 273–287.

Zollo, M., M. Minoja, L. Casanova, K. Hockerts, P. Neergaard, S. Schneider and A. Tencati (2009), 'Towards an internal change management perspective of CSR: Evidence from project RESPONSE on the sources of cognitive alignment between managers and their stakeholders, and their implications for social performance', *Corporate Governance*, **9** (4), 355–372.

Index